*An Iraqi Jew in the Mossad*

# An Iraqi Jew in the Mossad

*Memoir of an
Israeli Intelligence Officer*

*by* Joshua Horesh

McFarland & Company, Inc., Publishers
*Jefferson, North Carolina, and London*

British Library Cataloguing-in-Publication data are available

Library of Congress Cataloguing-in-Publication Data

Horesh, Joshua, 1920–
    An Iraqi Jew in the Mossad : memoir of an Israeli intelligence
officer / by Joshua Horesh.
        p.   cm.
    Includes index.
    ISBN 0-7864-0261-X (sewn softcover : 50# alkaline paper)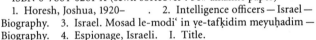
    1. Horesh, Joshua, 1920–      . 2. Intelligence officers — Israel —
Biography.   3. Israel. Mosad le-modiʻ in ye-tafḳidim meyuḥadim —
Biography.   4. Espionage, Israeli.   I. Title.
UB271.I82H67   1997
327.125694 — dc21                                                    96-51936
                                                                       CIP

Manufactured in the United States of America

McFarland & Company, Inc., Publishers
    Box 611, Jefferson, North Carolina 28640

To my wife, children, grandchildren;
and all unfortunate wives and children
whose husbands and fathers in this service
never made it back

Also, to all the volunteers and low ranking
operatives who made the Israeli Intelligence
and the Mossad one of the best in the world

# Contents

## Contents

# Preface

I was ten years old when I learned that a public execution by hanging was to take place one morning at the public square near our home in Baghdad. Such executions are still taking place in most of the Arab countries.

I was curious and decided to go out and watch. While there, I inquired what the condemned man had done and was shocked when someone said he had killed all his children because they disturbed his midday siesta. My informant added that the condemned man should not be hanged because, according to religious interpretations of "Shareea" Islamic law, his children were his own property and he was free to deal with them however he liked.

Surely, the Islamic laws do not condone such interpretations. The problem is that, in the Arab world, many leaders twist the words of the Koran (the sacred book of Islam) for their own purposes, and their followers — often uneducated, with no real idea of what their religion is all about — accept these misinterpretations because of their worshipful devotion to the interpreter.

Often, the result is a fundamentalism so saturated with hatred that less fanatical fundamentalists — and they do exist — are unable to attain any power that would allow them to bring reason to the extremist ranks. The fundamentalists lately sentenced to death an honorable Islamic leader because he commented that their explanations of the Koran were distortions that the masses, through their ignorance, were compelled to accept as truth. Another Moslem leader was condemned to die because he declared that words written thousands of years ago could not be a beaming light in the modern era. Demonstrations against him ended with his death when a crowd of his supposed rescuers chased him to the roof of his house and pushed him off.

Misguided believers can easily become terrorists, and terrorism nowadays is spreading throughout the world, especially in the Middle East. In the meantime most governments in the world, especially in the West, attempt to deal with Arab and Islamic populations as if they were Europeans, Americans, or Russians. But they are very different in religion, culture, and traditions. According to the late Dr. Elie Khedouri, a professor at the University of London and a native of Baghdad, democratic rule in the Arab countries has been a disaster, regardless of any good intentions. The Moslem Arab lands were under the control of the Islamic Ottoman Empire for over four hundred years; after their liberation by the West, they ended up following the worst of rulers. The Western ways are far from applicable to these countries, where the people have long been accustomed to autocratic leaders and passive obedience.

Historians tell of Genghis Khan (1160–1227), founder of the Tartar mongol empire, who wanted his burial place kept secret from everyone in the world. He accomplished this with a diabolical plan: Of the three thousand men who comprised the cortege to the burial spot, two thousand were killed by the remaining one thousand, who had been secretly ordered to do so. When these thousand returned home, they were killed in turn by another two thousand who waited for them and who never knew the burial place. The soldiers paid with their lives to carry the secret of their false god.

People unused to democracy willingly turn to such false gods, and often from there to terrorist activities. In today's Arab world, the leaders of such activities blame their favorite scapegoat, Israel. In turn, Israel compounds the problem by attempting to deal with Moslems as though they were Westerners. Also, in Israel, all the generals and high-ranking officers have been political appointees with little experience in military affairs. As government functionaries shaping the future of the state, they are the guardians of most of the secrets of the ruling parties. As a result, certain administrations and military campaigns have been disastrous.

In truth, this sort of disaster has visited all populations of the Middle East. For example, at the time the British were in control in Iraq, the Iraqi government was semidemocratic. Later, kings, prime ministers, generals, and other leaders were assassinated. Demonstrations became an everyday occurrence, and the rights of the individual tumbled into a dark abyss.

Growing up as an Iraqi Jew, over time I found it unacceptable that one group should dominate another within the same nation by ignoring that group's inheritance. Later, I realized it is even worse when the evil acts of a nation's intelligence and security organizations are condoned, sometimes even directed, by the ruling group — especially when that group considers its power a licence to act as it pleases. I am a former intelligence officer of the Israeli Defense Force and a former agent of the Mossad. Born in Baghdad in 1920, I left Iraq in 1938 as Nazism was spreading across the country. My first work in intelligence was voluntarily gathering information of military value for the British to aid in the allied invasion of Syria and Lebanon. Later, ostensibly a member of the British forces fighting the Underground, I secretly served the Underground with information about British actions and policies toward the Jews in Palestine. Following the 1948 War of Independence, I joined the Mossad and served in Turkey and Austria under an assumed Arab name, confronting Turkish secret police and the KGB.

When I returned to civilian life, I found myself unhappy in the socialist state of Israel and eventually resettled in the United States, where I live today.

It was never my intention to write a book about my experiences, until a curious thing happened. I saw a story in the *Encylopedia of the Defense Forces of Israel* that related some of the work I had done — except that where my name should have been, someone had substituted the name of another who came to the unit much later. My former commander wrote me a letter apologizing for having overlooked my name but also insinuating that I kept notes (unlike himself) that helped me to remember everything. This was completely untrue; nevertheless, the events of those years were still fresh in my mind. I saw that if my story was to be told, I would have to do so myself. I bent to the task, putting my work together from memory and comparing it to appropriate dates to bring all into proper sequence and perspective.

While in Israel in 1993, I was approached by an Israeli reporter who had learned about my past work and my connections and wanted to write an article about me. We agreed to meet, and at our meeting I gave him a copy of this manuscript. I had to leave for the United States the next week, and we parted on his promise that a wonderful article would be published the next weekend. However, no article appeared. I called the reporter, who admitted that he had encountered some difficulties but hoped to have the article published within the next two weeks or so. When that time had passed with no article in sight, I called the reporter again, even though he had advised me not to (he said he would call me). When I insisted on knowing why nothing had appeared, he said that my story was already told by government officials and the censor did not approve of publication of the article.

Before I left Israel, the reporter had sent a special photographer to take my picture for the newspaper. While the photographer was doing his work in my brother-in-law's home, someone joked that perhaps the Mossad had lost my photos and had concocted the whole situation in order to obtain new ones. I responded, "I hope so, because that would mean that at long last someone is remembering." That was the end of my hope that my story could be made public — until now.

I wrote this book because I believe that secrets need to be told. In my experience, the Mossad and the Israeli intelligence service acted independently and at whim. When the creations of elected governments act this way, that government's ability to rule is dubious at best. Meanwhile, our boys and others from all over the world continue to sacrifice themselves for peace. Throughout the history of Israel, most of its young men have participated in one war or another, including the Underground movement, the War of Independence, the Sinai War, the 1967 War, the Yom Kippur War of 1973, and many skirmishes in between. Veterans of all these wars live among us all over the world;

many others have died. Still others continue their lives as if nothing has happened, raising families in Israel and abroad while those who hold the reins of government, whether democratically elected or otherwise, are still showing off as if ordained by God to fashion the future of the country the veterans brought into existence.

I wrote this book to tell the secrets of the past, in the fervent hope that it will help mold a better future. I hope that my autobiography will shed some light on the problems that still dominate our lives in this world, and allow us to put some of our misery behind us. Otherwise, may God help us to avoid the consequences of mad acts in a mad world.

JOSHUA HORESH
*Fall 1996*

# CHAPTER 1

# Early Pedigree

I was fascinated by the story of Ezekiel, whose shrine I had the good fortune to visit with my parents when I was four or five years old. It is in the village of Chefel (which is a Bedouin dialect form of the word *kefel*, guarantor), not far from the site of Ancient Babylon, the famous old capital that prides itself on the Hanging Gardens, one of the Seven Wonders of the World. Its King Nebuchadnezzar sacked Jerusalem in about 600 B.C. and took our ancestors as slaves to Babylonia in what is now called Iraq.

I was born in Baghdad to Yosef and Taffi (Tuffaha Khebbaza) Horesh some seventy years ago. Yosef Horesh was born in Baghdad in 1889 at Kadi El Hajat quarters near the Shorja Bazaar. My family tree goes back to the period when Spanish (sephardic) Jews were driven out and scattered all over Europe and the Middle East. My father was the son of Sasson Ben Yehoshoua Ben Eliezer Ben Saleh Kleif of the Horesh Family.* *Horesh* is Hebrew for "ploughman." I have heard some claim that the name really comes from the Arabic name Atrash. Presumably when my ancestors fled Spain for Austria they were guests of the Atrash princes at Jabal El Druze in Syria, and somehow there was a change and they acquired their present name, which sounds like the Hebrew *Heresh*, meaning "deaf."

I personally disagree with this version. It sounds like a blatant attempt to Arabicise a Jew, my father, who happened to be the best singer of his day. It wouldn't be the first time this happened. Hundreds of years ago the Jewish poet Shmuel was Arabicised to Samowal. His poetry was taught in Arab schools until 1936 — but I'm getting ahead of my story.

My father was one of nine sons and two daughters born to Sasson Horesh. He became a well-known Makam singer (Makam is the traditional Iraqi music). He performed for premiers and other prominent figures — even the king of Iraq. My father sang privately for Om Kalthoum, considered the best Egyptian singer in the Arab world back then. He also sang in Arabic on Israeli radio.

*The book Babylonian Journey, *a history of the Jewish Babylonian population in Baghdad, written by Sir David Suleiman Sassoon of the Sassoon dynasty about a century ago and reprinted by Meir Benihoo, lists our name (the family name at the time) as Hirsch and in brackets, Horesh.*

My father served as cantor at the Alliance Israelite Universelle Synagogue during the Jewish high holidays. In return, I received a free education at this prestigious school, where I acquired my basic knowledge of Arabic, French, English, and Hebrew. My father and his father believed education was the key to everything. They rigorously applied this belief to us kids, and never stopped pumping into our brains the need to improve our life through education. Knowledge was our best survival weapon. Like Jewish kids everywhere, we believed our goal in life was to become lawyers, merchants, doctors, businessmen. But I'm getting ahead of my story again.

In 1914, the Jews of Baghdad were called upon to serve in the Turkish Army. Those who could afford to, bribed their way out of it. Others, less fortunate, went into hiding. The rest were drafted, and either served or ran away.

Many of the runaways became victims of Bedouin Razia, or were slaughtered by anti–Jewish leagues in the army, like the million or so Armenians who were slaughtered. Those who escaped death faced starvation or murder by Arab tribes in the desert. The survivors returned suffering from malnutrition, cold, and disease. They had shocking stories to tell about this *safer barr*, or *journey into the desert*. A member of my wife's family, Abraham Sharabani, related his ordeals in his book, *These Are My Memories*. The following excerpt has been loosely translated from Hebrew. I have deliberately not polished the translation so you can get the feel of Sharabani's thoughts.

> After being drafted into the Turkish Army we started walking before sunset on a Sabbath eve. At night, it became pitch dark around us and bitterly cold. After a few miles of walking, torrential rain came down, pouring as if all the fountains of heaven had opened. We became soaked by the downpour.
>
> We continued walking until we reached a Khan caravanserai, a shelter for animals. The next morning we continued until we reached a place called Fallouja where we rested and were permitted to visit and spend that night with local Jewish families.
>
> The next morning we continued our journey, occasionally riding a cart loaded with straw. At night we slept in the open, and after about twenty days we reached Aleppo in Syria. After resting for a while, we headed north toward Istanbul where we were told we would soon be sent to the front. I decided to desert.
>
> On the day before Yom Kippur (Jewish holy day of atonement), I was issued a one-day leave permit. I did not return to my unit after this leave. A Jewish family made arrangements to send me back to my family in Baghdad. The danger was great to all of us should I be caught because our fate would surely be death by firing squad or hanging.
>
> Somehow I managed to lay my hand on an ambiguous forged leave permit to travel on leave to Baghdad with other military personnel. Some of

the others sensed that I was different. Worst of all, I noticed that few officers were from the same unit.

I panicked and thought that, should they recognize me, it would be disastrous, leading to sure death. Therefore, I managed to withdraw and went back to Istanbul. In those days the city was tightly sealed, and no civilians, Jews or Christians, could leave Istanbul without a special permit.

One of the Jewish families, who laid their hand on a stolen blank paper with the letterhead of the Prime Minister Anwar Pasha, gave me one to write my own permit. Without knowing it, I became the first to test this dangerous venture, and should I succeed, it would be applied to others. Being familiar with the Turkish language and all the wording of official letters and documents, I filled the blank paper as a special leave permit to visit my people in Aleppo, Syria. In order to make it official, I had to have it endorsed by the military officer in charge of the railway station who, after some slow reaction, affixed his stamp and signature to it. In his private room, I had to urge him to do so before the train left and I was stranded in the station. In that station officer's room, I felt the deadly danger hovering over me, but luckily, after a little while, everything was all right. I headed toward the family who gave me the blank paper to tell them about my actions.

When I reached their home, I found it dark and deserted. After a while someone tapped me on my shoulder and asked how it went.

I recognized him as one of the family who gave me the blank paper.

"Everything is all right. I am leaving soon and came to say good-bye."

Out of nowhere all the family gathered around me to bid me farewell.

What had really happened was that one of them had followed me to the station. When he noticed I went into the officer's room, he went back and told everyone I was probably caught red-handed. As a matter of precaution, they hid themselves, fearing I would be back with the authorities after breaking under interrogation. When I came alone, they realized that everything was all right and came out from hiding.

They helped me get on the train at Haider Pasha Station in Istanbul. There were about forty other Turkish soldiers on leave at that time. We reached Kunia, a post on the way to Aleppo, where we got our meager ration of one loaf bread each. I managed to outwit the issuing officer and obtain an extra loaf by volunteering to fetch the whole ration for the forty soldiers. I collected their ration slips and added mine with an extra forged one which had to be endorsed by the officer in charge. Since he was very busy with other matters, I suggested he sign the slips on the back, which I had stacked for him, and thus save time. I would present the endorsed slips to the store keeper and collect the ration for everyone with the help of one of them who accompanied me for this purpose. He agreed, and I made sure that the extra loaf of bread from the forged slip would not fall into the wrong hands. I sold my extra loaf for a high price and kept the money for any unexpected eventualities.

(Sharabani's memoir, continued)

At the next stop we had our food at an army camp. A large karawana casserole full of rice and other vegetables was brought, and we sat round about eating out of it, either with bare hands or with spoons issued by the army to some of the soldiers. I owned my own, which was bigger and wider than all the others. I was almost lynched for eating more with it than the others could. I stopped in time and refrained from dipping it into the casserole, unless no one was watching.

In order to cross the border without being checked, I slipped under the seat on the train in the wagon where German soldiers were riding, since they usually crossed without inspection.

Arriving at Aleppo, I went straight to the nearest synagogue and informed the congregation that I was Jewish, just deserted from the Turkish Army, and seeking help. Three more Jewish deserters were already there. We were put in the basement of the synagogue. The place was neglected and filthy. It was full of roaches, rats and other insects. I did not sleep the whole night. I met an acquaintance of the family and requested his help. The needed funds were raised to pay a Bedouin Arab who was experienced in guiding people through the desert to Baghdad.

We put on Bedouin clothes and began our journey through the desert between Aleppo in Syria and Baghdad, Iraq. We were tense, and our fear of the unknown was appalling. We walked all night, until the rays of the early sun broke through the mists of the desert sky. Our eyes were bloodshot, but we were grateful for the new day.

Our guide left us in the middle of the desert, telling us to stay where we were until someone else arrived and took over. We had no choice but to listen to his instructions. We were left alone in the wilderness of the desert. We waited all day, but no one showed up. We began to suspect foul play, and we were at a loss as to what to do.

Before sunset, we noticed in the distance Bedouins racing toward us on horseback. We heard their shouts in Arabic telling us to throw down everything: "Throw down! Throw down!" We did not know what to make of the horsemen dashing toward us. We started saying our prayers, fearing the worst and that our end was near. We soon realized they were all armed with rifles, daggers, and swords, which clearly indicated they were not ordinary Bedouins roaming the desert to locate grazing land for their herds. They were robbers looking for victims.

We immediately felt the enormity of the danger surrounding us and our helplessness. First, theatrical shots were fired, then hitting and kicking ensued, until one of them, apparently the leader, shouted we were deserters and no harm should come to us. They ordered us to strip naked, took away our clothes and shoes, left each of us with one torn and filthy robe, and rode away.

We thanked God our lives were spared, and we waited in the same spot till dawn, when our guide appeared again. First he did not recognize us because of the robes we were wearing (probably he pretended that he did not because perhaps he sent the robbers to take our clothing). We strongly suspected the robbery was planned with him; otherwise, how could the horsemen have known our exact position in the middle of the desert?

The guide signaled us to move on. He brought with him a donkey, which he rode, and we followed him on foot. We constantly reminded him of his terms with our friends in Aleppo. We told him he had agreed to supply us with food and horses to ride. He became angry and denied it. That night we reached a Bedouin encampment, and the guide told each of us to go separately to a tent where we spent the night.

The Bedouins were well known for their hospitality. Any person who entered their tent was a welcomed guest. Food was served and a place to sleep for the night was offered. In the morning, the guest must leave. After finishing breakfast, the lord of the tent and family would eat whatever was left over.

We were given clothes to protect us from the cold and the severe weather of the desert as we continued our journey to the next Bedouin encampment.

The next morning, three sheiks, riding their horses, appeared. These were sheiks who were bribed by the Turks to remain on their side, unlike most of tribes who revolted against Turkey during World War I.

They soon noticed we were not Bedouins but Jews, deserters. They began to call us names and tease us. We were bluntly informed that they would give us to the Turks to get the reward. It was clear that we were doomed if they carried out their threat. We humbled ourselves and fell to the ground, asking for their mercy, and they let us go.

They were constantly riding ahead of us, hunting, and then turning toward us to order us to retrieve what they hunted, using us like retriever dogs fetching their game. They cooked whatever they hunted and gave us some to eat. All of a sudden they separated, and we continued alone until two or three days later when we reached another Bedouin encampment.

Our guide informed us that he decided to leave us there and go and look for someone else to take us along. Luckily one of the Bedouins, who had taken other deserters to Baghdad, agreed to take over.

We kept on walking from one Bedouin encampment to the other. We then reached one encampment headed by one of the three pro–Turkish sheiks we met on the road. He recognized us but ordered food. Knowing we were Jews, they brought us only boiled eggs and dates because, like Moslems, … we do not eat non-kosher meat, and the sheik respected that.

After feeding and lodging us, the sheik announced to his tribe that we were deserters and requested volunteers to chain us and escort us to the nearest Turkish police station in Dir El Zor to deliver us to the Turkish Army and bring the rewards back.

Familiar with Bedouin and Arab customs, I began screaming and telling everyone that since the sheik's food was still in our bellies and the remains

(Sharabani's memoir, continued)

sticking to our teeth, it would be only proper if the sheik himself took us out and shot us instead of handing us over to the Turks to hang us.

All of a sudden, a female scream went out from somewhere—"Yaboui! Yaboui"—telling the sheik if he did not let these people alone she would denounce him to all the Bedouins, telling how he did not honor his guests who ate of his food and thus betrayed them. The whole tent became silent. The sheik turned away from us, as if he was not watching. Those surrounding him signaled us to leave immediately because the sheik could not go back on his word.

We ran for our lives without stopping almost the whole night, fearing that the sheik would harden his heart and send his horsemen to catch us far away from his tent, in which case Arab customs would exonerate him from bringing harm to his guests.

When we reached the next village, we were afraid to venture into it. We were very hungry after marching on empty stomachs for several days. We had no money, and we were desperate. The guide looked at my finger and noticed a ring with stone I had been trying to hide. He grabbed it, painfully pulled it off, and said he would go to the village, sell the ring, and bring us some food.

We waited a long time for our guide to return, but to no avail. We slept where we were and in the morning realized that our guide was gone. We needed water because we were thirsty. In the distance we observed a sort of a small lake, and we began running toward it. To our surprise, the lake was distancing itself from us as if it were running away too. We realized the lake was a mirage.

We became disoriented, tired, hungry, and thirsty. One of us suggested we dig holes in which to bury ourselves lest we be left to be devoured by the desert beasts. We prayed and we became hilarious, and we expected a miracle to happen. We continued walking as long as we could without knowing where we were going.

All of a sudden we saw a valley where a lot of sheep were grazing, watched by a young shepherd. He approached us with joy. He hugged us, blessing us with the words "Ahlan Wasahlan." He announced that his sheep were his offering to us. He picked a lamb and gave it to us to eat. He killed the lamb and cooked it on a fire, but before it was cooked, we snatched pieces of its meat and ate it almost raw. The shepherd was very surprised to see us eating meat still hot from the hearth and before it was cooked. We behaved like animals, and when we ate enough we asked for water. He led us to a small source of water nearby. We drank and washed and only then realized we were still alive.

The shepherd gave us few sheepskins to warm us at night. In the morning we had breakfast again, through the generosity of the shepherd who prepared it for us. He directed us how to proceed on our way toward Baghdad, and we started walking again. After a few hundred yards, we turned around to wave farewell again to the kind shepherd, but we did not see anyone — neither the shepherd nor the valley in which we stopped.

We continued walking. Our leftover food dwindled, and at sunset we arrived at a small Bedouin encampment. We went into a tent and requested water and food. When we were invited to sit at the campfire, there were two Turkish policemen who later discovered that we were deserters and not Bedouins. One of them detected that we were Jews and called for us to be chained and brought to the governor for a reward.

The lord of the tent came out with his rifle and told the policemen that if they moved from this tent they would be killed. He said we were his guests. How, he asked, could they even think of taking us away from his tent? He called for another Bedouin outside by the name of Mohammed, telling him that he was in danger and asking him to bring in his rifle. He asked Mohammed to watch the policemen and not let them move until the sheik came back. He asked us to come with him. He accompanied us on the right tracks till midnight. He showed us the direction we should take, bid us the Arab blessing of "Allah Maakum" (God be with you), and returned back to his tent.

We started running again till dawn, and after walking many days we reached a sizeable Bedouin encampment. We were told we were in Ramadi, a small town not far from Baghdad, and the town was under the British occupation. We breathed deeply, sat on the ground and rested. We then realized that soon we would be home and free.

What a world I was born into!

# CHAPTER 2

# Coming of Age

When I turned thirteen, I discovered the best reason yet for being Jewish instead of Moslem. My being a boy might have had something to do with it. It's the bar mitzvah. At thirteen, according to Jewish and Moslem traditions, a boy becomes a man. At thirteen, one begins to bear the consequences of one's acts. The difference, at least for boys, is that the Moslems perform their *brit* (circumcision) on the males at this time. So you can understand part of my joy at being Jewish. Of course, there was more to it than that. Like all Jewish youngsters coming of age, I was happy — but also sad. Till that moment, I had felt completely free and uncommitted. My mistakes were forgiven; I enjoyed the love and protection of my parents. We always celebrated the *brit* of a new baby boy by singing our traditional *shebahoth* (praises). My favorite is: "Let there be peace in our camps — tranquility in Israel — It is a good sign that a son is born unto us — The savior will arrive during his lifetime...." I can become quite nostalgic about the good old days — maudlin, even. Who doesn't? But I'll try to keep it to a minimum.

An Arabic proverb says: "We are always conducted and are not the conductor in Life." So it was in my young life. I grew up with great awareness of the *goyim* (other ethnic groups), especially of those who sought our harm. I learned to run away from trouble and the wrath of our hostile Moslem compatriots. A Westernized saying that originated long ago among the Arabs became very real to me: "He who turns and runs away lives to fight another day." I learned unequivocally that there is no shame in running.

I was completely unaware of our fellow Jews in Europe and elsewhere. I firmly believed we were the remnants of the Jews brought as slaves to Iraq (Babylon) by Nebuchadnezzar some 2500 years ago. While the condition of our brothers in Europe was catastrophic, our fate in the Middle East was relatively survivable. While the Europeans' daily bread was pogroms and massacres simply because they were Jews, in the Middle East we were much better off. It was still a shock to us kids when we discovered that we were different, and that difference made a difference, if you know what I mean. It saddened us, of course, and made us apprehensive; and it maddened some of us, causing us to have rebellious thoughts.

My cousin at six or seven tried to put his rebellious feelings into action, boldly declaring that he would take care of the next wicked Moslem who maltreated us. One day, as soon as he stepped outside accompanied by his father, he hid behind him. When asked why was he hiding, he pointed to a lonely, miserable Moslem approaching them. He was terrified, all his bravado going up in smoke as soon as he confronted a single poor soul on the street.

When still a little boy, during summer vacation, I was invited by our neighbor Isaac to spend a day helping him in his tailor shop. His shop was located in a *khan* (a traditional caravan rest stop), a kind of shopping or business mall. The khan was built around a covered open space. It consisted of two upper floors of small rooms or spaces for business located around the perimeter of the building, something like a flea market, with a long gallery on both floors supported by wooden pillars overlooking the ground floor of shops and spaces. Isaac occupied a top-floor space. The space right under him was occupied by a friendly Shiite merchant.

The whole place fascinated me. At one point I was leaning over the gallery barrier observing the goings-on below me. I was sipping on a glass of water and spilled a few drops just as the Shiite merchant passed directly beneath me. I didn't actually get him wet, and I probably didn't really laugh either, but you know how kids are. He looked up and fixed his bloodshot eyes on me, and I did what any kid would do—I jumped back into Isaac's booth. I heard him ask Isaac if I were a Jew.

Isaac had no idea what had just transpired and answered, "Sure—what about it?"

All hell promptly broke loose. The Shiite bounded up the intervening steps two at a time with murder in his eyes. He struck me a flat-handed blow across my face that sent me reeling before Isaac intervened, begging him to spare the ignorant child—me, if you can believe it! Perhaps out of his friendship with Isaac, the old Shiite relented, but he added that if it were not for my young age he would finish me off for defiling him, and there wasn't a doubt in my young mind that he meant every word.

Not that I understood why, mind you. My head was still ringing from the blow, and I had no idea why a little water should inspire such fury. I was scared and bewildered. The defiled Shiite closed his business and went home, where he took a cleansing bath to purify himself. I understand he arrived back at his shop in a fresh set of clothing shortly after I left for home.

Later on I discovered the old Shiite's problem. It seems members of the Shiite Moslem sect have hated Jews for a long time. During the reign of Caliph Ali Ibn Abu Taleb in the olden times, the Shiites were conducting a vicious pogrom against the Jews, with a lot of looting and mayhem. A Jewish rabbi who had grace at the court of the Caliph begged his help to stop the pillage of Jewish properties.* His request was granted. The cagey caliph decreed that, according to the *Koran*, Jews are unclean, impure, and defiled. Any Shiite, he declared, who contacted a Jew or his belongings would become defiled. The ruse worked, and all looting and pogroms were stopped. And so it's been ever since. If you're a Shiite, you don't touch a Jew or his belongings. It was my water; I was Jewish...Q.E.D. Of course, I don't have any idea about what kind of defiling takes place when a Shiite slaps a small Jewish boy, but that's apparently another subject.

I soon learned that there was more to Islam than just Shiites. While the Shiites constitute most of the Iranian people, who are the modern-day descendants of the Persians, Iraq is only about 50 percent Shiite. The rest are mostly Sunnis. But whether Shiite, Sunni, or some other sect, to me their customs always seemed unfathomably strange.

For ten days each year, the Shiites celebrate the *Ashuraa*, marking the martyrdom of Hussein at the battle of Karbalaa in Iraq back in 680 A.D. Ashuraa is ten days of spectacular religious pageantry reenacting the event and consequent lamentations.

I was eight or maybe ten when I first witnessed the Ashuraa. Jews were forbidden to watch, of course, so we had to conceal ourselves. Fortunately, our houses were built in such a way that a portion of the upper floor of each house projected partway across the street so that persons leaning out the windows could actually shake hands. My uncle's house was along the path of the procession, and many of our family gathered upstairs in rooms that projected out over the procession way. It was like having my own box seat at the stadium. We had to be careful not to be seen, and we always locked our doors as an added precaution. In spite of the looming danger, I was able to glimpse that queer, almost otherworldly religious commemoration.

The organizers of the processions set out special watchers to ensure the absence of Jews and infidels. Their security was pretty bad, however, and we never were caught. Nevertheless, it remained dangerous, for had anyone of us been caught peeping, this violation would have aroused the wrath of the mourners. We Iraqi Jews could control our own behavior — even youngsters like myself — but we were deathly afraid of vicious Shiite mob action.

First came ancient mounted warriors decked out in armor with spear, sword, and dagger, their horses adorned with shields and banners, and draped with black sheets and flowers. Each rider held aloft a different colorful banner, and the horsemen's helmets bobbed and glistened in time with their

---

*The rabbi, whom we call Hakham (Wiseman), according to Dr. H. Haddad of New York, was Sheikh Isaac whose shrine, which I had many opportunities to visit with my late mother when I was 10 or 12 years old, is located in the known market called "Suk Hennouni" in Baghdad. The title of sheikh was bestowed on him by the caliph at that time.*

trotting horses. Following them were foot soldiers, decked out in similar attire, heavily armored. These warriors affected heavy, thick mustaches emphasizing their fierce, illustrious, and heroic characters.

Next was a group of people carrying an open coffin. White doves attached to the coffin with silk ribbons circled about without (to my amazement) getting the ribbons tangled. From time to time they landed on the coffin to peck at special seeds spread over the white-draped, red-stained body it contained — the murdered Hussein.

I will never forget the thousands of marchers following the cortege. They were dressed in black with backs bared, marching ten abreast. They held wooden handles from which protruded clusters of chain — I remember it to this day. In unison to the monotonous, melancholic beat of large drums, they flagellated their backs until they ran with blood. They were followed by more lines of people holding swords or daggers and pounding their foreheads with the handles until they bled.

I was most fascinated by the next group of mourners. They had to be specially trained, because they were swinging their swords, sharp edge first, towards their foreheads in unison to the beat of the drums. Each sword-swinging mourner was accompanied by an interceptor with a heavy stick who would swing his stick up just in time to stop the blade from splitting the mourner's head open. Their heads were shaved, and each had taken a purifying bath before joining the procession. Accidents happen — and this procession was no exception. I actually saw several mourners split their own heads. I later learned that when this happens, the family becomes blessed because the deadly strike is considered to have come from heaven — that is, the mourner died a martyr. It still happens today in both Iraq and Iran. The relatives become exalted, believing that their martyred kinsman is fortunate. (I would not doubt that more than one interceptor has been paid off through the centuries.)

Attendants with buckets filled with ashes lined the procession route, scattering ashes over the bleeding backs and faces of the mourners. All the while the droning, rhythmic, beating of the huge drums saturated the air and the overhanging rooms we occupied with its melancholic sound.

The riding warriors, the fearsome foot-soldiers, the bleeding mourners — it was an overwhelming spectacle. The women watching the macabre procession beat their breasts in unison with the drumbeats, wailing with a warbling screech that penetrated the very walls of our overhanging room. So long as I live it is indelibly imprinted on my mind.

Islam spread throughout the world after the conquests by the caliphs. In the tenth or eleventh century, an offshoot of the Ismaili sect took root in India under the leadership of Mohammed Agha Khan. Known as the Nizaris, they were reputed to partake immoderately of hashish, so that they were also called *hashshashin*. These hashshashin became well known for the carefully planned murder of enemies of their sect — hence the word assassin. These Ismailis developed a well-deserved reputation of being prepared to sacrifice themselves in the service and for the cause of Islam. They became the swords of the imams (Moslem priests) the world over.

In the early nineteenth century, the Ismaili imam received the official title of *Agha Khan* from the shah of Persia, harking back to the origins of the sect. This representative of Allah issued his assassin followers letters of introduction to the angel Gabriel in order to secure for them a good place in paradise.

This ploy has not been lost on modern Islam leaders — especially the late Ayatollah Khomeini of Iran and his successors — who routinely dispatch Ismaili assassins throughout the world, promising them a place in paradise. When you are a soldier of God Himself, guided by the hand of his holy imam, you are unlikely to be impressed by international decrees outlawing terrorism. Ismaili assassins are located throughout the world today, set to destroy target unbelievers upon a signal from their imams. The suicide car-bombing of the American compound in Lebanon or the killings of Israeli Olympic athletes are excellent examples of this activity. The danger is very real to anyone anywhere who publicly undermines fundamentalist beliefs and actions in the Moslem world.

Not all Moslems believe in self-sacrifice for their religion, of course, but a fundamental dictum of Islam dating back to the prophet Mohammed himself is that internally Islam is gentle and mild, while external enforcement upon others is by the sword: *Din El Islam Balseif.*

I cannot forget the Friday prayers at the mosques of Baghdad when mullahs (teachers) and imams incited the worshippers after the prayers to go out and demonstrate against the Jews and Zionism. Jewish deaths became routine; it was reminiscent of the tenth and twelfth centuries. I developed the understanding that my Moslem compatriots were helpless, unable to free themselves from their macabre traditions and from the rule of the little dictators who used and degraded them for so long.

When Adolf Hitler seized power in the early thirties while I was still in my teens, I became aware of a wider all-out war against the Jews. Thousands of German Jews fled Europe, and many settled in Palestine.

By then Iraqi newspapers were displaying headlines that clearly identified them with Jew-hating Arabs. Under the leadership of the mufti (Muslim lawyer) of Jerusalem, who was instrumental as early as 1929 in the massacre of Jews, Jew-hating became a religious doctrine, gaining momentum throughout the Middle East and the Islamic world.

One incident in Baghdad opened my eyes to the grim reality of our situation while I was still attending Alliance Israelite Universelle.

Our Moslem teacher for gymnastics and Arabic language, Mr. Abed El Rahim, fought hard to put our school on the Iraqi government official Boy Scout list. We were delighted when it happened, not knowing how reluctantly this placement came about. We purchased our uniforms and eagerly awaited the big Iraqi Boy Scout Jamboree.

Finally the day arrived, a beautiful summer day. We were told to come early in the morning to march through the streets of Baghdad with all the other schools. For some unexplained reason, possibly to keep us from public view, part of the parade was diverted from the street through which the main parade participants were marching. Somehow in the confusion, our troop joined the main line with all the pageantry, drums, and music. We were so proud to be Boy Scouts and part of the Iraqi nation. Unfortunately, such thoughts were short-lived. We were greeted with degrading insults and ugly remarks immediately upon being recognized as Jews. We were terrified of a group of Palestinian Arabs who shouted at us, "You are moths and must be exterminated!"

Our teacher intervened and encouraged us to disregard what the Palestinian Arabs were saying. He appealed to our Scout code of honor, held us together, and focused our attention on our lingering pride.

After the parade, all the schools gathered in a soccer field across from the royal palace. King Ghazi (the son of King Feisal, first king of Iraq) reviewed the final assemblage and made a short speech which made everyone happy. We accepted him and his words at face value, and in my childish frame of thinking, I respected the man, especially when he mixed with us and, here and there, chatted with a few. At that time, of course, I didn't know that his reign oversaw the worst massacre of the Assyrians in northern Iraq. This Christian sect claims direct descent from the ancient Assyrians whose capital, Nineveh, fell in 606 B.C.

Two years later, King Ghazi was killed in a car accident. Rumor had it that British Intelligence took him out because he was a Nazi collaborator. The elimination of King Ghazi came as no surprise to the Jews of Baghdad. They were well aware of British Intelligence efficiency in that part of the world. Mass-mourning processions in the streets of Baghdad were held despite the fact that the Hashemite Kingdom was imposed on the Iraqis by the British and was not to their liking.

The mourning processions were orchestrated by Nazis. Multitudes of people marched ten and twenty abreast, chanting lamentations and poetry about their dead king. It was a public spectacle, reminiscent of Ashuraa — with a major difference. The Jewish community identified itself with the grief of the nation. Although denied permission at first, Jews were later permitted to join the processional march.

The Iraqi rulers had no real idea what ruling was all about. Hate replaced rational thought. Hate begat hate, and the Iraqi Jewish community came to expect little of justice and freedom. Our twentieth-century lords and masters and most of their subjects were medieval in their outlook.

These throwbacks even beat drums and tin cans, and fired guns and rifles at the eclipsing moon. While the moon was in the shadow of earth, the people of the city relentlessly chanted. The chorus and the drums resonated throughout the city, commanding the wicked Leviathan to release the moon. Once the eclipse ended, everything would return to normal again. Many of my compatriots were strongly convinced that if it were not for the shooting of their rifles, and whatever, the Leviathan would not have released the moon. And this was the twentieth century.

You never forget the place where you were born and raised. For me that was Baghdad, beautiful, glorious Baghdad — of course, beauty is in the eye of the beholder. Among its many attractions, the Baghdad I knew could boast of a few bazaars.

There was Henouni, where every kind of food product grown in Iraq was available: wheat, barley (Iraq was a world exporter of barley), rice, string beans, red or white beets, and also fish, yoghurt, every kind of vegetable, and so forth. In the middle of the bazaar is a shrine to Sheik Isaac (a Jewish rabbi) who is buried there. It is visited by pilgrims as well as Jewish residents of Baghdad. On several occasions I paid homage to the rabbi, accompanying my mother.

Souk El Bazazin was a textile bazaar filled about eighty percent by Jewish textile merchants. All kinds of fabrics were sold there, imported from all over the world, especially England. Nearby stood dyeing factories famous for their fast single-color dyes, with ingredients dating back to the time of the caliphs. For centuries, this textile trade has been an integral part of Iraq's national character.

Shorja was (and probably still is) unique. Upon entering, starting from Rashid Street, next to the Jamea Morjan Mosque which is over a thousand years old, one immediately observed rows of spice stores, and was overwhelmed by the aroma of cloves, crushed lime, sour salt, cardamom, cinnamon, cumin, mint leaves, coffee, tea, pepper, mace, ginger, curry, turmeric (curcuma), myrrh, musk, and many others.

Next was a row of paper dealers who sold every kind of paper — for writing, school and office needs, and accounting. Further down the road were sellers of household china articles, crystals, and all kinds of glass.

Thereafter my youthful favorite: dealers in candies and sweets of all kinds. On nearby side streets, sweets and candies factories prepared orders for weddings, Brith Milas, engagements, and the Jewish holidays. Although the manufacturers were almost all Jews, the merchants were patronized by both Jews and Moslems. I used to love fetching sweets and candies for my uncle before Shabath in order to help myself on the way back to a *lukum* (a cubical patty made of jellied sugar and dusted with fine white flour) or *melabass* (almond with a caramelized sugar coating), or a *halva* or *helawa*, or even a *baklava*, all Middle Eastern delights dating back to before the Ottoman Empire.

After the candy stores were the fruit and vegetable merchants, selling oranges, numis (yellow-skinned sweet orange-like fruit), grapes, cantaloupes, watermelons, potatoes, and also dried fruits and vegetables.

Near the end of the street were shops selling Iraqi earthenware and hardware. At the very end of the mile-long bazaar were several coffee shops that were almost always filled with noisy shoppers. Some smoked hubbly-bubblys (water pipes); some sipped tiny cups of bitter black Arab coffee. This coffee normally is served in meager quantities, and the drinker is expected to pass the tiny cup back empty.

Several meat stores completed the milieu at the end of the road, which was punctuated by a police station at the very end.

Safafir was a copperware bazaar, and might well have been the noisiest bazaar in the world. The copper utensils—graceful Arab coffee pots, water containers, trays and teapots—were made on the premises in front of the passersby. They were fashioned and decorated mostly with hammers by a multitude of craftsmen, and because copper is hard and strong, the noise was deafening until dark, when the bazaar closed. Conversing while walking through the bazaar was next to impossible. I am certain that many of these artisans lost their hearing as result of this cacophony.

Down Rashid Street to the east of Safafir was a street ironically called Samowal, or Bank Street. It was the Wall Street of Baghdad, the location of foreign and Iraqi banks and businesses. (As I have already mentioned, Samowal was the Arabicsed name of a famous Jewish poet, Shmuel, who was a Jewish famous poet during the Ignorane [Jahelia] period for the Arabs.) I recently visited Cairo and noticed that despite the problems between Israel and Egypt, famous Jewish business names remained unaltered, although their owners have changed. For instance, "Sikurel" used to be owned by the father of the present first lady of Israel (Mrs. Herzog) and her sister, Mrs. Eban. (I knew Mrs. Herzog in the army because she served in the same unit I was in.) Shoshani, Aboudi (Iraqi Jewish name) Bahari is unchanged. The famous department store in Aswan, Ben Zion, remains unchanged as well. Maybe the Iraqis retained Samowal Street.

The late Israeli General Moshe Dayan wrote that in 1942 he hitched a ride to Baghdad where he stayed for one day. He was greatly disappointed at what he saw, or rather what he didn't see. He expected, as he put it, to see, if not the formidable palaces of the Caliph Harun El Rashid, at least the exciting bazaars of Damascus.

But even in a small village, you can see very little in just one day.

# CHAPTER THREE

# Spoiled Age Changes

With no ostentation or parties, as was the case with most of our community boys at that time, I was bar mitzvahed in a simple and tête-à-tête ceremony by my father. He taught me how to put on the tefillin every morning and to recite the morning prayers. He explained to me that I would be responsible for my deeds henceforth and that they must be good deeds — thus the appellation "bar mitzvah" (bat mitzvah for girls), meaning "son of good deeds." "You are now a man for a minian," he said. (A minian is a gathering of ten persons required to answer amen at a Kaddish "prayer to God.") He added: "I hope that someday you will be a pride to our people and remember that our religious performances are acts that keep our morals high during our lives and show us the way to understand the meaning of Good and Evil." His words reflected the importance of the bar mitzvah and how it makes us proud of our traditions and actions.

My thoughts began to take a new stride when I became aware of my Jewish faith. While Jewish boys become "sons of good deeds" at that age, more than 50 percent of the goyim followed different indoctrinations which had nothing to do with their religious beliefs, but which might classify them as the sons of bad deeds. They were learning how to hate Jews and how to harm us or even eliminate us. When I began to read Arabic newspapers, I hardly understood the doings of certain nations and the reasons for the bad deeds spreading throughout the world. I was unable to comprehend why people were against each other, nations against nations and most of them against Jews. Later I began to grasp the idea that Hitler's poison was pervading most of the world. I kept asking why this Hitler hated me — the young fellow from Baghdad, thousands of miles away from him — and for what? Was it only because, through no fault of mine, I was born a Jew? I could not figure out why the Moslems and the Arab world, with whom we were friendly, were supporting and rallying behind a man whom they hardly knew or understood. They were acting like sheep following the one that makes a lot of noise. It was obvious that Hitler was anti–Semitic and they, like us, were Semites. But, who would understand? Blind hatred feverishly ruled at that time; this was the topic in our community.

Growing up in Iraq was extremely hazardous and uncertain. None of us was sure of being alive the next day, month, or year. Danger lurked all around in spite of the relative calm in that part of the world: not realizing that a blinded corporal (with due respect to all the corporals in the world) would soon become the Führer of Germany. Then the sun over the whole world began to set into darkness. It was a new world to me, and I never returned to my old one. How would I know at that age how much of history is shaped by dark forces?

The youth of Iraq in the thirties were mostly pro–Nazi and anti–Jewish. In this new world, we did our best to perfect the Moslem dialect so that if we were confronted with aggression by Moslems on the streets, we could seem to be Moslems ourselves. This assimilation also served me well in my life away from Iraq.

There were many changes. We no longer had the innocent friendship we had once enjoyed with our Moslem neighbor of the same age; now he began to slap us in the face or hit us on the head when his Moslem friends were around to show off his boldness. We no longer had innocent visits to the neighbors, who used not to bother to have their women cover their faces in our presence. Now it was different since I had reached the age of thirteen.

A year or two before plunging into the realm of adulthood, I experienced a vision that indicated to me the forthcoming of a split world. I remember it vividly still: I abruptly woke up, as if a powerful ray of light was projected upon my face. In Baghdad, in the summer, we slept in the open on the flat roof of our houses. Lying there under the naked and clear night sky, I saw two bright, full moons, one of which was noiselessly and smoothly moving through the night sky while the other remained fixed as usual in its high place in the heavens. This was an occurrence that I interpreted as a cosmic sign that our world was being torn apart.

Puberty was not an easy state of mind and body. Incomprehensible developments throughout the world, especially in Germany, were taking place. Hitler became chancellor. The German Parliament was burnt. Hitler won a majority at the election and quit the League of Nations. Japan prepared to attack China.

My mind then could not digest the meaning of these events, but more and more we felt their repercussions in our lives. Hebrew, which we had always studied at school, gradually became a forbidden language, and one day it was ordered to be stopped altogether. Even our prayer books became the target for cover change because many had the Star of David printed on them. I was always fascinated by the star and wondered what threat it could present to the enemy of the Jews and the dark forces spreading throughout the world. I was told that it was forbidden even to draw it and if caught doing so, I would be punished. What a powerful combination of geometrical shapes! Still, I could not find any threat in it to anybody. To me it meant balance. No extremes.

It is said that when young David chose to fight Goliath, his slingshot was made of two strong strings or cords, each attached to a leather base in the form of a triangle. After David aimed and shot at Goliath, killing the fierce giant, he looked at his slingshot and discovered that the triangular bases were stuck to each other in the form of a star. He kissed it and proclaimed that this star would be henceforth his shield and emblem. Thinking of this, I realized why our enemies were always fearful of our star: It shows that the weak and small can conquer the oppressor.

As I said, the forces shaking Europe caused tremors in the Middle East, and the dark power pervaded Iraqi soil, giving rise to an anti–Zionist movement. All kinds of demonstrations were being organized, some with violent results. This was in spite of the fact that the wide population of Iraq did not really know what Zionism meant or even whose religion it was.

One such demonstration ended in the looting of Jewish stores and the death of one or two Jews. I listened to the mobs of Iraqis marching through the streets of Baghdad shouting slogans against the "watchmen." A man said that this was all against the watchmen and the Jews.

I could not understand what the watchmen had to do with the Jews. Then I realized that the word Zionism in Arabic is pronounced "Sahyonia," and the crowd had made the equivalent pronunciation, "paswania," which meant "watchmen." They made this noise because they were paid to make it, or because they wanted to loot stores, or perhaps because they were pursuing some bizarre fantasy — but most of them did not even know what their noise was all about.

It was time for the Jewish community of Iraq to rally against the anti–Zionists, anti–Semites and also anti–British. Most of the other youth became pro–Nazis, pro–German, and of course pro–Hitler.

Until that time, the Iraqi Jewish community did not really think much about Palestine or a Jewish state. Now we suddenly found ourselves driven to entertain such ideas as we realized that, should Hitler or the anti-Semitic Arabs win — and they were gaining strength at that time — the future would be bleak for us. We found that there was no alternative but to turn towards Palestine, the home of our ancestors, where we could either find refuge or, at least, perish together with Jews from all over the world.

In the meantime, in faraway places, things were happening fast. The civil war in Spain, which gave strength to the Fascist powers, allowed Mussolini to invade and conquer Ethiopia. Germany and Italy were testing their armaments on these battlefields for future use. I was seventeen, a storm was gathering, and I could hardly grasp the enormity of the situation.

The author (standing, far right) at the Alliance Israelite Universelle, College David Sassoon, in 1936 (author's collection).

Luckily, the Iraqi government was headed by Nouri El Said, an acquaintance of my father and fellow appreciator of Makam music. My father had the opportunity to appear with Om Kalthoum, famous for her songs throughout the Middle East and the Arab world and even among Europeans and all over the world. He sang in her presence, and she enjoyed his songs and appreciated the old Makam and Chalghi music. She sat by the musicians and savored every note. She agreed to be photographed with them, demonstrating solidarity between Jews and Moslems, at least in the realm of music, before any political poisoning took place.

My education in the Alliance Israelite Universelle in Baghdad continued without hindrance. I was so proud to walk to school through the narrow streets every morning and return in the afternoon carrying my heavy bunch of books in my hands, showing off to all around that I was a student. At one point, a few of the students refused to accept the heavy load of studies assigned to us and protested loudly to have it reduced. Our school principal, Mr. Laredo, gathered us in a class and lectured us on our need to survive, emphasizing the fact that a Jew needs many weapons to fight with — not real weapons, but the armor of intelligence. The protests ceased, and we continued with more enthusiasm.

Developments in my body unleashed excruciating feelings that began to overcome me, and at the slightest thought of the opposite sex my entire being was inundated with emotion. Seeing the shadowy form of a veiled female on the street, I focused all my imagination on her looks, trying to determine the shape of her body; then I would begin to dream of being alone with her, and more. In this exercise of the imagination, many a brother fell in love with the unidentifiable figure of his own sister. There were many fantasy romances without participation by either sex. It happened to a friend of mine and also to one of our neighbors. A male in my wife's family chased his sister when Jewish girls were forced to veil themselves on the streets. When she realized what was happening, she laughingly identified herself to her own brother, who was greatly embarrassed.

In spite of all that was happening around me, nature remained all-powerful. At the age of sixteen, my body's urges pushed aside everything else and ruled supreme in my thoughts. I always wound up with a dream of a beauty I saw only as a ghost. This was the emotion shared by all youths because of the segregation of sexes. Dire penalties, in some cases even murder, made love or loving or desiring the opposite sex very dangerous and also more powerful and exciting.

Reaching the age of 17 or 18 was both a blessing and a curse — a curse because of the turbulent times, and a blessing because I awakened to my faith and environment. I felt free and natural. Yet old emotions and behavior were starting to change, little by little. It became clear that things would not be the same any more. The happenings in Europe would soon affect us more. The natural beauty of the soul was being raped everywhere by Nazism. The people of the world who were, generally speaking, noble and good, were changing.

Luckily the beauty of the landscape remained the same. The Tigris continued to flow towards the south where Basra lies. Each year, when ice and snow melted in the north, the Tigris turned muddy and very rapid, overflowing parts of the city of Baghdad. Usually the government or the municipality mobilized people and resources to stop the flood. Unfortunately, nobody acted to stop the flow of Nazi propaganda into Iraq at that time.

Then came the period of growing into manhood in an Arab land. Our community was rather different from the others. It was unbecoming to be friendly with a girl of one's age unless one was under ten years old. Love was a very powerful sentiment which could be enjoyed only in marriage. The Moslems absolutely forbade one to look at a girl, not to mention shaking hands in greeting or, God forbid, kissing on the cheek. The Jewish community tried its best to accommodate the Moslems' feelings about this. We acted more liberally amongst ourselves only at our homes and gatherings on various occasions.

At that age, I fell in love with every second girl that I knew, and with the same fervor and emotion for most of them. My first real love happened at the age of 17. She was a distant relation to my mother and at the age of puberty. Her name is Dee. I can never forget when our eyes met and I became aware of our existence as opposite sexes. There was a special, invisible, silent, and, to everyone else, nonexistent liaison, diffusing in waves all around us. Thus began my love at the mere sight of her at that moment. I walked in a dream-like manner, tongue-tied in her presence. When I talked to her, my voice cracked. I suffered exquisitely when I caught sight of her walking through our school, which was used by most of the girls as a short cut from Laura Kedouri School for Girls. She appeared so poised and self-possessed. I don't know how, but I always sensed her affectionate tolerance for me. Her strict, old-fashioned upbringing and my own wild thinking imposed a distant behavior that made even touching hands impossible, no matter how fervently such touch was desired. Secretly, I managed to let her know my feelings towards her. On occasion, I visited at her house, and by intention or through fear of her mother and brothers, it became known that I had an eye on her; then all hell broke loose. All contact with her was forbidden. I was disconnected from the family until my departure from Iraq.

Gradually my thoughts started to take different shape. Understanding justice, equality, freedom, and also patriotism took me away from the paths I had learned in my surroundings, which were based on principles cleverly described in books but never actually applied as they should be. I was especially interested in movies depicting courtrooms, juries, the accused and defendants and their lawyers, bearers of the torch of justice. While such procedures became sheer mockery throughout the world, I was still a champion of American justice as I knew it from the movies.

I did not seriously think about Zionism and Palestine during this time until one day I learned that a friend of mine and his family had left for what they called the Holy Land, to start a new life there. I desired so badly to go to this land and feel free, but it was impossible, and the whole idea was forgotten. At that age, we were all full of dreams and good deeds.

One year later another friend and classmate, Herbert Somekh, left for the United States. On the day he departed after school, Herbert emotionally declared, "As soon as I am there and settled, I will make arrangements that you emigrate to the U.S., too." I became determined to leave Iraq for either Palestine or the United States. But how? Since 1935, Jews had been forbidden to travel to Palestine.

In 1936, there were disturbances in Baghdad and in Basra during which about ten Jews were killed. Apparently this was only the beginning, and more deaths would follow. I became restless and disturbed, realizing that I had nowhere to go and feeling like a caged animal. The fate of our Jewish neighbors in Syria was not any better because there, too, Nazi offices were established and anti–Semitic activities were felt more and more.

The peaceful land of 1,001 Nights, Ali Baba and the 40 Thieves, the Thief of Baghdad, and the flying carpet became the land of 1,001 Crimes, Hitler and the 40 Thousand Executioners of Jews, the Thieves of Law and Order, and the flying bombs. The same thing was happening in other Arab countries as well.

I turned 18 years old and continued living and schooling as usual. I was extremely happy when a trip out of Baghdad was announced by our school. For the first time in my life I was leaving Baghdad, the city, to travel north. Baghdad then was the whole world for me.

For a few nights before the trip I could not sleep; I lay awake fantasizing about the coming event. Then at last came the day we left the city, on a train pulling its wagons through flatlands where nothing existed except the sky and land. It was a narrow-tracked train, originally built by the British after World War I. We continued along; at night we fell asleep, exhausted and also lulled by the rocking train movement.

The sky of Baghdad is changeable. It can be clear blue, grey, or dark, and on many occasions red because of a sand storm bringing tons of dust from the desert nearby to cover the city. When I woke up on the train and looked up at the sky, I was disappointed because I saw dark clouds, and I thought the clouds would ruin our trip. I then realized that these were not clouds, but very high grey mountains in neighboring Persia (Iran). The picture printed in the back of my mind since that day still inspires a great reverential wonder at Mother Nature's majesty. The peaks, not human-made but the work of nature in all its raw splendor, seemed to be telling the whole world: "You do your things but I will remain eternal and unaffected by you. Go ahead, have your fun, your injustices, your good or bad deeds. Soon you will perish and be forgotten, but I will stay here longer, perhaps forever, undisturbed." That serene scene captivated my senses for a long time.

I lived near the Tigris, one of the two rivers going through Iraq, and I still remember how the sun, the same sun which shines over all our world, was reflected like silvery stars on the ripples of the breeze-stricken waters running eternally through the river's banks. I remember, too, how that sun passed overhead, making its daily rounds, and then disappeared in the evenings behind the multitude of date palm trees, making them look like blazing red fireworks in the sky. When the moon was full at night, the same sun sent out its silvery rays over the same waters. The palm trees made the scene look like a picture of paradise at night.

Summer nights in Baghdad are spent in the open on the flat roofs of the houses. It is cool and comfortable at night in the open air. I still recall the sublime tranquility which used to overtake my senses as I lay on my bed facing the millions of stars overhead. Some moved slowly, others were fixed, and still others shot themselves down to earth into oblivion.

On these summer nights, especially when there was a full moon, people used to organize small parties riding a *balem* (small boat) and drift with the current on the Tigris towards a small island in the east of Baghdad, which usually appears at the turn of the river in summer. This island is usually sown with cucumbers and taaruzi (a vegetable of the same family) because they thrive on plenty of water. Along in the boat, "bunny" fish are brought along or bought conveniently at the small island, and then cooked on the spot with all kinds of curries, paprika, and other spices to make them tasty. This is called Samek Mazgoof. The evening becomes a regale when music is added, and sometimes expert singers join to render the party unforgettably superb. Many of us still remember such feasts with Samek Mazgoof, specially prepared, which cannot be compared with any other gourmet fish in the best restaurants of the world. The scenery, the setting, the Middle Eastern music and singing, and the river with its environment cannot be duplicated. Such peaceful times in the land of the two rivers are both unforgettable and gone.

My entire life in Baghdad seemed uneventful. Still, I reached manhood in sobriety and in apprehension of my surroundings. Perhaps I was thinking ahead of my compatriots and looking forward, as a Jew is raised to do, to a better world wherever it might be, yearning to have a life of liberty, equality, and fraternity — those three wonderful words we learned at school that were used during the French Revolution. The theme of the Marseillaise reverberated always in my head, repeating its glorious words urging the people to defend the soil of their land against the brutal enemy who comes to slaughter their sons and daughters. Alas! Our enemy was within and we were helpless. However, life went on.

We competed in soccer, basketball, and other sports. Our school always played against the Shamash School and, in my recollection, always won. For that, we had a one-day holiday the day after the game. Our soccer players were in demand, and some of them were even loaned to Moslem schools to play for them. A classmate of mine became such a wanted player and was loaned to a Moslem school. His name was Latif Dabby, but a condition was made that, being a Jew, he would be called Abdul Latif in order to hide his religion.

It was 1936 when I received the certificate for Primary Schooling in Arabic and 1937 when I received my certificate from the French Consulate in Baghdad after I passed the test. In early 1939, I was given the certificate of the Alliance Israelite Universelle College Albert D. Sassoon–Baghdad for my studies from 1937 till 1939. Later, I continued in Beirut at the Pigier School of

Paris, France (Beirut Branch), my studies being in commerce, economics, administration, and some commercial law, till February 1941.

In 1938, my mother died. I was 18 years old and my two younger brothers — Mordechai (Nazim) and Naim — were younger by five and six years, respectively. We were left alone with my father, who was incapable of taking care of us as our mother had. I thought that my world was tumbling down over my head. I screamed; my little brothers cried; but all to no avail. I learned that this is the way of life and everyone will go through this sometime.

There is a saying in Arabic: The dead are the forerunners and we are the followers. With the death of my mother, my entire thinking and plans changed. Instead of continuing my education in Baghdad to be qualified for a respectable position, I decided that world events — and consequently events in Iraq — were forcing me to seek places where I could be free and also contribute to the spread of freedom throughout the world.

My father entertained the idea of marrying someone who would take care of my younger brothers, especially the youngest. (This marriage would happen after I left Iraq.) Of course, none of us liked the idea, and my desire to go somewhere else became stronger every day.

First I wished to go to Palestine, but it was forbidden by law for a Jew to leave Iraq and go to Palestine. On the other hand, I could get a passport to go to Lebanon as a student, with a guarantee put up by my father that I would come back when I finished my studies there.

(The bond put up by my father was somewhat overlooked after the failed coup d'état by the Nazi premier Rashid Ali El Keilani in 1941, but interest revived again in 1947-1948 at the establishment of the state of Israel. Then I heard personally on the Iraqi Broadcasting Station of my condemnation to be hanged if I did not return within a week. The same was also announced regarding many other Iraqi Jews who left the country like myself, including my brother Mordechai, who was by then with the Israel Defense Forces "Haganah." Many heeded the warning and returned to endure more persecutions later in their country of Iraq.)

I discovered that, before my mother died, she had been saving money for me to pay for my *badel* (a tax substitute for military service). Army service was mandatory for all Iraqis reaching the age of 18, unless one paid the badel. It was quite a sum of money in those days (over ten dinars), and was enough for more than one scholarship year abroad in Lebanon paying tuition, food, and books. I did not think too much, and my decision was made quickly. Instead of paying the money to the Iraqi government, I would use it for my own benefit.

Hitler had invaded Austria and then Czechoslovakia; Britain declared war on Germany; and now my family rose up in arms against me, telling me it was crazy to travel alone to another country at that time. All their endeavors to stop me were in vain. I had made up my mind. I got my passport and prepared myself for my first journey into the unknown, the unsecured future of an 18-year-old youth who was determined to decipher the Rosetta Stone of his life. After that all my friends and relatives would be cut off from my life like bus drivers, shopkeepers and policemen whom one meets and then tends to forget.

My first trip abroad started with buying a ticket from the well-known bus line in the Middle East — Neron — which ran the service from Baghdad to Damascus and back for many years. After packing a few personal belongings in one bag, I went to say my goodbyes to everyone. Their reactions, especially those of my relatives, were mixed. Some thought it was a good idea; others were furious; and a few even shed a tear or two, regretting my departure and, knowing my feelings, convinced that I would never return to Baghdad.

It was December 1939, and behind me were events which had plunged the whole world into bloody war. Poland was attacked by Germany in September. England mobilized, and there was no hope of averting war with Germany.

The bus was full, and we started our journey in the afternoon in order to save on daylight and to avoid the heat of the sun when crossing the vast barren wilderness of the desert between Baghdad and Damascus. In spite of the winter season, temperatures during the day could go up to almost 100 degrees and then drop down to 32 or less during the night.

The driver and his assistant were excellent navigators. They drove along the tracks of other vehicles or transports using the same road. There were no paved roads or highways in the desert at that time. If they drove off the track, the trick was to go in circles — small circles first, then wider and wider ones until the tracks were located. Otherwise, we would have been lost under the dark dome of the night sky, roaming aimlessly upon the flat surface of the deserts. We did lose our tracks, but located them after a short while.

At sunset the silhouette of the outskirts of Baghdad faded into the distant horizon. That night I was unable to sleep, and my thoughts were streaking through my head like shooting stars. I sank into my seat, thinking about world events and what would become of our future. Four months had passed since England had declared war on Germany, and nothing was happening. Perhaps the whole world was astonished that the two great powers, England and France, had done nothing since Hitler's crashing onslaught upon Poland. What really disturbed everybody was that the Russians occupied part of Poland in agreement with Germany in spite of the antagonism between the two countries. Could it be that Russia was no better than Germany after all? While I puzzled over what was what and who was against who, a bump on the road jolted me back to my real self on the bus to Damascus.

At dawn I admired the big red ball rising slowly in the East as if to tell everyone: "Hey! Don't worry! I am here and everything will be all right." I realized that it would be there to light up my life for a long time to come.

We crossed more and more stretches through the wilderness. After leaving Ramedi in the evening, we were about to reach Abou Shamat just before nearing Damascus. Exhausted, we started to pass some hills and then what looked to me like mountains, actually ridges, which gave me the impression that Damascus was a well-protected ancient city with narrow streets, bazaars, alleys, mosques, and Roman remains, lying in the center of a wide and fertile plain.

The story of Damascus suggests it was a beauty attacked by a beast. It is said that the existing dome that crowns the Taj Mahal in India owes its shape to Damascus, and to one of the most blood-soaked leaders in history before Hitler. Tamerlane, the 14th century Mongol responsible for hundreds of thousands of deaths, set fire to Damascus and sacked the Great Mosque. Thirty thousand women, children, priests, and old men who had sought refuge inside were put to death. Tamerlane then had the unique bulging dome of the mosque copied for his own magnificent tomb. Shah Jahan later built the Taj Mahal with a glittering white dome derived directly from the Great Mosque of Damascus that his ancestors had looted 250 years before.

## CHAPTER 4

# Beirut: The Zurich
# of the Middle East

I spent three nights as guest of a Syrian Moslem architect who was with me on the bus from Baghdad and who insisted that I stay at his family house in Damascus before I left for Beirut. They treated me with generosity in the best sheikly way (head of an arab tribe tradition), and they replenished me with snacks and other necessities for the road in my trip to Beirut. They knew perfectly well that I was a Jew on my way to Beirut to study.

In the next part of my trip, our bus crossed the Bekaa Valley, which lay between Damascus and Beirut. Climbing the Lebanon mountain, I could see the cedar trees all over extending to great distances beyond. Dense woods covered the slopes all around and the snow, a few inches deep, looked like white cotton. We continued climbing to the top to a place called Arz, where the snow was heavy and thick. When we reached the other side of the mountain, we began our steady descent until the Mediterranean sea came into view.

I was seeing snow and sea for the first time in my life. I became overwhelmed admiring the wonders of nature. The sky looked like a cupola and the sea waters seemed to be falling into the abyss beyond the horizon. Further down, I could see the Beirut harbor, and I was interested to see if the ships were small, as they seemed to be from up where we were — as small as ours on the river Tigris. When we approached the harbor, they looked like huge floating castles in comparison to our 20 × 100-foot boats.

We alighted from our bus with our luggage and, as was our custom back in Baghdad, I called a horse-driven coach and asked the cabbie to take me to the address of a classmate in the old country. That friend's hello to me was more than I expected. He had already secured a room for me for the duration.

Beirut on the cusp of the 1940s was not like Beirut in the eighties. The Levant ruled by the French seemed to me like Europe. It was a bit of heaven for people who were running away from previous rulers. The date was December 14, 1939, the beginning of my residence away from home in a foreign land and the beginning of my studies there. It was a new world. The people were

The author (far left) with French Officers in Beirut before the fall of France in World War II (author's collection).

nicely dressed in European styles, unlike the drab-looking gowns worn by the men and the "Abaya" black cloak by the women back in Baghdad.

There were many Frenchmen and foreigners, and the French language was spoken by almost everyone. My group in Beirut was made up of an engineering student at the Jesuits, an economic student at the University of Beirut who was killed by Arabs later in Baghdad, and, of course, my friend and classmate who was at the same school as me. They all were ex–Alliance school graduates from Baghdad.

Thousands of scholars and individuals owe much to the American University, which has produced top-quality students in spite of what has happened in Lebanon. Even when it used to be called American College of Beirut, it was the most renowned institution of its kind in the Middle East. Even in 1900 or probably before that date, all the medical practitioners scattered up and down the Middle East graduated from this institution.

My studying in the Pigier School was French-oriented, which I picked in accordance with my French Alliance School Israelite studies. The Jewish community in Beirut was very hospitable and accommodating. They treated most of us like family, and we did not really feel like strangers amongst them. We were invited to their homes often and shared their Simches "joys" (weddings, brits, or bar mitzvahs). At these parties they usually sang the Tiqwah (Jewish national anthem) fervently and standing, as if they felt, even then, that they needed protection in spite of the prevailing favorable atmosphere.

The Jewish community in Beirut was concentrated in Wadi Abu Jamil and mostly spoke French and Arabic. There were those who were ardent Zionists and talked always of immigrating to Palestine, but it was rather doubtful at that time because the rapport with the other ethnic groups in Lebanon was proper and normal. In contrast, today, only very few Jews are left in Beirut, and they are persecuted by the Shiite Moslems; those in Damascus and Aleppo Syria are under siege, pursued and harassed by the authorities.

The "Zurich of the Middle East" deserved the name in my day. Many rich and famous people from many countries, especially from the Middle East, visited Beirut at least once a year, and many had a second residence there. The inhabitants of Lebanon are essentially Maronite Catholics, Druze, and Shiite Moslems, who welcomed those rich and famous and also prospered by them. The Druze are a splinter sect of Islam who sought refuge from persecution in the Valley of Lebanon mountain ranges. They later controlled Lebanon and brought prosperity, which attracted others to the area. Later, the Maronite Christians rose because of conflicts amongst the Druze themselves, became prominent in Druze areas, and prospered under French protection.

In the eighties, Beirut became like Dante's capital instead of being the Zurich of the Middle East. Had I been told fifty years ago that the worst terrorism would spring out from Beirut and Damascus, I would never have believed it. I could have anticipated disagreements and smelled skirmishes, but not on such a large and deadly scale of destruction and killing as happened in the eighties, with deadly car bombs exploding against the various factions, and terrorists from the outside using Lebanon as a springboard for attacks against Israel and other countries.

When Beirut was still in its glory, the news and rumors about the Jews of Europe were very discouraging, especially what we heard from those who came under the yoke of Hitler's Germany. It frightened us, but no one would believe the rumors were true.

One day I discussed these rumors with an Armenian classmate and friend of mine. I did not know much about the fate of Armenians in Turkey during World War I. When I asked him if the disturbing news about the Jews in Germany's hands could be true, his face turned red, and he answered me agitatedly that his parents did not believe the massacre of Armenians was forthcoming in Turkey until they discovered that their entire family was wiped out. Over one million Armenians were slaughtered there. He looked straight into my eyes and said: "My friend! You better believe it before it is too late! This is what they call nowadays 'modern savagery.'" I became very disturbed at hearing the stories about the extermination of his people, but I kidded myself that the Germans were "an educated and civilized people" who would not commit atrocities the way those who were still distant from civilization did.

My conversation with my Armenian friend changed my whole way of thinking. On occasion I asked myself whether life was worth living. What's the use of living if such atrocities can happen? Is life worthwhile? I answered myself on this last question in the affirmative: Yes, it is worth living to the last minute of one's natural life and, in the meantime, one could do something about the evil. But what? What can I personally do to help? Well, nothing much, I thought.

This pattern of thinking kept nagging at me until I personally was convinced that the danger was serious and we Jews could be next. I brooded about all this for many days, probably months; but again the shadow of doubt crept into my mind, and again I believed that the news from Europe was exaggerated.

In the meantime, the war was being carried out at sea. The Germans seized Norway. France and Britain had been on hold while the world wondered. It was almost a year that the "super two" remained in France. In Egypt, there was little notice amongst the population, except for the Jews, and life continued normally as if nothing had happened.

An Iraqi Jewish student friend surprised us one day when he showed up at our congregating place, a cafeteria in Beirut, wearing the French army uniform. He explained that the situation was so bad that he was drafted because he carried, in addition to his Iraqi passport, a French passport. His mother was French.

In 1940, a rapid series of catastrophic events was taking place in Europe during the months of April, May and June. Winston Churchill called it "the end of the beginning." His speech was very encouraging insofar as holding on to whatever was left. The British were fighting the Germans alongside with the French on French soil. In a matter of one week, the front in France crumbled. Within two more weeks, the French army collapsed and the British were hurled, or rather they pushed themselves, into the sea. Six weeks later, they were left alone against triumphant Germany, and all Europe became open to Hitler's power.

At the moment the fall of Paris was announced on the radio, my friends and two French officer friends of ours were all at a dining club. The music stopped, and the sad announcement was made. We turned to another radio set, as if the first one might be lying, but the same news was coming from all the stations. Both officers slumped into their seats; one started crying like a baby, and the other joined in for a little while. When I approached them saying that it was not all over, the reaction of the first was swift and definite: "My friend, you don't know the Germans!" He added that all his friends, family, and neighbors back in France now were in real danger. He could not predict when this would all be over, and if he stayed alive, whether he would be able to see them all again. My thoughts turned to enormous concern for our people. If this French Christian person was so worried about his family and friends, I thought, then the Jews must be in greater danger than we ever thought before.

The following day we noticed that the Moslem Arab population in Beirut was jubilant at the news. They did not hide their feelings, but there was no aggressive attitude towards the Jews as yet. The Druze were rather different, as were the Maronite Christians and others of the Christian faith, except for a few who wrongly believed that there was no danger from the Germans if they won the war.

The Iraqi Jewish oldtimers considered our being away from home as folly in those days. Of course, every family was concerned about their children in times like those when the forces of righteousness, as we Jews perceived them, were on the run and the dictators were winning. The naked truth was that most of the free world was half-blind, and when they did see what was happening they were only half-ready. We students were not aware of the consequences of what was going on. As usual, most of us were prepared to go home for the summer vacation, though our plans for the next year were rather vague. The Arab population in the Middle East became rather bold and showed their anti–Western feelings publicly. The Western democracies, fearing for the worse, tried to appease them, especially in Palestine, and never brought up the dangers to Jews in the Middle East and Europe, nor the dangers to other sects living amongst them.

When I returned to Baghdad in June for the summer vacation, I discovered that anti–Semitism had become stronger and more open. I went back to Beirut in the belief that, in spite of what happened to France, anti–Semitism there was less felt than in Baghdad, and so thought most of my student friends who came back as well. My relatives and friends in Baghdad insisted that I was wrong and that Lebanon would soon be under Nazi administration through Vichy, which would make it worse than Iraq. The Vichy government after the fall of France started to give in to Nazi Germany after the Armistice. German agents who had been interned were released, and many more arrived; with lots of funds, they proceeded to arouse anti–British and anti–Zionist feelings among the Arab peoples of Lebanon.

My second year at school in Beirut was the last of my studies. I had to make a choice whether to return to Baghdad or stay in Beirut. I decided to stay. In order to do that I had to go to the Sûreté Générale (State Security Department). I presented my passport with my application for extension to the policeman at the desk and then waited a long time. Uncertainty and fear were creeping into my mind, and I was afraid that my request would be refused or worse. Vichy personnel were in charge now, and soldiers from the French army occupied most of the posts in the Sûreté Générale. Other Iraqi students had been refused extensions. I began to think of ways to join the free French or the British army in Palestine. I was also eager to find a way to join the underground, if any, should I be refused an extension or ordered back to Iraq.

A policeman woke me up from my planning dreams and asked if I was Mr. Horesh. I answered in the affirmative. He motioned to me to follow him.

I was tense and nervous and was almost sure that I would be taken straight to the bus line to be sent back to Baghdad. German Nazi officers or their representatives were already there, probably knew that I was Jewish, and would send me to where I came from. The short walk seemed to last forever, and I began to sweat. I was ushered into a room, and a young French officer came towards me. He was shorter than myself, but he looked like a Middle Eastern person. I felt a little better because I believed that he would understand me and perhaps help me.

When we were alone in the room he looked at me and asked in perfect French, "Are you a real Horesh?" I did not know what to answer. I thought perhaps it would be better to deny it in order to save my skin because Horesh is a 100 percent Hebrew name, but my pride in my family name and my religion prevailed and I answered, "Surely I am a Horesh and my ancestors are also Horeshes for a long time." I noticed a little smile on the side of his face, and he continued to question me rather cautiously as if to protect his interests, too. "Where are you from? Baghdad or Basra?" Surely, I thought, he knows about the branches of the family because we do have a branch in Basra. I wondered if he already knew about my plan to fight from a conversation I had had with someone from Palestine many days before. I said I was from Baghdad.

Surprisingly, he smiled broadly with some noticeable relief on his face, as if he were the applicant and not me. He stood up and asked, "Do you know Kelly Horesh?"

I nodded my head in the affirmative because I had met Kelly back in Baghdad while on vacation. His wife had escaped Paris before the Germans captured it. My mind flashed quickly back to our meeting. I remembered that the father left Basra for France before I was born. Could this French inspector be one of my father's cousins from France?

Before I could finish my thoughts, he stood up and extended his arms to greet me warmly, saying that he was a Horesh, too. I did not know what to say, whether to cry or be happy meeting a lost kinsman in a time when being a Jew was becoming a real problem. After we made our acquaintance and discussed where we fit among the various relatives, I understood that a brother of his had been taken prisoner back in France and was at that time in a concentration camp, though we would know little of that bad news until after the war. He was listed as missing in action and most probably perished with the rest of the six million Jews in Europe.

I kept our encounter strictly between ourselves, and we promised to meet again. It seemed that no one knew that this Horesh (who would later die in Brazil) was Jewish when he occupied an inspector's position in the regime of Vichy, France.

The Iraqi Jewish students in Beirut in 1941 managed very well, and even latecomers stayed till the end. As soon as classes ended in that year most of the students obviously preferred to leave for home rather than stay in Beirut under Vichy. However, I chose to stay to join whatever war efforts were available to give my share in fighting the forces of darkness.

# CHAPTER 5

# World War II —
# Unsuspecting Spy

It is a known fact among the world intelligence communities that a good spy is one who is unaware he is spying for a secret controller. The controller can be a close friend, an employer, a neighbor and so on, planted there some time ago for this purpose. The knowingly spying person must always be aware there are borders to cross and official eyes to satisfy; he knows that with each move the odds of his being watched and detained (or, as it is called in intelligence terms, "burnt") could be multiplied. He usually has no name or country of his own nor a home address to receive his own mail while operating. In contrast, the unknowingly spying person acts naturally and fears nothing because he is himself, has a country and a home with an address and relatives. His life is quite normal — except that, without knowing it, he is spying for his secret control.

At the time I did not know that one had to take certain precautions to protect oneself. I did not bother to find out, because at the beginning I was unaware that a certain acquaintance called Albert Hakim would use me as a spy. It struck me first that his requests were like a small child's game of hide-and-seek. I was not a professional, but I had some idea of the purpose, which seemed irrelevant, and I accepted his requests. Therefore, I became, as I found out later, an unknowing spy for him.

While strolling with Mr. Hakim along the seashore of Beirut one day, I noticed that he was memorizing the French army vehicles, their marks and numbers. He was also taking note of the people entering and exiting the Hotel Normandy, which was used as general headquarters for the Vichy French forces in Syria and Lebanon. Among the people at the hotel, along with the high-ranking French and Nazi officers, were civilians and Arab notables.

After a few days, he asked me if I could do this sort of observing for him. He explained that he needed the information in order to compete with other suppliers of food and goods to the French soldiers at camps throughout Syria and Lebanon. He said he did not want the competition to take over other camps not known to his firm.

At the start, I believed his story, and I fiddled with the idea that some-day I would be able to join his firm or work in the supply business. Whether by accident or by design, someone I knew very well assured me that he was Jewish and a Zionist, and had business in Palestine where his main office was. This information calmed me a little, but also sparked a light in my mind that maybe Mr. Hakim could be a spy. I did for him what he wanted, and even better.

There were strong rumors that forces from Palestine were about to invade Syria and Lebanon. A great part of the inhabitants of Beirut left for the moun-tains nearby where it was safer. Every year a lot of them spent the summer up there in Aley, Bhamdoon, and Dhoor El Shweir, but this year their number was increased.

I made it a habit to stroll along the seashore across from the Hotel Nor-mandy once or twice a day and slow down just in front of the hotel entrance. Acting casual, I would memorize and sometimes even write down everything and everyone military entering or coming out from there, just as Mr. Hakim did. Then I had an idea: Instead of memorizing, I brought my camera and started boldly clicking my camera, without realizing that what I was doing was dangerous. I took photographs of everything that approached the hotel, including, as I was requested to do by Mr. Hakim, the building of the hotel from various angles and sides until the whole structure was photographed.

One day as I was doing my work at the hotel, I was approached by one of the sentinels posted there, with threats in his eyes. He asked me what my business was in being there all the time. Luckily I was without the camera, and I pretended that I did not understand his question. I showed him where I lived, which was nearby, and with gestures and intentionally broken French I tried to explain to him that I usually strolled every day along there and near where I lived, which was true. He seemed to accept my explanation and let me go, with remarks to the effect that I should not stay long where I was stand-ing and I should choose another spot.

Shortly afterwards, it seemed Mr. Hakim had all the information he needed, and I ceased to operate on that target. I told Mr. Hakim that I was broke and needed money, and he introduced me to a restaurant owner in a French military camp, and I got a job there as a waiter. The owner of the restaurant in the camp was a landsman, an Iraqi Jew married to a Lebanese Jewish girl and living in Beirut for some time. Mr. Hakim probably had two purposes in mind: one, that I earn some cash on my own, and two, that I could watch all happenings in the camp itself.

The military situation became serious, and British troops were moving in from all directions towards Syria and Lebanon. We began to hear air raids by the Royal Air Force. We did not know that activities had also started in

Iraq after Rashid Ali, the pro–Hitler leader of the coup against the British there, requested the help of the Germans. An Australian division was ordered to Palestine after arriving to advance into Syria and Lebanon because the German air force was already established there and by the end of May it was hoped that the British forces would enter Baghdad.

The operations began simultaneously against Beirut, Damascus, and Rayak Airfield in the Bekaa Valley. In June the advance began, and while the French started to resist the British, aircraft sorties over Beirut and other targets increased. We were becoming used to such attacks, which were mostly concentrated on the harbor of Beirut, especially at night. One night after we went down to the basement of the six-floor building that was used as a shelter, I became aware that there were planes overhead instead of by the harbor. One particular noise made me jump up, and everybody else jumped up with me as if they realized, too, that a bomb was coming down on us. I yelled to everybody to get down on the floor in the four corners of the basement to minimize the hit of the bomb. It was coming down over the building, with the hissing noise becoming louder every second. At last we heard an explosion, but nothing happened to the building. Soon I realized that the bomb was intended for the Normandy Hotel where the Vichy French headquarters were — a fact I had helped Mr. Hakim establish. Luckily the bomb fell in soft ground around our building, but other bombs damaged the hotel and its surroundings. That was my first experience under fire from our friends in whom our hope for the future was entrusted.

The next morning I watched as a British bomber on its way to its target — probably Rayak Airfield in the Bekaa Valley — was intercepted over Beirut by Vichy French planes while R.A.F. fighters were escorting it. It was a dog fight that we all witnessed for two or three minutes until they all disappeared in the east. The sounds of the guns blasting between the fighter planes was music to our ears.

Beirut became empty and only a few people stayed, including myself. I went to live with a friend, an Iraqi Jewish student across from the American University of Beirut, where I believed it would be safer.

We had a somewhat pleasant time together. He shared with me the little he had left for everyday sustenance and even helped with cash, when necessary, in accordance with the customs of his Kurdish Jewish community, and I am still very grateful to him.

A few days later, an armistice was signed. Syria and Lebanon passed into Allied hands. The facts became known later that Jewish fighters also participated with the advancing British troops.

Soon after the occupation of Lebanon by the Allied forces, I called on the British Consulate and offered to enlist but was politely refused because although a score of countries were listed on my Iraqi passport, Palestine was not among them. Visas were issued only for countries listed on the passport — these were the international regulations at that time — and so the British consulate could not issue me a visa to travel to Palestine, the only place where I could enlist.

After they reviewed my application and qualifications, I was offered employment attached to the British army in Lebanon working as a clerk-interpreter because of my knowledge of four languages. I did not hesitate to accept, and so I started my first job as interpreter with Australian divisional headquarters stationed in Aley. It was summertime, and the town was crowded with people from Beirut who had stayed after the end of hostilities. I was billeted in a camp nearby. In the evenings I visited my old friends who were there, too, and was told about the fall of Baghdad and the pogroms against my Jewish landsmen and family by the Arab population before the entry of the British troops into the capital.

Later, I received news that my brother, my father, and my father's new wife had fled to our best long-time neighbors. Reluctantly, after threatening to kill my folks with a gun, my childhood Moslem friend and neighbor took them in after his mother intervened, and they were saved from sure death. Our home was looted in an Arab Razia traditional style. Nothing was left. Thank God no one was hurt; in other Jewish quarters there were killings, rapes, and other unspeakable atrocities, such as slaying infants and babies and carrying their severed heads and limbs through the streets of Baghdad with thousands of demonstrating crowds. I also learned that two of my former classmates had been butchered.

Armed Arab Hitler scouts were roaming the streets. The Jewish population of Baghdad did not realize then that the British forces were actually on the run on all fronts except in the Middle East, where they were determined to make a stand and eventually score a victory with the meager forces they could use there.

What disturbed me most to learn was that other sects joined in the beating, killing, and looting of Jews in Baghdad. The police, who were supposed to protect them, fired at Jewish homes and houses instead of at the pillaging, murdering crowds. The men who were supposed to keep law and order also took part in the traditional Arab Razia. The advance of Rommel's armies in the western desert in Egypt was brought to a standstill for nearly five months. I was working then for the British Army in Baalbek. Other Jewish Iraqi young men also joined forces in Palestine before the Jewish Brigade was formed, including my brother Mordechai, who falsified his age and clandestinely immigrated from Baghdad (unbeknownst to me) to serve with the British Army.

I was assigned to the Royal Engineers of the district commander's headquarters, with an objective to build a line of defense to stop the Germans if Egypt and Palestine were overrun and overtaken by the German Army.

The greater part of the occupation involved Baalbek and the surrounding Shiite Moslem and an unorthodox sect of Islam called the Metawallis, which has a reputation for fanaticism. Only one Jewish family lived in town. The Christians were continuously threatened with eviction and seizure of their properties, just like the Jews used to cope or grapple with Moslems back in Baghdad. I thanked God I was with the British Army and there only for a short while.

During the first month after my arrival in Baalbek, a group of Arabs entered our headquarters and asked to see the commanding officer. When I asked them why they wanted to see the commander, they pointed at one of them in the group and explained that he was a public figure here in Baalbek and wished to obtain a building contract in the construction in which the British Army was engaged in the district. I figured that the request was more political than professional so I asked them to sit and wait a few minutes while I communicated their request to the commanding officer.

An interview was granted and, for the sake of avoiding trouble amongst the Arab workers, the commanding officer, Col. Edwards, promised to give a reply within a few days. In the meantime, he requested that I find out who the public figure was exactly. I was elated at being given an investigative task for our unit; and also frightened by the fact that I would be discovered as a Jew asking questions about someone who was well placed in the community of Baalbek. How would I proceed to furnish our commander with precise information so that he might act? Well, I said to myself, "Follow your instinct!"— a phrase that we Israeli Jews were well familiar with back home. Every resource in me had an immediate use. Because the target was feared and venerated in Baalbek, the best plan for me was to talk with others about his exploits. It took me a short time to realize that the public figure was Public Enemy Number One. He was the real boss in town and nobody dared oppose his acts. His hands were stained with the blood of tens of known murders. Once, in revenge, he extracted the heart of his victim, broiled it and ate it. This report was communicated to my officer, who was aware of Arab customs. His main objective was to put up the defense line as quickly as possible. Should the commanding officer refuse the public figure a contract, he knew that he would have labor trouble in his district, maybe worse. Although he realized that construction work would suffer and delays would ensue, he decided that the public figure be given work in some unimportant area and be paid as other professionals working in his district. After communicating this decision to the public figure, I became well-known in town. Because he believed that I was instrumental in obtaining the work for him, I was also well-protected. I realized that should the British Army have turned him down, I would have been in danger because he would have suspected me. However, since his request was granted, I was treated like a king in town.

This reminded me of a scene back in Baghdad when I was in my teens. One evening, I was returning home and at the alley leading to our house I noticed a horse-driven coach with a policeman beside it talking to someone who was lying on the floor of the coach with blood and stab wounds all over his body. I heard the policeman asking him who did it and he faintly mentioned Mousa Ibn Abu Tabra's people. Mousa was a feared criminal in Baghdad and considered Public Enemy Number One. One day he was assassinated and it seemed that the person in the coach was either the assassin himself or instrumental in Mousa's death. He was eventually executed in revenge for his deed. And so the circle goes on forever all over the Arab world.

Captain Colin Smith of Gloucester, England, of the Royal Engineers, became my officer in charge. We worked together in the field for most of my duration in Baalbek, especially taking care of our Arab Public Enemy Number One. Captain Smith dedicated a photo of himself to me with these words: "Thanks for your help in the past and hope you have good fortune in the future." I was delighted because for the first time in my life someone appreciated my work. In nearly eight months of working together, he never asked where I came from or what my religion or background was. One day before I left, I mentioned to him that I was a Jew, and his reaction was: "What? Christian? Jew? What difference does it make?" Captain Smith had a liberal state of mind when anti–Semitism was at its peak, even in the Allied countries fighting Hitler.

During the course of my duty in Baalbek, an Arab nightwatchman shot and wounded a would-be robber of another sect. The watchman who was employed by our unit was arrested instead of the robber. The watchman was about to be sentenced by the district judge; Captain Smith did not like the fact that the watchman was arrested in the first place.

I suggested to Captain Smith that he see the judge before the trial. The captain could not believe that he could see a judge before trial to influence the judge's decision. I explained to him that Baalbek is not like England and, besides, by doing so he could avoid bloodshed between the two sects involved in the incident. He agreed to do so, although he kept saying that it was not proper and nobody could see a judge about a case before trial. I accompanied him to the judge's chamber. I translated the captain's speech and the judge responded in direct English, promising to render judgement in our favor.

In the evening at the officer's room, Captain Smith was telling his fellow officers how amazed he was in influencing the judge's decision to free our watchman. "Well, this is the Middle East; not England," one of the officers duly commented. Captain Smith and myself were invited on many occasions to Beirut nightclubs as guests of our Public Enemy Number One. Even girls in his service were present.

All this was to try to obtain some work and of course make more money in participating in the construction of a defense line in that region. This line of defense was to assure that Turkey would not be left open to Germany's armies should the desert western front crumble. The news from the eastern desert and Egypt was rather alarming. German armored formations and aircraft in Tripoli were a direct threat to the British forces and to Egypt. A new German warrior, General Erwin Rommel, appeared on the world stage. Ironically, in 1940 Rommel narrowly escaped capture when the British counterattacked at Arras, France. Also Rommel's thrust towards Lille in France would have cut General Montgomery's division if not for a restraining order from the German High Command. As fate would have it, General Montgomery reached England safely and faced Rommel again in the western desert theater of the war. The British general beat Rommel's advancing armies, turning the tide of the entire war. The news of victory was exalting for us after so many defeats.

From time to time I visited Beirut on the weekends, and on a few occasions stopped at Zahla along the way. This small town is a kind of paradise between two mountains in the Bekaa Valley. It was usually crowded in the summer and was understandably famous for its locally brewed *arak zahlawi* (Middle Eastern alcoholic beverage). Once one tastes its flavor, one becomes addicted to it.

Many of the officers and men of our unit used to frequent Zahla's cafés near the stream running through the middle of town amongst widespread greenery, shade trees, and shrubs. One could relax in the cool summer breeze beside one of the arched foot bridges and forget the worry of war. I ate at one of these outside cafés where, like others in Lebanon, with the order of a drink, ten to fifteen kinds of hors d'oeuvres were served on the table. I savored the delights of crushed chick peas (*humus*), cooked pattied eggplant (*babagannush*), bread, many kinds of vegetables, *tabula* (old-fashioned salad dating back to the time of Israelites in the desert), cooked beets, lettuce, cucumbers, farmer's cheese with olive oil, olives, and so on. I sat peacefully listening to the murmur of the stream nearby and the singing of birds overhead in the multitudes of native trees.

When Mussolini declared war on Britain after the fall of France in 1940, the Italian Empire in North and East Africa had a majestic appearance. But this would soon change. Already, skirmishes were in progress between Italian troops and rebellious British and Sudanese forces. General Wavell enacted a policy to support the patriot movement in Abyssinia, making the position of the Italian troops impossible to detect, and eventually reconquering the country. The operation to clear the Sudan was also very successful. The Italians evacuated Kassala and Gallabat, leaving the Sudan. They were pursued up to Keren, midway between Asmara and Agordat on the Sudan borders. After a successful assault on the troops in Keren, in which Palestinian Jewish transport units participated, the road became opened to Asmara, the capital of Eritrea in East Africa.

Sudanese troops and Abyssinian patriots were under the leadership of Colonel Orde Wingate, who later trained the Jewish Haganah in Palestine in partisan warfare in case Egypt fell and the British troops would withdraw to new defense lines in Lebanon. Colonel Wingate made it possible for Emperor Haile Selassie to reenter his kingdom. By doing so, he also made it possible for many troops to be freed from Syrian and Lebanese fronts.

It was ironic that I was fated to serve the British in fighting the patriots — who were later called "Shiftas" — in Eritrea and then against the British with the Haganah in Palestine. But, I am getting ahead of my story again.

At work, everyone was doing his best for the war effort, working feverishly well into the night to beat the clock in erecting the line of defense. In June 1942, a request for volunteers to serve in Occupied Enemy Territories Administrations (OETA) was circulated through all British units in Syria and Lebanon. The volunteers were needed to replace officers and men who left for new theaters of war or the front lines.

I volunteered and soon was invited for an interview with a colonel in Beirut who checked my papers and also tested my proficiency in different languages. He told me that I was qualified for service in East Africa, which was free and occupied by the British forces. Eritrea, East Africa, was an Italian colony and my interviewer asked if I knew any Italian. I answered, half-heartedly, "But I know French very well and Italian is similar." Then he asked me in Italian if I understood his question, which I did by converting in my mind the words simply into French pronunciation. Then by doing the opposite — converting French words into some kind of Italian pronunciation — I answered him in Italian in the affirmative. The next question became easier. It took him a few moments to accept me for the assignment. He handed me a note and asked me to go and see the British vice consul who would take care of my departure within the next two days to Asmara, Eritrea. I was issued military papers and vouchers to travel by train.

# CHAPTER 6

# Journey into the
# Unknown — Travelogue

My journey through Egypt to Eritrea would last nearly one month. I was thrilled because I would be in Palestine for one day and get a glimpse of the land of my ancestors. Our bus to my first stop, Haifa, was full of Palestinian Jews returning home on leave for a day or two. They spoke Hebrew and another still unknown language to me, Yiddish. What thrilled me most was to see young Jewish people in British uniforms speaking Hebrew. It was the middle of the afternoon and the trip could take at least a couple of hours to reach Haifa. One British-uniformed, Hebrew-speaking fellow asked the bus driver in Hebrew whether we would be able to make it in time before *Shabath* (Saturday) to be home for *Oneg Shabath* (Saturday Pleasure). This conversation filled my heart with joy and sent chills down my spine.

I could not believe that I was in the country where our Holy Language is spoken. The people who spoke it were like visitors from another land. The idea of belonging to them took hold in my mind, and I decided that when the war was over, I would settle in Palestine. I kept my composure during the whole trip and nobody around me realized what was going through my mind. Nobody knew that I was Jewish, either. During the trip I kept saying to myself, "Oh what a joy! They are real and are here." I figured that no one would call me a "dirty Jew" or some other degrading name. The short trip was pleasant and I enjoyed the dream-like scenery.

We reached Haifa just before the beginning of *Shabath*. I was taken to an army camp near the shore and was issued blankets and biscuits for the night before being taken to my room. In the morning, I woke up early to see as much of Haifa as I could because the following morning I would leave for Egypt. I got a pass and started walking towards Haifa. First I visited the lower part at the foot of Mount Carmel; then I climbed to Hadar Hacarmel. I could not walk to the top of Mount Carmel because I became tiresome and the sun was about to set, signaling the end of another day of our journey.

I went back to town, slept overnight, and early in the morning took the

The author dressed in occupied enemy territories administration uniform in Eritrea after the occupation by British forces (author's collection).

Orient Express, which then connected London and Paris and ran through Europe, Istanbul, Turkey, Syria, Lebanon, and Palestine until reaching Cairo, Egypt. The passage through lively orange groves and small modern villages and towns along the seashore contrasted sharply with the Arab villages when the train later took us inland to Palestine. We passed Tulkarem, Gaza, and El Arish where, like in Iraq, date palm trees were everywhere. We stopped for a short time to restock coal for the engine and water for the journey ahead through the Sinai Desert. The railway station was full of vendors hawking all kinds of food and drinks, with thousands, if not millions, of flies around. The buildings were primitive, with very few made of brick, and most were made of a mud-straw mixture. After crossing the Sinai, we reached Qantara where our papers were checked. We then went over the Suez Canal into Egypt, via a drawbridge. In the evening, we came to Cairo's main railway station. Unlike other stations in the Middle East, this was a huge structure, the only one of its kind in that part of the world. Because no sleeping compartments were available, I had two days until everything was arranged for me to ride the train to the Shallal.

My uncle (my father's brother) and his family, whom I would be seeing for the first time, were living in Cairo. I had his address and called on him the next day. Needless to say, they were very glad to see me and I hastily accepted to stay with them during the next two days and nights. I greatly enjoyed being with them and their two beautiful and very sweet daughters. My aunt was very hospitable and kind, and they all took me on a quick tour of Cairo.

In the past, like all the Arab nations, Palestine was positively influenced by Egypt's literature and pro–European parliamentary government. I read a lot of their Arabic newspapers, which were then moderately-priced and very interesting, full of sophisticated articles. One was *Al Ahram* and another was *Musawar*, which was like *Life* magazine. Throughout the tumultuous Middle East, countries looked up to Egypt for leadership and its fine Arabic literature. Many students from the Arab world filled Egypt's universities. The attitudes of Egyptians are something to be envied. They are joyful all the time in spite of all the miseries around them. They are full of spiritual feelings and have a special ability to turn sad events into joyous laughter. Their music and songs are the best in the Arab world. They can make jokes at any time and on any occasion. They were the first to make movies for Arabic-speaking countries to watch and enjoy. In short, they are polite, spirited, and accommodating. Many of them speak several languages, primarily English and French.

I did not have enough time to visit all of Cairo and to enjoy its museum and the other exotic sceneries around the Nile. Everyone is impressed by Cairo, especially if he is from the Middle East. Its buildings were higher than other Arab capitals in those days, and for someone who came from Baghdad like me, Cairo looked different — almost European. It was full of Allied soldiers and Rommel was knocking at its doors, planning to take it away from the British. Air raid alarms sounded once or twice as if to remind us of the war.

Egypt could have fallen any day while I was there. The Jewish community was very much concerned with the situation and relied on some Egyptians for individual protection. Most of those who could afford to left Egypt for Lebanon, leaving behind their businesses, wealth and so on, believing they would be safer in the Shuf Mountains of the country.

The news from the western desert was not encouraging at all. Rommel had already attacked with his Africa corps and a powerful air force. Rommel's plan was to open a direct assault on Cairo from Tobruk, Libya. Bir Hakim, encountered before Tobruk, was strongly defended by the Free French and at first held firm. Rommel first concentrated on Bir Hakim in order to open his supplies route. The Free French were evacuated, and the capture of Tobruk reverberated around the world. The fall of Cairo was imminent.

During the period I was traveling to Egypt on my way to Asmara, the British sustained a succession of misfortunes and defeats in Malaya, Singapore, Burma, and Tobruk. The British rapidly retreated to the western desert with many casualties and vast masses of artillery, ammunition, vehicles, and stores lost to the enemy. Rommel was pressing forward in captured British trucks, fed with British oil supplies and firing British ammunition. Hitler and Mussolini were about to enter Cairo, or its ruins thereof, after only a few marches. The Nazis' fifth column in Egypt was extremely active, finding support from many highly placed officials in the government like the Quislings of Europe. Also the university students were successfully led astray in their belief that Germany would fulfill their national aspirations. Many of them became the leaders of Egypt in its unpopular war against Israel. The negative effects on the Allies and the world could not be measured. Jewish hopes in the Middle East never sank so low after the fall of France.

Amazingly, in the midst of all this, the British government was still functioning democratically. Members of Parliament made a motion of non-confidence in Mr. Churchill because of the events in the western desert. The motion was designed to remove him from office because some believed that he could not do the job. I wondered that while Hitler was giving direct orders without opposition and winning the war, the western democracies were still debating whether the Prime Minister was effectively doing his job. Mr. Churchill, then, had to fight on two fronts — one political and the other military — to achieve any progress; fighting one at home and the other abroad to regroup and bring victory to his people against the worst tyrant the world had ever known. What a world after all!

General Auchinlek, Commander-in-Chief in the Middle East, was relieved of his command and General Alexander, along with General Montgomery, assumed the plan of facing Rommel. Transport ships, lent from the United States by agreement with President Roosevelt, were rounding the cape of South Africa to reach Egypt with fresh troops and materials for the Eighth Army.

On the second day, I boarded the train after a cabin was secured for me, and I was on my way to the Shallal, the first waterfall in Egypt (or rather the last from the Blue Nile). I shared the cabin with three other servicemen, one of whom was a flight officer joining his squadron in the Sudan. We left the station in the evening and slept rather comfortably during the night.

I woke up at sunrise, opened the window and looked outside. I could not tell where we were exactly, but the scenery and morning breeze fully stimulated my senses. I watched the distant pastures going quickly by and the date palm trees receding to the end of the train. A ploughman or two were working the field and the delta of the Nile passed by like in the movies. Here and there, a lonely buffalo monotonously circled a waterwheel to bring up water from the Nile to irrigate the field. When we were nearest the water, I watched the far away *felukas* (sailboats) spreading their white sails like white doves ready to take off, gliding silently over the water while carrying people from one bank to the other. There were plantations of wheat and sugarcane, and a line of camels and donkeys moved along and among the palm trees and tamarisk. There was hardly a moment when a village was out of sight. The birds had a tame and unhurried air — like the people — whether they were herons or storks. The train rushed through villages, each having multitudes of vendors of all kinds of food and drink, with clouds of flies all over. The people wore black or grey *gelabiyas* (men's robes) and one could hardly see any European-style dress on anyone. Often one could hear Arabic music and singing in the distance and also the *muezzin* calling the faithful to prayer. The villages along the White Nile were all made up of farmers, and most people were illiterate.

There was a story about a young man from a village who left to enter the University of Cairo. Three years later, he returned to the village wearing European clothes and was received in public by the *omda* (a kind of mayor) of the village. Casually, the *omda* asked the young man what he studied at the University. The student replied that he learned languages like English, French, and others. The *omda* interrupted him and said, "Allah, I know English, too." The young man was perplexed, knowing that the *omda* was illiterate, and asked if he could test the *omda* in his knowledge of English. When the student got his approval, he asked the *omda*, "What would you say in English to an Englishman to let him join you inside your room?"

"Simple", said the *omda*, "I just tell him in English, 'Come here.'"

"Fine," said the young man, rather surprised. "Now, what would you say to the same Englishman if you wanted him to leave the room?"

Without hesitation the *omda* said, "I would go out of the room myself and tell the Englishman to 'come here'."

That was how illiteracy was treated in Egypt — with humor and a presence of mind.

I was by then completely cut off from any news from the outside world; my mind was completely absorbed in my new environment. I found out that the people of Egypt were very polite, fast-talking, and sociable. They were always ready to help, wherever possible, and were great conversationalists. Their special Arabic accent was pleasing to the ears. It contained a treasure of expressions as well as poetry in Arabic that allowed a poem to run a hundred pages or more, ending every verse with the same rhythm.

No matter where you were in Egypt, you would hear the *nay* (flute) being played by someone. Our train continued puffing smoke and struggling with its heavy load of long wagons full of people and materials through Koul and Aswân, finally reaching the Shallal. We disembarked and my belongings were transferred to a waiting boat nearby on the Nile River. I was assigned a room that would be my home for the next three days and nights. A boat was standard transportation on the Nile before the Shallal was connected by railroad with Wadi Halfa in the Sudan. Ours had two decks and about 20 or 30 cabins on the second deck which were considered first class. The first deck had a wide single hall where second-class passengers could lie on the floor and sleep.

The boat lifted anchor and the Mississippi-type old steam-wheeler started its journey against the muddy current toward the borders of the Sudan.

The first day on deck, with the African sun reflected into my eyes off the surface of the wide brown water of the Nile, I felt like I was travelling through paradise. We were passing thick bushes, perhaps jungles, along the banks of the Nile. After hearing the excited shrieks of some passengers, I went up on the top deck. Sudanese Egyptian, probably Nubian, youngsters, were lining the shore of the Nile on the eastern side of the river and people on the deck were throwing Egyptian *piasters* (coins) into the dark murky waters of the river.

Several of the boys dove deep into the waters to retrieve the money, swimming quickly back to shore afterwards. The Nile in that part of Egypt was infested with crocodiles and hippopotamuses. As soon as a *piaster* was thrown into the waters, a crocodile would move fast to catch the retrieving youngster for his meal. But the boy was much faster and would be on shore before the crocodile was ten yards from him. What courage! What a swimmer! How could the boy pinpoint the money in the river, pick it up from under the deep water, and get back so quickly?

Further upstream, I noticed an island the size of about one square mile in the middle of the river, covered with all kinds of birds. Land and greenery could not even be detected. There were storks, starling-like birds with gleaming feathers in different shades of blue, black ibises (the famous birds of ancient Egyptian god Thoth), pelicans, darters, and giant hornbills which, with their enormous bills, looked like extinct birds from the dinosaur era. When our boat approached the island, they all flew away in unison, creating a cloud overhead which eclipsed the sun for a short while. What a spectacle; this could only happen in Africa. Drinks were served on deck under the shade of a tarpaulin cover, and I had a lot of ginger ale, my favorite drink. We passed slowly alongside Abu Simbel, the temple of Ramses II's wife Nefertiti. It is cut into the face of the rock and colossal statues guard the entrance to the temple. At Wadi Halfa, we were cleared to enter Sudan and our belongings were transported again to a train to take us to Khartoum, the capital of Sudan. There was a stretch of about 250 miles before reaching Abu Homed in the bleak and sandy Nubian Desert. The railway line which crossed the desert was completed back in 1897 by the British for Kitchener in his drive to Khartoum to oust the rebellious Mahdi. There were three or four stops in the desert which could only be numbered because not a living thing there had a mark or name. These stops were made so that water from deep wells could replenish the engine of the train. Traveling through this barren region of sand and sky was like being in another land. The sands and blue skies all around, the blazing sun during the day and the bitter cold during the night — this all made me feel as if I were on the moon. It never rains in Sudan and no greenery or grass can be found anywhere.

The author with his Australian spitfire pilot friend in Khartoum, Sudan (author's collection).

After Abu Homed, the train ran along the Nile again. In contrast to the bleak desert, bushes and trees and what appeared to be jungles were seen on both sides of the train. Through the window of the train I caught a glimpse of running wild animals such as giraffes and zebras. The trip through the jungles was rather exotic, but soon we arrived at Khartoum, where I had two days to stay until catching my next train to Kassala on the border of Eritrea. I heard nothing new about the war around the world and it seemed that, while there, nothing else mattered except the quiet life of Africa while others throughout the world were at each others' throats.

My friend, the flight officer, and I went out to the city to explore the markets and people. It was Friday and in one store we struck up a conversation with its Jewish owner, Malka. Upon learning that I was Jewish, too, he invited us both (the flight officer was Christian) to dinner and *kiddush* at his home. We gladly accepted and spent a pleasant evening with his family, whose house was full with others, Jews and non–Jews, to celebrate the *Oneg Shabath.*

Just like it used to be in Baghdad, people in Khartoum slept outside at night. Spending a night under the open sky made me nostalgic for my childhood days. The stars above shone brilliantly and when they started to dim, the stillness of the surrounding desert was shattered as life began to return to the city of Khartoum. The Blue Nile appeared to me while the sun was rising along the river. In the west, the two Niles flow around the two islands to become one vast heavy stream. The white-sailed *felukas* came out from the banks. The heat was 90 to 100 degrees and intolerable.

*Khartoum* in Arabic means "elephant's trunk" because the Arabs were the first to trade with ivory there. Sudan (then Anglo-Egyptian Sudan) was under joint British and Egyptian rule until 1956. The inhabitants were nice-featured Africans wearing *jellabas* (long robes) and like other Arabs were traditionally hospitable.

The second day, I visited Omdurman, also called the city of the Mehdi. It is rather different than Khartoum. Its bazaars are full of fine-crafted works of art, especially ivory, and I bought a two-inch exquisitely carved miniature elephant. On the bus, a man struck up a conversation with me, asking what country I came from. He could not figure out what I meant when I mentioned Palestine, and after I explained in more detail, he exclaimed, " Oh! You mean *Bar E Sham* (the Damascene Desert)."

I enjoyed Khartoum during my stay there and forgot about the ferocious war in Egypt, North Africa, Europe, and around the world. Early the next morning I boarded the train again, headed to the Sudanese border.

More jungles, sand, and small deserts passed until we reached Kassala, where we disembarked and rode a bus into Eritrea to the towns of Tessenei and Agordat. Later, I was destined to spend over six months in the line of duty in Agordat. The Italian train that took us from there to Asmara was rather comfortable. We traveled at night, climbing high mountains while passing through Keren. The moonlight gave us a faint view of the passing terrain, and during a few moments we could see high peaks jutting up like hills. The air became scantier every hour until in the morning we reached the city of Asmara. It had taken me one month since leaving Beirut on July 16. On August 16, 1942, I reported to police headquarters in Asmara for my assignment.

# CHAPTER 7

# Introduction to Democracy — Occupied Enemy Territories Administration

During the passage to my new post, there were a lot of activities and arguments between the Prime Minister of Britain, Mr. Churchill, and his general staff in Cairo who remained unabated. While the United States was predicted to concentrate its war-time actions in the Pacific, it seemed that its President was determined to hold onto the Middle East and hit Rommel at his back door in North Africa. General Montgomery was appointed commander of the famous Eighth Army in the Middle East. In the meantime, with the whole world at one another's throats, war was ferociously and bitterly going on everywhere. The threat to Egypt was still existent but with different expectations.

After my first day in Asmara, I was sent to a camp about 15 miles from the city and 4 miles from a village called Adi-Ugri. The camp previously had served the Italian forces and now was a training ground for native recruits in jungle warfare. The officers were a mix of South Africans, Rhodesians, and Palestinians of the British administration. My unit was called the Eritrean Police Striking Force. The commanding officer was a veteran of the British Army who had participated in Spain's civil war.

My unit was actually fighting a native rebel and his men who were trained by Colonel Orde Charles Wingate. They had been referred to as the Patriots before the occupation by the British and had helped to fight the Italians before the British invasion. They had been supplied with arms and ammunition under the condition that they would surrender them back when victory was achieved. In return Eritrea would achieve independence.

Incidentally, the same Wingate was also sent to Palestine to train the Haganah and organize similar guerrilla forces to fight both the anti–British Arab marauders and guerrillas and later the Germans if the British were forced to withdraw after abandoning Egypt and the Suez to make a stand at Baalbek.

When Ethiopia and Eritrea were liberated, the British government demanded the return of all arms issued to the Ethiopian and Eritrean patriots to the British administration there. Some of the patriots did; others held on to theirs. Fearing that the British would keep Eritrea for the throne of England, they stipulated that the return of arms be conditional with the leaders being given an immediate say in the administration of the country. This request was obviously turned down. Ali Muntaz, the head of the rebels, went into the jungle with his followers and started harassing British officials and troops as well as natives who refused to accept his demands to sustain his movement and his little army of guerrillas. He was very ruthless in that respect and the task force of Adi Ugri was assigned to chase down and capture Ali Muntaz with the rebels and end his insurgency. We had our informers and members of Intelligence who continually furnished us with up-to-date information of his whereabouts, and we used to respond as quickly as possible with all the command cars, trucks, arms and equipment needed for such a jungle operation; in a few cases we even used camels. His informers, though, were always faster and sent the signal for him to escape, sometimes just before we arrived at the village where he was hiding. Before he left, he managed to massacre the whole village — old and young, males and females — in a horrible bloodbath, under the false assumption that the villagers were themselves the informers.

One day, a Rhodesian officer was having trouble with his tommy gun, which was apparently jammed. He was trying to release the magazine by hitting it hard on the table. The barrel was pointed directly at me, but luckily, the gun didn't fire and I moved aside. Then, he turned the tommy gun again toward me in my new position and hit it again against the table. I became sure that he was trying to kill me and make it look accidental. Luckily, nothing happened again and when he continued this act, I rushed toward him, grabbed the gun from his hands and threw it to the ground. When it hit the ground, a bullet was discharged. I accused him of attempted murder and a fistfight ensued. Because of the fight and the commotion, other officers rushed forward and separated us. A complaint was filed against him with the commanding officer, which was procedure. The commanding officer very strongly rebuked the Rhodesian officer, but for lack of strong evidence of his intentions, the case was dismissed. Later on, I learned that this officer was a hater of Jews, natives, blacks and other ethnic groups. Here were two human beings away from home fighting for the same cause and putting their lives on the line, and one contemplated killing his fellow struggler for the mere reason that he was a Jew. The incident shook me to my bones, because before I had believed in British justice and the fairness of its people. Henceforth, I became more aware of my race and origin.

A few days later I was instructed to report to a place called Agordat near the borders of Sudan and Eritrea, a crossroads for the rebels in these countries. Again I was moving to a new place, but I had no choice. I handed over my job to a native sergeant of the unit and made sure that he understood the responsibilities well. This was the policy of the administration to transfer gradually all functions back to the natives of the country for democratic rule.

In 1954, many years later, I travelled back to Eritrea with an Israeli passport and presented it to the C.I.D. — Criminal Investigation Department — for a permit to stay in the country for a certain period. I was requested a few minutes later to go in and see the deputy chief of the C.I.D., which also deals with visas, passports, and other permits. Did staying for a little while necessitate the approval of the deputy chief of the department, I wondered? After shaking hands with a nice-looking Eritrean, he smiled and asked me if I recognized him. I did not. Then he mentioned his name and added, "I was your sergeant back in 1942 in Adi Ugri with the Police Striking Force to whom you handed your job." Then I remembered him and was very glad to see him again.

During our conversation, I inquired what happened to Ali Muntaz, the rebel leader whom we were always pursuing but never capturing. He recalled that Ali Muntaz became a member of the Eritrean Parliament after the country became independent. I realize now that our efforts in introducing democracy did not fail vainly.

So far, I had been in a cool climate, situated on a plateau 10,000 feet high. Agordat is at sea level and full of forests infested with malaria-carrying mosquitos. It has a tropical climate and the heat in the summer passes the 100 degree mark and in winter does not go down below 85.

I arrived at the Agordat Police District Headquarters, where I was to spend approximately six months as interpreter and assistant administrative officer to the district commander of the area. Our headquarters were established in a nice building belonging to the previous Italian administration, across from a complex with window-like openings all around. It was a typical accommodation in a year-round hot climate like other parts of Africa. There were no windows to close or shutters and no separations between rooms except a three-quarter inch mat wall divider for every one or two beds. The climate being equatorial, the length of days and nights was almost equal during the year round. This structure, with its solid roof and brick and cement periphery, was like a hotel in the midst of the Safari with modern amenities, a bar, and a neat restaurant.

I had to stay there for a while until a better and home-like building was made available for me. The place was clean and the service was good and it was owned by an Italian. Other officers and soldiers were living there, too.

The next day, I reported to the commanding officer for duty. Stewart was a captain from Dar Es Salam in Tanganyika and an ex-officer of the Palestine police force. He gave me a very cool reception, behaved indifferently, said nothing and entered his office after our introduction. I was sure that he already had my papers before I arrived and knew a lot about me. For many days, I barely spoke to him. I was not given any instructions and he satisfied himself with brief orders only. In the meantime, I managed to get along with the work in spite of his hostile attitude. I tried to become friendly with him as well as with the other personnel.

One day, I met a soldier in a British Army uniform who spoke English with an accent. Later, I found out he was a Palestine recruited truck driver who transported materials through Eritrea for the army and reported to our headquarters. Without realizing it, one day I greeted him with "*Shalom*" and to my surprise he returned my greeting, adding one or more Hebrew words that he translated for me. His name was Yisrael. I told him about myself and we became friends in that wilderness. Through him, I began to hear the catastrophic news about our brothers in Europe under the tyranny of Hitler.

Captain Stewart's attitude toward me made me angry and bitter. I was working for the same purpose, without personal gratification — and I was being offended and disregarded for no apparent reason. I became determined to do my job and ignore his attitude toward me. One day I learned that Captain Stewart served for some time in Palestine and was probably in contact with mostly Arabs. Therefore, he probably liked Arabs more than he did the Jews from Europe. The Arabs were also better "yes" men than any other ethnic group. Remembering our behavior back in Baghdad with the ruling nation, I started treating him likewise, calling him Major on purpose to please his ego and serving him coffee and drinks (he loved drinking beer).

One day, the Inspector General from Cairo came down to our headquarters to check and report to the general headquarters of the Middle East. I could not believe my eyes when Captain Stewart brought him into my room and introduced me, explaining my work. I, the discarded member of the unit, was meeting, talking and shaking hands with a brigadier general from general headquarters. A couple of months later, the general's report was received at our headquarters and Captain Stewart purposely left it on my desk for me to read. In that important report, I was described as hard-working, conscientious, and efficient. I then realized that Captain Stewart was not an anti–Semite, but simply antagonistic because he was not treated well while serving in Palestine. Henceforth, it was an about-turn. Our relationship improved and I began to somewhat like him in spite of his mild mocking of a Jewish inspector's name in Tessenei under his command.

One day in Agordat while I was still staying in the hotel, I woke up in the morning to discover that there was no roof over us. While I was sound asleep, a tornado blew the entire roof a few miles away.

During the period I spent in Agordat, I learned that most of the tribes and people of the East African coast have beautiful features: a tiny nose, wide beautiful eyes, delicate mouth and lips, and beautiful figures wrapped up by bright-colored fabrics. They have pinkish chocolate skin which blends well with all kind of hues.

One day when we were instructing new recruits in camp, a newly-arrived major was watching a girl nearby and said loudly, "I wish this girl was of a lighter skin." We turned our heads and saw a young beautiful girl talking with a likewise nice-looking young man. She was clad in a transparent colorful fabric through which her entire naked body could be seen. She was not ashamed of this display and either did not realize our awareness of her or did not react to it.

Her shameless feeling was probably due to the fact that most of the females on the east coast of Africa, including the Sudan, are circumcised. This is done by clipping off the clitoris or by cutting away sections and sewing back the vagina, leaving a small opening for urination. Sometimes this operation causes later pain and dormant sexual feelings. Therefore, I figured that exposing their nude bodies did not shame them. Although this is not a religious practice, and many mothers resist such clipping and cutting, the elders insist on maintaining this tradition. It is not a Moslem religious practice like the circumcision of the male, but it is more likely a widespread tribal tradition dating back to the pharaohs and Queen Sheba. Infibulation and circumcision of the female was practiced prior to Islam, but this fact was ignored by Islamic authorities. I was told this knowing that Islam strongly forbids public exposure of the female body and in some countries even the face.

Agordat is surrounded by jungles crowded with monkeys, gazelles, wild boars, wildcats, and wild rebels. It was very hard for us to chase and catch the rebel leader up in those jungles. He was agile, wilted, and extremely dangerous; therefore our force was no match for him. Occasionally, I used to go around the market with a policeman in search of clues or rumors about the rebel leader and his whereabouts. Languages spoken there are mostly Tigrini but also Amharic and Arabic, and of course Italian.

On one of these tours I entered a store and found the owner, a light-skinned person, and two girls. I did not speak with any of them, except to extend greetings, and I scanned the shelves and hidden corners in an attempt to spot something that might help our search. I noticed the end of a *tzizith*, a

Jewish prayer shawl, protruding from one of the corners of the shelves. I approached the spot and pulled it out. At first I thought that some robber deprived a Jew of his religious article or, worse, that it was loot from an unfortunate Jew who was assassinated. But no Jew, as far as we knew, lived there. When I confronted the owner about the origins of the shawl, he replied that it belonged to him, bought for his use in prayers. He said, "Sir, I am a Jew." In a protesting tone, he added that he had lived here for the last decade or so. I calmed him with a smile and added that I was a Jew, too. He said that he was surprised to find another one in this place. He was from Yemen and made his living in the wilderness of the Bassopiano Occidentale.

Later, he introduced me to some Falashi Jews who visited the region, which made me aware that Jews come in different colors, shapes, and backgrounds and are scattered all over the world. Before that I had the notion that all Jews must be of my kind wherever they lived. I recall that my introduction to the Falashis made me change my stereotypical thoughts about our people since childhood. I realized there are blonds, browns, blacks, and yellows, just like talls, shorts, mediums, heavies and lights. I also understood that the Falashis were brought up exactly the same traditional values that a Jewish mother would give her son or daughter. Like other sects of the Jewish faith, they differed somewhat in their liturgy but the basic principles of Judaism are adhered to. I must admit that reverence is given to the sanctity of the ritual of worship with intense fervor and passionate praying in liege of others. Amazingly, they stuck to their religion and traditions in spite of the dangers surrounding them for over 2,000 years.

After a few months in the area, I fell very sick with tropical malaria. The Italian doctor of the district, who was also a prisoner of war, treated me as if he was an affectionate father and actually saved my life. He visited me while in bed two or three times a day until he was sure that the danger was over. He explained that I suffered from a kind of malaria that was usually fatal. I pulled through and could not thank this doctor enough.

My friend Yisrael, the military truck driver who came to see me now and then, had disturbing news about the Jews of Europe. Rumor had it that many thousands of men, women, and children were being put to death in concentration camps in various places in Europe, especially in Poland and Germany. The German war machine was assisting in the killings. This news immediately brought to mind the story of my Armenian friend at school in Beirut who told of a million or more Armenians killed. The horror of it overwhelmed my thoughts. On one hand, I believed it must be true. But on the other hand, I believed the Germans to be too civilized to carry out such an act, unlike the Turks. I could not know what to believe. Yisrael, who was also worrying about his family and friends, asked me what the Jews of Palestine could do in this situation. It seemed as if nature itself opened its gutters and a mighty volcano was consuming everything helpless in its path. We did not know exactly what was going on inside occupied Europe, and we could not validate the rumors, which after all were just rumors at the time.

Later, we went hunting and on flat land we chased a bunch of gazelles. We picked up speed to at least 65 or 70 miles per hour but the gazelles were faster, probably running 80 miles per hour. Then we let them go and abandoned the chase. Childishly, I thought, perhaps the Jews in the concentration camps could do likewise to survive — escape, run away with all their might to freedom like those gazelles did. It seemed like a simple solution, but we did not know how efficiently those concentration camps were sealed off and guarded. In spite of that, after the war we heard of stories of just such escapes by hundreds of prisoners who risked their lives.

A couple of months later, I was transferred to the city of Asmara. But before I left Agordat, I received the surprise of my life — a farewell party given by Captain Stewart himself. I'd had a few drinks and one of the British inspectors jokingly reminded the captain that I was a Jew and that he was not sympathetic to my people. He said that I was not a Jew and laughed, rebuking the inspector in telling him what to do. Everybody laughed and the captain admitted that while in Palestine he was dealing with Arabs only, which probably poisoned his thoughts about the Jews. He thanked me profusely for my assistance to him, especially in his military trials, where he sat as judge and had to communicate with the defendants or the accused through interpreters. (In some cases there were two or three translators because of the many dialects and languages; I was usually the last to translate everything into English.) He even asked the other officers and ranked officials to sing to me, "For He's a Jolly Good Fellow."

The city of Asmara at that time was considered modern and on par with any small town in Italy, if not Europe. It had clean, wide streets for two-way traffic and the houses and buildings were pleasant to look at. It boasted of a few modern theaters, French-style cafés, nightclubs, and movies. It had first-class hotels and beautiful houses and villas not only in the city, but in many villages and small towns over the country. If it were not for the race discrimination imposed on the native Eritreans, I would say that it was as beautiful as any other modern city in the world.

The port of Massawa, unlike Asmara which is built on a plateau with an altitude of 10,000 feet, is at sea level, as every port should be. Its climate is hot year round, while in Asmara it is always cool. One gets very hot quickly in the sun and very cool in the shade. Massawa had the facilities for big cargo boats and cable cars from the port to Asmara, which was the quickest and perhaps also the safest means of transportation.

The road from Asmara to Massawa was extremely dangerous and many cars and trucks with their cargo and passengers crashed down the 100-to 200-foot cliffs while on their way down the serpentine road running through the mountains to the seashore. There was no other road like it and it was probably the only one of its kind in that part of the world. The road down to Agordat is less dangerous. Both directions were also connected by *ferrovia* railroads serving modern bus-type cars carrying passengers. When riding these cars, the scenery all around was breathtaking in its natural beauty and exotic picture-painting. I was glad I was finished with the stifling, malaria infested, tropical climate. I was still safe and sound in spite of the many dangerous moments during the course of my duty.

In Asmara, I was posted at the C.I.D. Immigration Department headquarters. From the date I arrived in Eritrea, the changes in command of Middle East forces took effect and there was ceaseless training in Egypt. Both the Eighth Army and the R.A.F. were enormously strengthened for the coming offensive against Rommel. The preparations for the attack were meticulous and secret.

In October 1942, over 1,000 guns opened up on enemy batteries and tanks, in addition to the concentrated air bombing. A heavily armored counterattack by the Germans and Italians gained no ground, and the R.A.F. intervened on a devastating scale.

As a result of this bombing, the enemy's attack was thwarted. The Russians at long last succeeded in halting the German advance. They were victorious in Stalingrad and the German Army was trapped with General Romulus in command. Romulus later surrendered, making it known to the world that the Germans were not invincible. Then the battle of El Alamein raged in the western desert.

In October, the battle in Egypt began with the participation of United States Sherman tanks and equipment manned by British personnel, which added to their powerful self-propelled guns. The R.A.F. fought brilliantly and prevailed over the enemy air force. Rommel was in full retreat and many Italian soldiers were taken prisoner because their German friends gave themselves top priority for vehicles and transportation. The German Air Force had given up the hopeless task of combatting the superior R.A.F.

The British were masters in deceptive tactics and methods which were factors in them surprisingly winning battles. The landing in North West Africa by the Allies surely lessened the pressure on the Russian front because Germany had to remove thousands of troops from Russia and send them to Africa. Again the Australians managed to swing the whole battle to the Allies' favor with their bitter fighting. Enemy retreat was reported by November. The Indians also fought bitterly and their brigade launched a successful attack which cleared the way for the British armored division to pursue the German forces across the open desert ring up North Africa and destroy them. This clearly saved the Middle East from the forces of darkness.

Indians, Australians, and the British defeated Hitler for the first time. The whole future course of World War II was now changed.

While this news poured out from radios and newspapers all over the world, Jews were still very tense and very aware of our co-religionists imprisoned in Europe. I could only smile when Montgomery's success was reported and one of my British colleagues remarked with his cool and determined attitude, "This will shake Hitler." I wanted to grab him by his hair and shake him, telling him that what Hitler needed was the cutting of his throat, not shaking.

The mood of all of us began to change and the American troops in Asmara invited us to a show in which stars from Hollywood — Jack Benny, Larry Adler, Lucille Ball, Dinah Shore, and others — were to perform. It was a night to remember listening to Larry Adler, the famous harmonica player, delighting everyone with his tunes and melodies. Jack Benny tried to play the violin but never did, because he either interrupted himself or someone else interrupted him with questions and jokes. Jack Benny bragged that he and Lucille Ball were like this, and he showed three tight fingers together high above his head. One of the players remarked that Jack and the girl make two, but that he was showing three fingers together.

"What is the third finger in the middle there for?"

"Oh" replied Benny. "That's her husband."

The shows kept coming, we were always invited, and the Americans were almost everywhere. They had plants for various war materials and aircraft and their personnel were all over. I very much enjoyed their company because, unlike the British who were somehow rather conservative, the Americans were liberal and friendly.

In Asmara, I was in charge of the records of people working with the Allied forces, and I also issued temporary visiting permits for those who arrived in the country for various reasons. Some were allowed to stay while others were turned down by the head of the department, Captain Podesta. Captain Podesta, who was not an admirer of Jews, gave preference to my coworker, an Egyptian from Cairo. At that time, Jewish refugees from Europe and other places affected by the war were arriving almost daily. Captain Podesta was more interested in bribes than fairness, and he turned away or restricted almost every Jew applying for a permit, not allowing them to stay for more than two weeks.

I personally was very happy to see them and, whether Captain Podesta approved or not, I used my authority in granting them the time they asked for — in some cases over six months — saving them some roaming and wandering, looking for some temporary refuge. This caused some antagonism between us.

There were messengers from the Jewish agency in Palestine who arrived to take care of these unfortunate people. That is how I became known to them later when I settled in the Holy Land. My colleague, the Egyptian from Cairo, did likewise, granting such Jews their wish whenever I was absent or busy on some other duty, without benefit to himself. I admired him and also thanked him secretly. We talked about the plight of the Jews in Europe and he always said I had better cling to the hope that they will be freed in time, unharmed. I hoped so, but stories were indicating otherwise.

The help I was extending to my fellow Jews made any relationship with my superiors stiff and unpleasant. Added to this, an Italian girl who worked with the paymaster downstairs and who befriended me platonically was suspected of having an affair with me. Captain Podesta and Captain Price, the paymaster who exploited the girl, became my arch-enemies because of her. Later in 1954, I met her again and learned that the paymaster had married her and then suddenly left her with a child and she never heard of him again. She was forced to become a prostitute after the war was over and the Allies had left.

As I said, my relations with Her Majesty's officers became very stringent and impossible; therefore I requested a transfer to Egypt. Amazingly, it was promptly granted and I had two weeks to hand over my work to another person. The day before my departure from Eritrea, some of the Polish Jews whom I had helped to stay and three others who were employed as guards with the Eritrean prison system came to say goodbye to me. We promised each other that we would meet again in Palestine.

One of them asked me innocently if I were a *Frank* (Spanish Jew). Not understanding his question, I thought that he wanted to know whether I came from a franc currency-dominated country. My reply was: "No, I am sterling." Another fellow who understood what was going on started laughing and explained to both of us the meaning of the question and answer — none of us realized its meaning except him. That was the best laugh we had before leaving, although I was bewildered why my friend should have heard such a thing.

The next day, I took the train to Tennesei and then to Kassala and back the same way I had come; as opposed to going through Cairo, Egypt, where I went to report to general headquarters. I knew that my papers would be there with notes made by Captain Podesta and the paymaster of the Eritrean police force, and I expected the worse.

# CHAPTER 8

# Novice Spy in Cairo—
# Jailed Experience

When I arrived in Cairo again, I went straight to my Uncle George's home. He had lived in Egypt for over 30 years and was married to Aunt Sophia. They had two sweet daughters and a son. The next day I reported to general headquarters–Middle East for my next assignment, probably in Libya. My file had not arrived and I was told to report again in a week after enjoying a brief leave.

The Allies recorded a victory in Italy and the leaders met in Cairo for a conference attended by the three heads of state from the United States, Britain, and China before heading to Tehran for a three-powers conference, this time involving the United States, Britain, and Russia. Cairo was bustling with security forces. The British Intelligence was in full gear protecting these heads of state and their generals, admirals, and hundreds of other officials and dignitaries who came for the conference.

My next visit to general headquarters was disappointing again. This time I was requested to cooperate with British security in Cairo until other arrangements were made. They emphasized the confidential aspect of my activities in such a way that I could not talk even with my uncle about it. Then I was handed an address in the business center of Cairo, along with a name and introductory note. I was told that this person would tell me what to do next.

The next day I went to this address and was flabbergasted to read "British Intelligence Agent" on his business sign after his name. When I went inside I met a Jew who confirmed his identity, claiming that the sign was good for business promotion. I was referred to an Egyptian officer who was blond, tall with blue eyes, wearing an Egyptian police uniform and a *tarbush* (headwear). He could not speak Arabic because he was born in London. This was the best Purim (Easter masquerade) Intelligence gear I had ever seen in my life. He gave me the address of the headquarters of the Royal Engineers in Cairo and told me to report to the commander of the camp.

Another officer interviewed me and, after telling me a little about security, requested me to frequent the Sigurel department stores in Cairo and surrounding areas for clues about suspected persons, much like I used to do back in Agordat.

Later, I insisted on receiving a permit to stay legally in Egypt like the others to avert suspicion as an employee of the Royal Engineers. At first I was refused. Finally, it was agreed to issue me one with a statement that ran as follows: "Shoua Horesh: [Shoua is my Arabic name] This clerk's services can be utilized by this formation, and he would undoubtedly prove useful, provided that permission can be obtained for him to remain in Egypt. Signed H.I.A. Nov. 4, 1943, Brigadier C.E.M.E." This note is still in my possession. I was told that they could not do this officially and were not certain that it would work. It was up to me to get the required permit on my own to stay in Cairo.

When I heard this, I thought my papers had probably arrived and either they wanted to get rid of me because of a bad report from Eritrea, or they had the intention of making me a resident agent for their services if I succeeded in getting a permit. Resident agents, or what intelligence communities call "sleeping agents," seek to live and work as regular and work as regular citizens in enemy territory or other territories. They are activated only when needed by the employing country or people. It could be months, years or decades until the agent is summoned to serve his employers. This assumption weighed heavy because I was left with no choice but to start doing what I was told. My uncle and his family knew nothing of what was going on, and I continued to be with them, but I could not act normal because I worked as someone who does not "exist." I mobilized my uncle's assistance without informing him why I really wished to stay in Egypt.

He approached the right officials in the Egyptian government and I was allowed to stay for a short while. Endeavors for the real permit continued. Every time I asked some high-ranking official who promised to help, I received the same reply again and again. Using their glorious gestures and eloquent speech, they told me ceremoniously that I might as well consider my request as granted, and that in a few days I would have the required permit to stay. Even when bribes were offered, I received the same assertions over and over again and was told that I had nothing to worry about. This went on for a couple of months while I became more and more nervous.

Meanwhile, I toured Cairo and visited the colossal, enigmatic Pyramids and the Sphinx near Mina House, where Churchill and Roosevelt were staying, as well as many other dignitaries who came to Cairo for the Allied Conference.

So much literature has been written about the Pyramids; all I can say is that they are one of the Seven Wonders of the World. The Sphinx has been standing around nearby at Giza for who knows how long. It has the face of a

The author (second from left) at the Pyramids in Giza, Cairo, Egypt, December 1943 (author's collection).

pharaoh, probably Khafre, and the body of a lion. The combination represented the power of the ruler at that time. It stands about 70 feet high and 240 feet long. The Museum of Cairo contains the proof which indicates that Egypt was a nation of long-gone dynasties with a great history and culture. The vicinity of the Pyramids was bustling with troops and anti-aircraft guns, and cordons of military personnel guarded the approaches.

President Roosevelt, Churchill, and others flew to Tehran to meet with Stalin. From the landing in Alamein until the end of the battle of Napoli in Italy a year later, the British and Americans had virtually unbroken successes. Italy was on the verge of collapse and there were many desertions. General Eisenhower was appointed chief of staff for what became known as "Overlord"—the invasion of Europe at Normandy. My work with the army in Cairo became insignificant as the Allies began to win the war on almost all fronts.

By January 1944, all my efforts to stay in Cairo had failed. One last attempt was made after learning that a beautiful Jewish girl acquaintance of my uncle's family had connections with the chief immigration officer in Cairo and was willing to help me. I visited the officer with her and he promised to approve my application. He ceremoniously mentioned his friendship to the Jews and how friendly he was to our people. He asked me to come back in a day or two to have my papers approved. All my worries then disappeared — the chief immigration officer himself had promised that it would be all right.

The Egyptians were becoming more rebellious, especially among the younger generation. One day I was watching a motorcade of King Farouk drive by when degrading words were shouted at him from nearby. Some onlookers applauded while other hurled more derogatory remarks at the King. In the meantime, most of the army materials and personnel were being reduced drastically, either to be sent to Palestine or home to England in anticipation of the invasion in Europe.

The next day I went to our friend the Egyptian officer at the appointed time, and there I was immediately arrested and accompanied by two plainclothes policemen to a prison in Cairo. In prison, I was stripped of my belt and shoelaces, and all my pockets were emptied and handed over to the warden, who seemed to be an Englishman.

I was locked up because I had overstayed my permit. My protests — that it was with the consent and permission of the chief immigration officer who granted me a few days and who requested that I be at his office again to renew my extension permit, which he personally had promised to approve — were shrugged off. Then I said that I was employed by the British forces here, but this statement was also met with indifference.

I was led to a cell and the doors were locked behind me. There was a mattress on the floor and the only communication with the outside world was through a small window on the door of the cell. A bucket served as the men's room. I was allowed to go outside twice a day. The rest of the day I was entirely shut off from the world. I had no way to inform my uncle or to find out what had happened.

Wild thoughts raced through my mind. Did the officer or someone else in the government know what I was about to do? I had done nothing serious yet. Or, perhaps the British wanted to get rid of me? I knew that some Egyptians, including government officials, had fought the British rule for some time. Perhaps the Egyptians locked me up to prove that they were the boss. What went wrong? What had happened? There was nothing I could do but wait and see.

The first day ended with lousy soup and a hard piece of bread pushed to me through the window door, which I did not eat. Also, I had a supervised five- or ten-minute walk through the prison corridor. I noticed that a few non–Egyptians were locked up in other cells on the same floor, but I was not allowed to communicate with them. Needless to say, I could not sleep that night.

I heard people reciting the *Koran* almost all night long. In the morning, I understood from the shouting and arguing in Arabic, that also imprisoned were the *Akhwan al Muslemine* (the Moslem Brotherhood), who were anti-government, anti-western, anti–British, and basically anti-everything.

Day after day passed, monotonous and meaningless. I forced some distasteful food into my mouth so I wouldn't starve to death. I talked to the sympathetic ear of the guard nearby, even though he never answered me. I unsuccessfully tried to explore the reason for my detention. Knowing many Arabs since childhood, I feared a bad ending and started to have nightmares. All my admiration for the Egyptian people, their literature, and their semi-democratic rule fell apart. Then it crossed my mind that other civilized people in Europe were doing worse to my fellow Jews. Here I discovered the difference between statism and real democracy: the latter rejects totalitarian rule. The dignity of the individual in Egypt was at its lowest, and I wondered if it was under the Nazi yoke.

For four days, I was incommunicado. On the fifth day, I was called downstairs, handed all my pocket articles, watch, belt and shoelaces, and was told that I had a few hours to go to my uncle to pick up my luggage and leave. Two plainclothes policemen or agents accompanied me. When I was in my uncle's house, my little cousin, who was about five years old, rebuked me, saying, "*Shoua*! Don't you ever fight on the streets again so that no one can put you in *kalabush* (local jail)." So much for an innocent child; she said it all.

We tried in vain to figure out what happened. Personally, I suspected that perhaps the girl who intervened on my behalf was on more intimate relations with the chief immigration officer, and that my continued presence might threaten this relationship. Or, perhaps the Egyptians knew about and decided to end my relationship and future plans with the British. Or, perhaps my letter stating that I was needed by the army made them mad, and they wanted to show their independence by kicking me out of the country before I got stronger recommendations. Or, maybe it was simply because I was a foreigner and a Jew. I have still found no sure answer.

According to my agreement in Beirut, the British Consulate in Cairo issued the necessary vouchers for me to travel back to Beirut where I had been hired. Ironically, the consul refused to give me a few days to stay in Palestine to visit my other uncle, insisting that I get only 24 hours transit despite all my arguments and pleas.

After I said goodbye to everyone, the two plainclothes agents accompanied me to the main train station. We took the train to the Egyptian-Palestinian border, where I went through the usual formalities to cross into Palestine.

# CHAPTER 9

# The Beginning of the End — The Start of a New Era

A Palestine British officer glanced at my papers and remarked that he would see to it that I would be out of Palestine. Further, because he was in charge of this train until the Palestine-Lebanon border, he would check me out at every stop. Listening to all this and remembering what happened in Cairo, it felt like I was a dangerous criminal. The difficulties by the British Consulate in Cairo and the attitude in Cairo and the attitude of the British police officer on the train made it clear that no Jew who ever entered Palestine would ever stay there.

On the train ride through the country, I did some thinking. I feared that I would be denied a new post in Beirut, and I would be forced to proceed back to Baghdad, where I did not wish to go. The police from England looked upon me as a wog.

Allied armies were victorious and soon Europe would be invaded and the war would be over. The news about the extermination of Jews was foremost on my mind, and I made my decision.

On arriving in Tel Aviv Jaffa, I decided to be more useful in the struggle for the Jewish cause. It was time to actively serve an ideal rather than continue to be mistreated by others with whom I had nothing in common.

At the train stop station in Tel Aviv, I ran, before the British police officer could notice, to the open gate where lots of passengers and other people were freely exiting. I dashed out to the street and started walking briskly towards a crowded sidewalk of Allemby Street. Mingling with the people, I was safe.

What a pleasure: Hebrew was being spoken almost everywhere and ordinary people like me were arguing, talking, dealing and wheeling in our Holy Language.

I filled my lungs with Holy Air and pulled out my uncle's address, asking passersby, amazingly in Hebrew too, where I could find his work-place. I was in Allenby Street near the main post office, looking for the *Shouk Hacarmel* (Carmel Market) when one guy said, pointing, "Go west; you won't miss it."

Very soon after greeting Uncle Shaul, I was taken to his room to stay for a few days. Before long, I was issued an illegal Palestinian identity card with my Hebrew name on it — Yehoshoua — instead of Shoua. Then I felt like a real Jew in a Jewish land — that's all that mattered at that moment. I was penniless and the landlord where my uncle lived refused to let me stay a few more nights with him in the room. All reasonably-priced living spaces were scarce because of the refugees from Europe.

An acquaintance of my uncle offered me room in a narrow space under a staircase on Carmel Street. I quickly accepted, at least for the time being. The small space — where a bed could barely fit — was about six and one-half feet by five feet, and five feet high. I was even unable to stand straight, being five feet, ten inches tall, but I did not mind this for I felt quite comfortable there.

I went looking for work, unsuccessfully. I then decided to take a risk and call on the British Army, despite my fears that with my credentials I might be turned down. I called the recruiting office of the Jewish Brigade, which was being formed after a long struggle with British government politicians and ministers who stalled on the idea for a long time. They did not want to accept a Jewish unit to fight Nazism like they did in the first World War against the Turks. Many Iraqi Jews were already in British units, including my brother Mordechai whom I had not heard from in some time. He was with a unit that was called the Buffs, stationed somewhere unbeknownst to me in Egypt. Many other Iraqi Jews were also serving in various units and capacities, and I wondered how many more Iraqis of the Jewish faith stepped forward to serve a noble cause, besides those in France, England and the United States. In relative terms there were quite many.

My request at the recruiting office for an officer's course commission was subtly and stubbornly rejected because such commissions were limited and already filled by those who were politically entitled to it. Deciding to do it on my own, I approached the British Army, showing my credentials. I was immediately accepted and sent to Ghaza to fill a vacant post with the security identification section of the special investigative branch of the Intelligence Bureau.

In Ghaza, I was billeted in an army camp belonging to the Royal Engineers, along with 30 other Jewish employees of the army. They were engineers, architects, drivers, clerks and a representative of the agency for Jewish affairs in the Palestine administration of the government. His name was Abraham Maloul, and later he became a judge. Mr. Maloul taught me the basics of Jewish politics in the Holy Land.

I was the only person who worked with the British security, but there was another Jew from India who worked with the military police, the "Red Caps." I was surprised to find a Red Cap British military policeman in Tel Aviv who was a Jew from Baghdad. I could not believe it because such posts were usually reserved for the British.

During my first month in Palestine, January 1944, the Allies had already landed in Anzio, Italy. The road to Rome was open, the fighting at Cassino was raging, and the German counterattack was stopped. Hitler resolved to defend Rome with the same obstinacy displayed at Stalingrad and other places. Troops were brought down from France, and if not for Hitler's insistence in throwing the enemy into the sea (an idea and resolve lately adopted by the Arabs), five divisions of their elite troops would have been sent to northwest Europe at the time of the Normandy landing. Mussolini escaped to Germany and Badoglio surrendered Italy to the Allies. Hitler placed the Ciano family under house arrest after they fled, too. Mussolini let loose a wave of calculated violence and the Fascists who voted against him were brought to trial, including his son-in-law Ciano.

The death sentence was carried out against all of them, including the 78-year-old Marshall de Bono, a colleague of his in the march on Rome when they took power. They were each shot in the back of the head while tied to a chair. Mussolini's submission to Hitler's vengeful demands brought him shame and punishment from the people of Italy.

In February, the attack on the Monte Cassino monastery began. In the end it fell to the Indian division of the British Army.

My work in Ghaza was to check that no criminals, foreign agents or undesirables were hired by the British Army. Dealing with Arabs was a very hard task in this respect. Many employees and laborers had many or similar names on their identity cards. Fingerprinting was not used because it had not yet been efficiently developed. The only clues I had were photographs of the applicants or the employees and bodily descriptions. I personally devised a procedure by lining a transparent cellophane sheet, with various sizes of squares, on various sheets. By placing these squares on a photograph and studying the features of the face in comparison to the other photo, square by square, we were able to identify whether the new applicant was the same person or not. Of course, mistakes did happen, especially if the method was applied by new personnel unfamiliar with the technique of the job.

The people of Ghaza were the same as other Arabs in other places, except more troublesome. They were stubbornly anti–Jewish, and there were many criminals and murderers among them. In fact, it was not safe to go from home to work in town every day, and I often encountered someone looking to make trouble.

One day while I was walking by a cafe, a young Arab threw a stool at me, barely missing my eyes. He called me a Jew in derogatory terms. Without hesitation, I picked up the stool and threw it back at him, telling him in Arabic what I would do to him next time if he would not behave. He seemed confused and quietly let me pass.

The days went by monotonously. The only distraction was when some kind of election was taking place in camp for choosing the party that would safeguard the interests of the 30 or so people working with the British in Ghaza. There were about five or six parties to choose from, including Communist, Labour, Right Wing, Middleway Labour, and Socialist. Everyone was campaigning for his or her favorite party. Thirty persons were doing all this as if they were electing parliament for many millions of citizens. I was impressed, and being an anti-totalitarian, I felt I was an integrated part of what was going on even before the state of Israel was established.

I did vote for the Labour Party, but there was a bigger task ahead of us — to make sure that Germany was beaten and the Jews saved. Then we could start the job of our salvation.

Still, I kept thinking about the Arabs who would be opposing a Jewish deliverance. No one envisioned an eternal struggle with them: some predicted that they could be transferred, others believed that they would not be a threat and would accept us as benevolent neighbors. Unfortunately, both schools of thought were, and still are, wrong because of the complicated nature of Arabs who cannot react or act like Europeans and will always be antagonistic. The Jewish people have to always bear this in their minds.

The idea of serving the Jewish cause, irrespective of the political views held by various parties and people, grew stronger inside me. It was presumed the Jewish struggle would begin when the war ended. Nothing could be done until then because our youth were serving abroad. For my part, I could only watch for information vital to the future of the Jewish cause.

Heavy air attacks over Europe intensified. Essen, Hamburg, and Berlin were bombed, creating widespread havoc and consternation throughout Germany. The German leaders increased their use of forced labor from occupied countries in order to maintain their arms production. Even this labor dwindled because of starvation and mass executions.

In May 1944, the confrontation of the Allies against the Germans in Italy, who numbered about 23 divisions, against the Allied forces' 28, was memorable. What was so special about the Allied divisions that rallied against the forces of darkness? They were comprised of soldiers from many nations — Britain, the United States, Poland, India, France, New Zealand, South Africa, Italy and Canada.

Approximately 2,000 guns were opened up in a violent barrage of fire.

The Germans were forced into general retreat, and the Allied entry into Rome on June 6, 1944, was a major victory against Hitler and Mussolini. But, it was not over yet.

On the Russian fronts, the Germans had been driven back and the Russians stood on the borders of the Baltic states. The Russians forced the Germans back towards the old Polish frontier, pressed against the Black Sea. The invaders were in full retreat, but the orders were to stand and fight it out — without withdrawal or concessions. The mass following of a deranged leader has been repeated time and again in the Middle East.

Another event of major importance was taking place during that eventful month of May 1944: the preparations for D-Day. Thirty-five divisions and 4,000 ships were assembled, and troops embarked for the first wave of attack. Eleven thousand planes were sent into action. The greatest armada of the Allied navies and air forces set out for the coast of France. By then, Africa was completely cleared, India had been defended from invasion and Japan was disillusioned. All danger to Australia and New Zealand had passed.

Mankind, especially the Jews, paused in thankfulness, hoping for final victory and for the safe deliverance of family and children facing death in European concentration camps, the scope of which was still virtually unknown.

Our N.C.O. (Non Commissioned Officer) in Ghaza who had survived the war in Italy was killed in a freak accident while riding his motorcycle on the road from Ghaza to Ashkelon. Headquarters in Sarafand sent another officer to replace him. In the meantime, I was requested to fill the vacant post in Sarafand. It was a break for me because I had not, as yet, really lived in a real Jewish or Palestinian community since I left Baghdad. It was about time that I was amongst my people. I had some hard times until I shared a room with a friend in Montefiori quarters. I found lodging at a hotel on Jaffa–Tel Aviv Road and Nahalat Benyamin belonging to an elderly Iraqi lady named Gourjiye, who ran it mainly for Iraqi Jewish refugees but also for illegals who were later ferreted to *kibbutzim* (agriculture settlement) or *moshabim* (Jewish settlers village) around Palestine. If a person came penniless, Gourjiye accepted the promise of future payment of rent.

My roommate and I joined the Haganah as soon as I arrived there. Our commander was an Iraqi Jew from Baghdad. My work at Sarafand was somewhat similar to mine in Ghaza. My colleagues were mostly Palestinian Arabs, and while there were also Jews, I was surprised to discover that most of the Arabs were senior employees, unlike the Jews who were filling less-important positions. The Arabs were the Jews' supervisors and the Jews were under their control. I was under the deputy to the commanding officer, a Christian Arab, and an Iraqi Jew from Baghdad. Most of the Arab employees were Christians, but none of them were friendly with their Jewish colleagues.

The author (standing, far right) poses with his Security Identification Section Unit in Sarafand, Palestine in 1945. The eight Arabs were in charge of the eight Jews in the unit, which featured a British intelligence captain (author's collection).

My task was to check new applicants, as before, except that I was now doing this in the Holy of Holies where top secrets and confidential materials were handled. Naturally, most of the secret materials were handled by Arabs only. Only the British commanding officer and his Arab deputy were allowed to consult or deal with secret papers, which were locked afterwards in a strong safe in the commanding officer's office.

Everything went rather smoothly, and I gained the confidence and cooperation of my Arab colleagues. It was not so difficult for me because I spoke their language and understood their feelings and sentiments. However, I felt stronger ties and a common destiny with my Jewish friends; in this regard the Arabs were completely oblivious. The Arabs were rejecting me, as I learned the hard way, as an Arabic-speaking person only because I was a Jew. Nevertheless, they did remove the thin curtain separating us in the office and became somewhat friendly.

I met a girl named Hava (Eve) of my age whom I started to date rather infrequently because of the situation. We went out on several occasions to take our minds off the events going on around us. She accepted me as I was, but we never thought of having a long-term relationship. She had better things on her mind, as far as money was concerned, and she got it at the end without our losing any of our love for each other.

The seashore of Tel Aviv was our favorite spot and later became like a shrine to us as we visited it every weekend and holiday. We often relaxed at one of its cafes, full of people and friends. It was our only distraction in those days besides the movies, which we frequented very often. The youth of Tel Aviv always scheduled their meetings under the famous, now gone, clock in front of the Moghrabi movie theater on Allenby Street near the seashore. There was another spot for the more affluent in Tel Aviv society — the dance floor of the café near King George's Park. Also at the seashore, Hebrew music made me feel very proud and sentimental.

Hava was good-looking with fair skin and black hair, while I was discounted by my fellow Iraqi Jews as dark and unattractive. To her, I was tall, dark and handsome, which gave me confidence in plans to marry sometime. Our friends bragged, and Israelis usually still do, of having a new girl every now and then. We stayed together and enjoyed our commitment to one another.

I met many of my schooltime friends and acquaintances. Most came illegally; very few came by legal means. By then I realized that a sizeable Iraqi Jewish community was already there. A very few joined the *kibbutzim* (agricultural settlements), and the rest lived in the principal cities of Jerusalem, Haifa and Tel Aviv. The settlements were made possible by the early settlers of the second *aliya* (immigration) from Russia and Poland who played a major part in the establishment of the State of Israel. Though socialist and communist in their philosophy, these founders also thought in nationalist terms concerning the role their settlements would play in determining the borders of a Jewish State.

The early settlers, like our ancestors in the desert, suffered from Bedouin marauders who regularly plundered the settlements in the old *ghazoo* (pillage or looting) style. This forced the early settlers to create some system of self-defense, embodied by the *shomrim* (watchmen).

The first of these settlements was Mikveh Yisrael, then followed Petah Tiqwah, Rehovot, Gedera and Hadera. These settlers stressed the bond which united settlements on the land and military training that was continued until the forming of the Haganah in 1930.

A parallel Jewish fighting force actually began in Egypt. Jewish refugees were exiled by the Turks, and Zeev Jabotinsky, a journalist, was amongst them. He was also a gifted orator and politician who joined forces for the establishment of defense units with Joseph Trumpeldor, a former officer in the Czar's army. Over 600 men joined the British in Gallipoli, where the bloodiest landing in the history of World War I took place against the Turks.

The Zion Mule Corps transported arms and ammunition to the front. After the Balfour Declaration (in which the British recognized the right of the Jews to establish a national home in Palestine), three units were formed to become the first Judean or Jewish regiment, which later became the Jewish Legion. Among the recruits were David Ben-Gurion and Yitzhak Ben Zevi (second president of Israel), both of whom had been expelled from Palestine by the Turks. Many of its veterans subsequently contributed to the development of security forces for the *yishuv* (settlers). While the first Jewish soldier was killed in Gallipoli, pogroms began threatening Jewish lives.

Trumpeldor, who originally founded Bene Zion, commanded the Tel Hai border settlement before later meeting his death in an Arab attack. Tel Hai became a symbol of Jewish self-defense. Jabotinsky was arrested by the British, deported by the authorities, and never returned to Palestine. Later, Arab riots spread and the Jews were stunned by the outbreak of violence. The British were not at all eager to honor the Balfour Declaration, in spite of the Jewish assistance during the war to oust the Turks from Palestine. When the Hashomer (Watchman and subsequent name of the Shomrim Watchmen) became inadequate to defend the Jews, the Haganah was formed. Because the British forbade the Jews of Palestine to bear arms, the Haganah remained a clandestine organization.

The third *aliyah* at the end of World War I gave the Haganah its moving force — mostly immigrants from Russia and Poland who were profoundly influenced by the communist revolution. They were young, single, and eager to establish what they couldn't in Russia — a socialist communist state.

Between the two world wars, Arab hostility erupted in three major outbreaks of terrorism, in 1931 and 1936–1939. Many Jews were massacred in Jerusalem, Hebron, Jaffa, Petah Tiqwa, Hadera, Safed and other settlements.

Armed with the lessons they learned, the Haganah established a clandestine arms industry of its own. The commanders continued to be idealists rather than military leaders, preoccupied more with ideological debates than strategic preparation. The Haganah remained controlled by the left wing. The pro–Nazi Grand Mufti of Jerusalem, Amin El Hussein, exploited the situation by mounting antagonism toward the Jews and easily enraging Arab emotions. Then Fawzi El Kawoukji, an Ottoman army officer dispatched by Syrian nationalist extremists, stepped up the Arab terrorist actions in Palestine.

The Nazi threat that was growing in Europe and among right-wing Arab political groups in Egypt prompted the British to quell the rebellion.

A rival to the Haganah was another underground group, *The Irgun Tzvai Leumi*, founded in reaction to the Haganah policy of restraint. After the British government's 1939 White Paper severely restricted Jewish immigration to Palestine, the Etzel moved against the British authorities and the Arabs. When the Arabs felt that it was very costly to face the British and the Etzel, a relative peace (or rather armistice) was achieved in the spring of 1939. The Arabs had scored a political victory via the White Paper.

By 1937, the Jewish population of Palestine was 400,000; it reached over 600,000 when I joined the struggle.

During World War II, the Haganah joined the Allied effort and the Etzel suspended its activities against and even prepared to cooperate with the British. An Etzel commander, David Raziel, was killed in Iraq while opposing the pro–Nazi Kilani Rebellion.

In opposition to the Etzel's cooperation with the British during the war, a splinter group headed by Abraham Yair Stern broke away and established the *Lochamei Herut Yisrael* (LEHI, or Fighters for Israel's Freedoms). With them, there was no ceasefire against the British. Stern was killed in a British police raid in 1942. Later, LEHI assassinated the British Minister for Middle Eastern Affairs, Lord Moyan, in Cairo. (The killers, Yacob Ben Zur and Albert Hakim, were caught by the Egyptian police and hanged.)

The Etzel also resumed its activities against the British early in 1944. Menachem Begin, then commander of the Etzel, and Yitzhak Shamir, commander of LEHI, both became prime ministers in due course.

Reports of the extermination of the Jews in Europe filtered through to Palestine, but the British still refused to permit the refugees of the Nazi Holocaust to enter the country.

The Etzel harassment steadily increased, influencing the British government to terminate its mandate over Palestine. During World War II, 28,000 men and 4,000 women of the Jewish community volunteered for various units of the British army. Some attained the rank of officer, and many became senior commanders with the Israel Defense Forces. These volunteers acquired experience in air force, infantry, commando, artillery, and engineering units. When Rommel approached Egypt, a retreat from Palestine further north to Baalbek was considered. The Haganah established *plugot mahatz* (smiting groups later known as the *Palmach*) to employ guerrilla warfare against the Germans behind the lines.

Many of the young immigrants from Iraq joined the LEHI and the Irgun instead of the Haganah. Others remained true to their ancestors' tradition and engaged in business — importing or exporting — while still conscious of the dangers around them and their duty to participate in some way. Others succeeded in establishing solid, mutually beneficial business ties with the neighboring Arab countries. I felt somewhat at home, relatively speaking, because here there was a larger and more significant percentage of Jews than in Iraq. What surprised me most was that they became quickly acclimatized and also absorbed into the Jewish community of Palestine, especially the *kibbutzim* (settlements). They adapted many customs from the Jews of Europe but failed to realize that our heritage carried with it a weighty past that could not be ignored. In some cases it was hard to recognize a covert Iraqi Jew because of quickly-acquired European manners and fluency in Hebrew. Many of them intermarried and had beautiful and wonderful *sabras* (offspring).

It puzzled me that very few got themselves involved in the Jewish politics of the *Yishuv* (Jewish population). Was it because they were a minority or because they were unenthusiastic about politics? We had our Jewish representative in the Iraqi parliament, but why not here? The Iraqis were represented by the *Hitachdut Olei Babel* (Union of Babylonian Immigrants), but they were not as influential as the Chief Rabbinate, who stood up in matters pertaining to Jewish affairs back in Baghdad.

It would take the Allies another year to end the war in Europe, plus another three months to end it in Asia. The invasion of Normandy started on D-Day — June 6, 1944 — and it was the real turning point in the most devastating war in history.

The Polish resistance movement in Warsaw ended with the ill-fated uprising that involved our Jewish brothers there. The Warsaw ghetto was completely destroyed, and every man, woman, and child was killed then or later slaughtered in a concentration camp.

The Russians, instead of helping the Polish underground army, stood still and did nothing. The Germans burnt entire streets of houses and shot all men, women, and children in them. A movie documentary filmed by the cruel Germans themselves shows people in flames jumping from windows to their death on the streets.

The news in Palestine was catastrophic to us. Not only was the ghetto destroyed, but the Jews were shockingly abandoned to their fate and annihilation without a finger being raised by any of the great powers, especially Russia.

It was of slight consolation when we learned that they fought bravely and bitterly against their mortal enemy to the bitter end, realizing Samson's resolve of *Temut nafshi am pelishtim*—"to destroy myself with the Philistines."

Upon hearing the news, the Jews of Palestine and the rest of the world fell into a deep mourning. Enlightened Arabs were also disturbed; there were no words to describe the tragedy of the European Jewery. Refugees who succeeded in entering Palestine were telling horrible stories unlike any heard before.

It is still being argued how so many millions of Jews were slaughtered without anyone raising a finger and why they went like sheep to the German slaughterhouse. First, it is untrue that there was not any resistance. Many thousands escaped and joined the partisans, maquis, guerrillas and freedom fighters in various lands. Besides, the innocent were tricked by their captors. During World War I, the Germans, arriving where the Jews were concentrated, forced them to take showers and deliced them to combat the spread of diseases when mingling with or working for Germans. In World War II, the Germans used the same procedure, knowing that the Jews would not suspect their true motive or put up any resistance. Instead of water, gas was pumped in, killing bunches of them at a time.

There was an attempt on Hitler's life, which failed, and when he got up, shaken but unharmed, he commented, "Who said that I am not under the protection of God?" He did not say what god. A few officers who were with him were killed. This act aroused his fury against suspected conspirators, including his best general, Rommel.

Later there were crossings on the Seine River. On August 24, the first detachments moved into the city of Paris. The main thrust was made at night, when a vanguard of tanks entered the square in front of the Hotel de Ville (Town Hall), and soon the capitulation of the garrison of Paris was signed in spite of Hitler's orders to scorch the city.

Paris was free again. The joyful French people regained their pride as they chased the murderous invaders out. Upon hearing the news, I remembered two French officers back in Beirut who cried like babies when Paris fell, and I wondered whether they were still alive to celebrate this joyous event. The same was with all the other liberated cities of Europe. In Tel Aviv, cautious celebrations took place because everyone knew the full details of the Holocaust were still unknown.

On April 12, 1945, President Roosevelt died suddenly during the supreme climax of the war. His poliomyelitis wore heavily upon him, and it was a miracle that he bore up against it through all the many years of tumult and storm. Harry Truman became the new president.

At this time, all of Palestine was still in the dark, observing a blackout with no lights allowed to burn on the streets or in the windows. It was a kind of romantic setting and people had gotten used to it after four years of open-air night clubs, dancing, and dining in cafés that enticed people to frequent them and relieve the tension of the war. People became more intimate, and many youth hastened their decision to marry. Crime was at its lowest rate and people even left their apartment doors open for fresh air without fearing the consequences.

Meanwhile, the advance of the Allied armies continued with increasing momentum. The Allies eventually met the Russians at Wismar, Germany. Everywhere in Europe, masses of refugees and disorganized soldiers fled from the Russians to surrender to the Allies.

After the capture of concentration camps in Buchenwald, Dachau, Meidenek, Triblinka, and Sobibor, the Nazi atrocities, which were so barbaric and animalistic, were made gradually known to the world. The human race never in its history reached such a low level of abominable acts. When the war was over, people rejoiced in the streets of the world, but Jews thought of observing another *Tishaa Beau* (Ninth of Av) — the date of the destruction of the second temple in Jerusalem — to mourn and memorialize the befallen Jewish people.

A rebellion in Syria and Lebanon resulted when de Gaulle sent French troops there. The French shelled gatherings and houses in Damascus and Homs. They occupied the Syrian Parliament, after killing or injuring nearly 2,000 people. A ceasefire was ordered upon intervention of the British commander in chief; the French withdrew to a camp outside the city.

After the victories of the Allies, it was said that it was time to enter a golden age of prosperity and progress. After the drop of the atom bombs on Japan, all world-wide war activities ceased. The dropping of the atom bombs on Hiroshima and Nagasaki saved hundred of thousands of lives for the Allies, but also destroyed hundred of thousands of innocent lives in those two cities. The Allies acted in self-defense and the innocent citizens of Japan fell victim to their rulers' grandiose dreams and demagoguery.

# CHAPTER 10

# Underground
# Double Action

The British Labor party that won the election took over the government from Churchill's Tories. Before the election, Labor members proclaimed that if they won they would support Jewish self-rule in Palestine. But, they did just the opposite, refusing residence to refugees from concentration camps. Other countries acted in the same manner, leading me to wonder if the world was becoming crueler after the war. The victorious governments chickened out because of the Arabs. We Jews knew that the war was not really over yet.

I was not surprised to hear on the radio and read in the papers that underground Jewish fighters attacked the Labor Party in England. However, the attacks were carried out after proper warnings were given to save lives. By then, everyone was aware that the British government would not keep its promises made the Jews of Palestine. Our dignity and liberty as human beings were still at stake, and we had to save it ourselves.

At work in the military camps, I noticed a lot of activity upon arrival of the Red Berets, whom we nicknamed *Kalaniot* (Anemones — Wind Red Flowers), troops from Europe fully armed as if they were going to another world war against another enemy.

We continued working as if nothing was happening in spite of the fact that the two underground groups — the Irgun and LEHI — were becoming more and more active in their struggle against the British. The Haganah, too, at this point struggled against the British, and they blew up bridges on the Jordan borders. After I made contact through my Haganah commander to the right wing of intelligence (the *Shai*) things became different with me and I felt I was finally working for myself and the Jewish people. It was the famous Hebrew saying that inspired my actions: "Am ain ani li mi li." (If I am not for myself, who is?)

In the beginning, I became interested in all activities at our headquarters. There were many confidential documents about arrivals of new units and the like that I either copied or borrowed for the evening if they could be valuable to the underground. My contact worked in Tel Aviv as a reporter for the *Jerusalem Post*. I began to see Mr. Garfinkel (possibly an alias) after work almost every evening because the information I was giving was very important to Haganah intelligence. In today's terminology, Mr. Garfinkel was my controller. In addition to this service, I was active in the Haganah Patrol in our Montefiori quarter in Tel Aviv which safeguarded against any unexpected attacks by British police who were then engaged in acts of terrorism against the Yishuv.

Anti-Semitic British officials and their Arab collaborators were also actively hurting innocent Jewish civilians in retaliation for the *Irgun Zvai Leumi* and LEHI activities. We used to drive through our neighborhood and the streets of Tel Aviv, sometimes carrying one or more handguns. We often had to hastily discard the guns in any of the lawns surrounding the houses (making sure to remember the exact spot in order to retrieve it later on) when we were being followed by police who wanted to search our car or interrogate us.

The *Shai* was the intelligence network of the underground prior to the establishment of the State of Israel. In Hebrew, *Shai* means *sherut yedioth* (information service). Its achievements were quite impressive. Among other things, the Shai gathered information about the British administration, its military activities and above all, changes of policy concerning Palestine. The *Shai* also eavesdropped and broke secret codes.

At that time, I never knew who my superiors were. I did not care much as long as my information went to worthy Jewish sources. My objective was to furnish them with as much information as possible. My previous experience helped me understand how vital such information could be in saving work and lives on both sides. Moreover, this information would tip off Israeli leaders before vicious acts of violence against the Jewish population and its leaders could take place. I was working on my own and did not belong to any faction; I remained so even after the establishment of the State of Israel.

At work, I needed protection from the risk of being exposed and possibly harmed. I was actually smuggling things from our security headquarters to my controller on the outside. One evening before going on patrol, our Haganah commander ordered me to put on a darker shirt, pointing out that I needed to camouflage myself from my surroundings to do my job. I also realized that to camouflage my thoughts and behavior in the office would keep any suspicion away from me while I was doing my clandestine work. Henceforth, I made sure that my Arab and Jewish colleagues remained convinced that I was either pro–Arab or at least neutral about what was going on in the country at that time. I convinced them that being an Iraqi Jew, I had nothing to do with any of the fighting factions. As soon my work was terminated, I would go back to Baghdad where I belonged. That at least calmed them down and assured them that I was not their enemy. They were initially surprised by my statements but later took them at face value, based on my past work abroad in Beirut. Later, we became more friendly and cooperative. I hoped someday to tell my Jewish colleagues the truth. Only one Jewish colleague, Mr. Candine, did not believe me because he knew exactly what I was doing. He never told anyone, but I suspected he might because of the way he smiled at me. Since he was Jewish, I wasn't overly concerned, but I was still apprehensive about the whole situation. On one occasion, when I was busily searching through the files for names on the Black List, he entered unnoticed and warned me that someone was coming, saving me from being caught in the act. Upon discovering my true intention, he explained, he began to watch and protect me from being discovered and caught. I thanked God for putting Mr. Candine here so that I could continue my work unhindered.

The attacks on British troops and police were intensified, but proper warnings were made every time to enable innocent civilians to save themselves. But the warnings were ignored on July 22, 1946, at the King David Hotel in Jerusalem — site of the British army headquarters and home to the secretary general of the Palestine government. The army, the hotel reception, the French Consulate and the *Palestine Post* newspaper were warned of the imminent explosion that would occur in 39 minutes. Because no one took the warning seriously, nearly one hundred people were killed, including many Jewish civilian workers.

The hunt for the LEHIs and the Irgun was intensified. Entire Jewish quarters were surrounded and citizens aged 16 or older were rounded up for questioning. I was picked up, along with 30 to 50 others, and put on a truck one early morning. I told one of the soldiers that many of the people he was guarding were soldiers who served his Majesty's government, but he just bent his head down and continued to blankly watch his cargo.

We arrived at the barbed-wire detention enclave and were ordered to go into the first big circle. There were three circles, each smaller than the one before, plus a very small enclosure for questioning. The British police were assisted by the Red Berets in its scrutinous interrogation. After more than an hour, a British policeman came in to "sort us out." Most of us who looked like Europeans were sent home and the rest were ordered into the second circle. After another hour or two, all who looked like Middle Easterners were detained and the rest were released and sent home. There were about five or six of us left. We were told to enter the smallest of the barbed-wire circles. We waited in the sun for nearly an entire day without food or drink. Finally, it was my turn to enter into the small room for my interrogation.

Needless to say, I was extremely worried by then and was prepared for anything to happen. I could not help but think that the Labor government in Britain that took over the destiny of Britain after World War II was trying to harm the Jews of Palestine while the world believed that the conflict was actually between Arabs and Jews. I began to realize that my employers — the British — could not be my friends and I decided there on the spot to disregard the idea of telling them that I was working for the British Security Identification section.

I went in and they made me stand in front of a policeman who was sitting at an improvised desk. First, he asked me for identification, which I immediately presented to him and which was deemed kosher (proper). I noticed that he wore a regular uniform, which was unusual because interrogations like these were usually carried out by an inspector or officer. Sure enough, one of his Arab aides slipped up, calling him "Sir" in spite of the fact that he was also in a police uniform. His manners and speech further confirmed my suspicion that he was an officer and not a regular policeman.

I was tired after the intentional long wait. His first question was whether I was an Iraqi-born Jew. I answered in the affirmative. The next question was rather ambiguous: did I know another Iraqi Jew by the name of Nouri or Nouriel? I said I did not know him. My interrogator smiled and asked me to let him know if I heard of his whereabouts, knowing very well that I would not do this. I just smiled and nodded my head and he let me go.

Later, this same Iraqi-born Jew was actually caught and hanged. All this was being carried out under the false assumption that Palestine was a land for the Arabs — in addition to their immense and vast territories in the Middle East — and their protectors, the British, who stood by and fought for them irrespective of the Arabs' past actions or the promise made to the Jewish people to establish a homeland in Palestine. The struggle from now on would be ugly and inhumane.

The Arabs were so confident they would rule Palestine that they did not think they would have to fight for it. They felt so sure that the country would be handed to them on a platter that even the ordinary man on the street behaved as if he was the ruler of the land.

A story appeared in the Arabic newspapers in Jaffa, which illustrated the current state of thinking. According to the story, a Jew issued a six-month loan to an Arab. Seven or eight months later, the still-unpaid Jew took the Arab to court. The unemployed Arab explained to the judge that when he was employed and had money, he could not find the Jew to pay him. The Arab then arrogantly asked the judge to jail the Jew instead of him so that he would know where to find him when he came up with the money.

The *Palmach*, an elite full-time military formation that was first active against the British, went into action just like the *Irgun* and the LEHI. They blew up railway bridges on the borders with Jordan and inside the country. Other similar operations would have probably continued if not for certain information I made available to the leaders of the policymakers that made them change their policy towards the British administration from an active struggle to a passive resistance.

At work, it was most difficult for me to go into the commander's office without a legitimate reason. Every time the military mail arrived, I was nearby to assist or at least to glance at the envelopes, especially the ones that were marked confidential, secret, or top secret.

All the mail subsequently went to the Arab assistant who carried it to the commander. The regular mail was given back to the Arab assistant and the rest was opened inside. One day I happened to be inside when the secret mail was being opened and I noticed one particular envelope marked for the commanding officer's attention only. Of course, I became curious but could do nothing except to remember the kind of booklet which was inside that envelope. Later, I formed a pretext to get into the commander's room and noticed the small booklet lying on his desk. After making sure that no one was watching, I slipped the booklet inside the privy part of my body and left the room.

No one mentioned that the booklet was missing. Either the officer thought he mailed it back after making notes or he knew that it was stolen and decided to keep quiet about it. At the end of the day, before contacting my controller, curiosity got the best of me and I read the contents of the booklet, which was about three by five inches with ten to fifteen pages. It contained complete instructions on how to deal with the underground movements or organizations, where to look for them, information about their ideologies and political views, ways and means to fight them, and other information. The instructions given to the officers of his Majesty's Government regarding the *Haganah* received my keenest attention. While the get-tough policy against the *Irgun* and the LEHI was emphasized in this booklet, it was specifically mentioned that the *Haganah* was not the real enemy and could be considered somewhat friendly.

In the evening, I handed the booklet to my controller, who quickly went through its contents. He appeared as surprised as me but said nothing. He took it over to the leaders of the *Haganah* for their perusal. A few days later, I could not believe it when I heard on the radio that the Jewish agency that actually controlled the *Haganah* announced that operations against the British forces were ceased and efforts would be made to help the authorities in the restoration of law and order. The *Haganah* then stopped all acts of violence and condemned such acts committed by the other two groups. This about-face action came about as a precautionary reaction to the widely oppressive suppression by the British administration. Many people, myself included, were eager to see more action from the *Haganah* in the struggle to liberate Palestine. Unfortunately, the *Haganah* went silent and let the other two groups do the work instead.

I was glad to learn, later on, that before the *Haganah* stopped it had helped liberate the illegal immigrants who were interned in Atlit Camp. Before it ceased such acts, the *Haganah* also blew up railway bridges and train tracks and sunk the British Coast Guard boats that intercepted illegal (as they considered them) immigrants from the ruins of Europe and the concentration camps. Unfortunately, the Jews of Palestine were not united. The three anti–British underground military groups worked independently of each other, according to each group's political viewpoint. There were very sharp clashes — verbal, political and sometimes physical — between the two splinter groups and the *Haganah*.

While continuing to supply actual or copied documents, which was vital to the underground, I made a goal to copy the Black List of the British administration. It would be the toughest job I faced in my entire life. I knew that absolutely no one could even glimpse at this list except Major P. Hogg, our commanding officer, and on rare occasions his Arab deputy.

The rooms where all the records were filed contained many tens of thousands of files. They contained most of the records of legitimate employees, Arabs as well as Jews and others who worked with the military in the country, including the British administration. There were names of contractors, suppliers, and even agents. I had free access to those files and had no problem going into the rooms for a reasonable duration of time. The alphabetically-arranged information, including photographs, filled the two rooms because our unit was the center of such information in Sarafand. This section was also used by the British special investigation branch. Neither Arabs nor Jews were allowed to work with this unit, not even Jewish British military personnel. The filing rooms, one large and the other smaller annexed to it, had eight walls with drawers filled with small envelopes, plus three or four shelves standing in the middle of the two rooms also stacked with drawers filled with more envelopes.

Among the tens of thousands of envelopes, one absolutely empty with a name in red ink indicated a person on the Black List. We were told that such envelopes should go straight to the commanding officer or the special investigation branch of the army in Palestine. I told my controller about my discovery and he was very pleased. The next day he gave me the green light from the people in charge of information intelligence (*Shai*).

I made it my daily routine to write down every name written in red ink. I delivered a daily quota of 40 to 50 names to my controller; at that rate, it would take a few months to complete the operation. I always had something to check in the filing room and always went in with legitimate papers and a small, long piece of paper hidden underneath onto which I copied the names in red ink. I did not miss a single day of laboriously writing down all of the Arab and Jewish names. Nobody noticed anything except for a Jewish colleague who realized there was no legitimate reason for me to be in that room for more than a few minutes. Sometimes he smiled at me in a meaningful way. We did not speak, but still he kept watch outside. I began to worry that he would betray me, because there were such traitors even then during our struggle. But, Mr. Candine kept his watchguard vigil. I was convinced later on that he was probably sent by my people to protect me until I finished the job.

Because of the many security leaks and possible smuggling of secret documents out of the Sarafand camp as well as the stealing of arms, security measures were beefed up around the camp and various agents tried to catch the smugglers and spies.

I usually had my breakfast in the morning at the *tnuva* (dairy) restaurant inside the camp. One day while the place was still empty, a Red Beret soldier sat right beside me and started a conversation. He said that he was pro–Jewish, and that made me immediately suspicious of him. How did he know that I was Jewish? I could easily be mistaken for an Arab, Christian, or any other nationality. I was familiar with British soldiers, but this one was different. His refined speech was unlike that of the ordinary cockney soldiers and his manners were conspicuous. I therefore began to suspect that he was not an ordinary soldier. He repeatedly mentioned that he was ready to help the Jews after all they had suffered through. I kept listening and smiling, answering with a terse "yes" or "no" whenever necessary. I also answered him as vaguely as I could under the circumstances. The same week I saw this soldier entering the special investigation branch offices in a captain's uniform.

One day after work, our military truck was stopped and we were ordered by the British and military police to line up near the gate of the camp. As usual, I was loaded with secret documents as well as my quota of black-listed names. Two tents were erected nearby and two British policemen of each sex started searching the bodies of both women and men inside each tent. My first reaction was to turn back and stay the night in camp if necessary and go home the next day. But who could guarantee that the search would not be conducted the next day as well? Besides, I thought, a civilian being caught in camp after curfew hours would be a worse fate.

Luckily, we were isolated from the tents so I instinctively decided to separate myself from the line by walking backwards. As soon as I was five or ten yards behind the line, a British police officer tapped me on the shoulder and asked, in Arabic, why I was there. I looked around and discovered that we were completely surrounded by soldiers and British policemen. As soon as I heard his question in Arabic, I answered as a miserable Arab would in Arabic: "I don't know, *Ya Sidi,*" which means "my master"—preferred by Englishmen when addressed by Arabs. I added, "I want to go out but I see a commotion and don't know what to do." He told me in broken Arabic that it was meant for the Jews, not me. A slight kick from behind sent me running towards the gate, and the British officer gave specific instructions in a loud voice to the gate guards to let me out. Calmly and nonchalantly, I walked through the wide-open gate like a prince.

I crossed the road, took the first bus to Tel Aviv and went straight to my controller. When he heard my story, he smiled and said that Jews are still working miracles. If I had been caught with the "hot" stuff I delivered, I would have surely been sent to jail for a long time, not only because I was working for the *Haganah* but because I might be suspected of belonging to other groups. That night I recited the "*Shehiyanou ve Kiyemanu Ve Hegianu Lazman Haze*"—"Blessed be He who kept us alive and sustained us and brought us to the present time."

One afternoon while on patrol for the *Haganah*, I was told to take the main road to the Yarkon River from Montefiori Quarters. I was also told to come back before sunset by following a path in the fields near the Templar colony, which then was a type of a military fortress in the area of Tel Aviv. It was surrounded by barbed wire and high watchtowers manned by Arab and British guards who shot upon sight any intruder on that field after curfew. The area was considered a restricted zone and no one could come within 200 meters of the perimeter without being shot.

My Haganah commander and I were not exactly aware of how much time it took to get back home before curfew. It was a rainy day, which made walking more difficult. Everything went well while photographing the turrets and towers until the sun sat in the west and darkness settled in before I could make it out of the restricted zone. All of a sudden, just before passing the last watchtower, I was spotted by a strong searchlight and ordered in English to raise my hands and stand still. I then heard a rifle being loaded. I disregarded the order and was about to continue moving when I heard a voice in broken English say, "Sir, maybe he does not understand English." The order was translated to me in Arabic and the Arab guard begged me not to move; otherwise I would be dead. Again my Middle Eastern features helped. I thanked him in Arabic and waited while doing just as he instructed. With the searchlight still on my face, the British officer in charge ordered the Arab to ask me where I was from and where I was going. I had ample time to think of my answer because I understood the question in English. I told them I was from a certain Arab village beyond the Yarkon River and took a shortcut through the fields on my way to Jaffa. When asked where I lived and whether I knew anyone in Jaffa, I promptly gave the name and address of someone I met a few months before. This reply seemed to satisfy them and they let me go with the warning that I should avoid Tel Aviv, especially in the evenings. They bade me "*Maa el Salama*" (Godspeed).

I was urged to complete the black list because so far the names on that list were known figures, Arabs as well as Jews, who were considered either dangerous or active underground members suspected by the British Intelligence. The *Haganah* had been unaware that the British knew about them. The discoveries demanded reorganization of activities and changes for those suspected of working for the administration in Palestine. It became necessary to assign others and change planning and activities in the future.

Before the mandate was ended, the British administration decided to arrest the known military leaders of the *Haganah*. But before the intended arrest, the military leaders had fled and the political leaders and other functionaries were arrested instead.

The effects of the arrests were minimal. Arab leaders were not touched, and by now it was clear that Britain falsely acted as an honest arbiter desiring justice for all concerned. The British were in fact active participants in the confrontations between Jews and Arabs. The British and the Arabs were allied in preventing the establishment of a Jewish State.

In appreciation for my work, I was presented a book about Hanna Senesh by the heads of *Shai* through my controller, Mr. Garfinkel. The book was dedicated to me by some of the leaders in the *Haganah*. Hanna Senesh was the girl parachutist who was dropped behind German lines in Europe to participate in intelligence activities for the Allies. She subsequently was caught and executed by the Germans. I very much cherished this dedicated book, but it was unfortunately lost when someone who borrowed it was killed in action.

Violent acts against the British administration became a daily affair and on many occasions I watched the chase of kids posting pamphlets and underground news. Members of the *Irgun* and LEHI held up British banks to finance their struggles. For everyone at that time, these were the moments to act, but now this principle is outdated. The Arab disturbances were just a myth.

The Middle East remained quiet for the duration of the war with or without the white papers restricting survivors to immigrate to Palestine. After the war, the British sought to classify all Jews as natives of their respective lands, a theme still being reverberated by the Arab nations, but they failed to understand that Jews had lost their self-esteem, national longing and human dignity after what Hitler and Germany did to them. The Holocaust had taken away any belonging to their countries, and their sole interest, like other Jews in other lands, was to come together and stand up in unity to survive. The splinter factions, knowing what was brewing in the British political camp, did

A commemorative monument was built on top of the small bunker where the author intercepted telephone calls made between Jaffa and Ramle. The bunker is located at the entrance to Mikve Yisvael, the first *kibbutz* (settlement) in Palestine (author's collection).

not wait until the war was completely over and, in August 1944, plotted to kill the high commissioner to Palestine, Harold McMichel, and in November they executed Lord Moyan in Cairo.

When the struggle against Britain intensified, the Jewish-populated areas were searched and the police and the army often erected roadblocks for stopping and searching vehicles. Britain intended to substitute Palestine for Egypt as its main base in the Middle East.

The Arabs stood still and did not take any action against the British during that period. They were not exactly nonbelligerent, but they organized themselves by purchasing arms and training themselves. National pride and anti-colonization in the neighboring Arab countries intensified. In Syria and Lebanon, the French rule came to an end. In 1947, the end was near when the United Nations voted to establish two states in Palestine, one Jewish and the other Arab. The *Shai* (*Haganah* Intelligence) dealt only in local and Palestinian matters and had no idea what was going on in the Arab countries.

After having terminated my work with British Security when the unit moved out, I was sent by the *Shai* to eavesdrop on the telephone calls made

between Jaffa and Ramle and the rest of the country. The telephone intercep-
tions were set up in a small bunker that still stands today, near the main gate
on the Jaffa-Ramle road at the entrance to Mikve Yisrael, the first *kibbutz*
(settlement) established in Palestine. There were five or six interceptor telephones and speakers. Besides me, another Iraqi Jew, Naim Kuweity, worked
at this bunker. There was no tape recorder so we had to write everything down
as fast as the conversation went. There were three or more of us at a time listening carefully to all calls, sometimes made in languages other than Arabic
or English, picked according to the judged interest of the *Shai* leaders. We
usually watched for any plan or action intended to harm the *Yishuv*. There
was a lot of information which was carefully scrutinized and forwarded to the
parties concerned. It seemed that we were doing a very good job; otherwise,
Mr. Isser Harel (later, chief of the Mossad Security Service of the State of
Israel) would not have visited us so often — in some cases a few times a day.

We learned about various movements of British troops and Arab irregulars, and all kind of activities taking place inside Jaffa, Ramle and the rest of
Palestine. Unlike today's communications, all calls went through wires passing
in front of the settlement, and tapping into it was not difficult. The most difficult
task was to follow the essence of the conversation and write most if not all of it
in comprehensible notes to be later translated into Hebrew and submitted to
those who would act upon its subject matter. I later became an expert in Arabic speed writing. It was fun and, above all, very interesting. On many occasions, we picked up messages of British police ordering an ambush or raid. Some
of the intercepted messages were in code and later had to be deciphered.

In one instance, we learned that Iraqi irregulars would soon be pulling
out their arms, armored vehicles and equipment. Other gangs were also
ordered by their military sponsors to leave Jaffa. The *Etzel* was at their heels
at the border of the twin cities. For several nights, the *Haganah* blew up all
the houses bordering Jaffa and Tel Aviv, planning that if the partition was
implemented and Israel accepted its borders, then troublesome Jaffa and its
snipers would be separated from Tel Aviv. The leaders at the time believed in
genuine peace and the blowing up of the border houses was just a precaution
for the future. The inhabitants of Jaffa were scared of the demolitions that
were taking place. Even I, not knowing at the time what was going on, lost a
few nights' sleep. The explosions were carried out and a permanent border
was established between Jaffa and Tel Aviv. (A tourist in that part of the city,
especially at the end of the Carmel Market, can see the open space between
the two cities that was created at that time.)

The unit of the *Palmach* in charge of the area received orders to ambush
and destroy all the Iraqi irregular units who were coming out of Jaffa at the
Mikve Yisrael settlement on the main Jaffa-Ramle road. Apprehensive and

very nervous, we all laid low in our bunker and in the surrounding field. Almost five minutes before zero hour, a specific rescinding order to abrogate the ambush was received. Immediately after the order came a confirmation of the cancellation, and this was transmitted to all units just a minute or two before zero hour. We then witnessed an unforgettable parade of humanity marching along the main road: military trucks, armored cars, tanks, mortars, machine guns, hundreds of irregulars with their rifles and equipment. The people of Jaffa were a mixture of old men, women, children, maimed and sick people, some carried on stretchers, some on armored cars or tanks. It reminded me of the movie *Les Misérables*. It was impossible to imagine what would have happened if we opened fire on these miserable refugees, who didn't know they were actually protecting the Arab gangs.

A few days later, I went into Jaffa itself. All stores, businesses, and public places were empty and not a single solitary soul could be found on the streets. There were no cars, except *Palmach*, nor animals except for cats and dogs roaming aimlessly about the empty city. I met an old man casually walking in the middle of the main street, so I asked him about the situation. I was not surprised when he told me that all the inhabitants of Jaffa had left out of fear and that the Arab countries had told them to leave everything behind because they would return with their victorious Arab armies in a matter of weeks.

This happened despite the Arabs of Palestine knowing that the Jewish settlers would not harm them. The demolition of border buildings and houses had created such a panic in the guilty consciences of the Arabs in Jaffa that, fearing revenge, they heeded their foreign saviors and fled. They believed that those foreign Arabs, self-professed saviors of Palestine, would reconquer the land and bring them back to their homes. Those people had followed their traditions and the preaching of their spiritual and political leaders who continuously brainwashed them into believing that revenge is sacred and hatred is noble.

The United States was about to suggest another mandate when it became known that all seven Arab countries were going to attack the newborn infant. It was unbelievable that the greatest nation on earth, the one that dropped atomic bombs on Japan, was afraid of the Arab demagogue leaders and their ominous, but ultimately unsubstantiated, threats.

Later, it was announced that all *Haganah* units, including *Etzel* and LEHI, were to be drafted into military units of the declared State of Israel because of the impending peril from the seven Arab countries marching toward Palestine to rid it of the Jews. The bunker at Mikve Yisrael became obsolete and we were told to join the Israeli armed forces and prepare for war. As one of the first men drafted, I was sent to a camp north of Tel Aviv called Camp David. I took leave for a day or two to wrap up a new export-import business I had just established.

# CHAPTER 11

# Sacrificing the Baby at Birth

In the following days, all communications with the Arab world were severed. We were completely isolated except from the sea. When the Arab nations declared war on the newly-born state, it seemed that they (as well as the Jewish people) had forgotten their own history and the famous sayings of their ancient leaders. The ancient Arab general Tariq Ibn Ziyad, who conquered Spain and whose name was still remembered as Jabal Tariq or Gibraltar, was situated at the extreme southern part of Spain, separating it from Morocco over the high rock where the Mediterranean Sea joins the Atlantic Ocean and separates Europe from Africa. There he had burnt the ships on which he sailed with his soldiers and told them at the shore of Spain they had two choices: the enemy in front of them or the sea behind them.

The Arabs did advance in hideous onslaught, mimicking the shattered Nazi war machine with its dandified officers and brutish soldiers plodding on like a swarm of crawling locusts. Behind all this was a small group of villainous Jew-haters, men who planned to launch horrors upon Zionism and Jews.

Again, I bade farewell to all my friends and relatives and became an Israeli soldier defending our ancient traditions, religion, and land which had flourished in the past. Above all, I was fighting to finally regain our dignity and freedom. Jerusalem was besieged and surrounded by the Arab legion commanded by British officers. Fighting in Haifa was fierce, though beginning to wind down. The last British soldier was leaving Palestine. Ben-Gurion was ready to make his announcement, despite objections from many nations and members of his own party. He had the guts to do it and it is no wonder why he was later nicknamed a "prophet with a gun." The State of Israel was declared on May 14, 1948.

For over 2,000 years, the Jews suffered unlike Poles, Iraqis, Egyptians, Russians, French, or any other nationality. Their agony was not uniform. In Yemen, for example, the Jews lived as second-class citizens for over 2,600 years. Like the Jews of Iraq, Syria, and Egypt, they were subjected daily to

The author (center) with friends on October 15, 1947, before active service in defending the new State of Israel (author's collection).

restriction, discrimination, and humiliation; this had not, as yet, come to an end. They were not massacred or expelled on a large scale like the Jews of Europe, but the danger to their safety was so evident that there was no other way but to leave and come to Palestine. The expulsion from Spain because of the Inquisition 500 years ago left more than half a million Jews destitute. They roamed North Africa and the Middle East looking for a place to settle and were dispersed in that part of the world, becoming known as the Sephardic Jews (Spanish Jews). Others went to East Europe where a substantial community already existed; they became known as the Ashkenazi Jews. In the Middle East, there were and still exist many strange tales of violence and looting and murdering of Jews in the Arab lands. In Syria, for example, the doors are closed in their face to prevent their escape.

Most gruesome of all was the Jewish experience in Iraq and Egypt, considered civilized countries by the west. Repression of the Iraqi Jews has approached the excesses of the Nazi Regime in the thirties. There have been violent searches, vandalism, confiscations, extortions and torture — all legal under martial laws. To make it specifically anti–Jewish, a crime called Zionism was added to the law. If two witnesses testify that someone is sympathetic to Zionism, that person could be hung. Jews were ousted from the Iraqi government service and deprived of medical licenses. Schools and universities were cleansed by deliberately and systematically making sure the Jewish students failed their exams. I was a victim of this practice, which had been going on since 1936. Restrictions were imposed on Jewish merchants and banks. It was a capital offense for a Jew to leave the country. Jews who disobeyed the order to return to Iraq within a few weeks were hanged or imprisoned, or had their property seized.

Even I, born in Baghdad but having left Iraq around 1938, was tried *in absentia* and sentenced to be hanged because of not returning within the given time as proclaimed by martial laws. The verdict was announced on the Iraqi Broadcasting Station in Baghdad and repeated many times. I heard it myself after a cousin told me it was being announced on the radio. In the Kelet (Recruiting) Camp David, we were sorted out and sent to various units. I was not, as yet, assigned to any unit and was granted permission to visit my office and take care of a few things which were still pending.

We had a lady, a survivor of the Holocaust, who served us tea and cookies. She was healthy and charming and somewhat attractive in her 40s. Her only son, 17 or 18 years old, was exempt from serving in a fighting unit. I was very sad to learn that he disregarded his military status, falsified his papers and joined the *Palmach*. A few days before I came back, she received word that he had been killed by Arabs on the front line. The lady was devastated; in one week she aged 50 or 60 years. Her face became quickly wrinkled and a melancholic voice replaced her joyful and friendly one. It was heart-breaking. There were no words to comfort her on the loss of her only son. She told me that he could not stay behind while others fought for our existence.

He was not the only one who met his death after surviving the Holocaust. When I met my friends in Tel Aviv, I was saddened by more bad news. My friend David, an Etzelnik from North Iraq, was killed at the front. We had good times together and to this day I cannot forget his smiling and joyful face. Our last time, in Tel Aviv, we went to the movies and parted, expecting to be seeing each other again soon. That was the last time I saw him again. Later, my friend and ex-classmate Yehuda Ezer, who was an officer in the artillery, was also reported killed only a few days after we met in Tel Aviv. My future brother-in-law, Maurice Sharabani, was also killed sometime around this same period, I learned later. There were many other Jews from Iraq, Shami, Ovadia, Yeheskel, Moshe, and other areas who died for the same cause.

The Arabs were, and still are, miscalculating the willingness of the Jews after the Holocaust to fight for freedom and to resist to the end. Our faith turned to a higher law and we endeavored to live like the One who made us. Telling our children and grandchildren about the War of Independence today will sound as remote to them as World War I did to us. What would these youngsters, in their graves all these years, have to say today? I am sure they would tell us to keep our heads high and be proud. We should also resolve to make our country better than our enemies ever thought it could be.

The boys in Camp David were disappearing every day and new recruits were replacing them. I could not remember such enthusiasm for being drafted into the army. We did not even have enough rifles for them to fight with. One day, I watched a truck unload hundreds of Czech rifles, which were immediately distributed to everyone on the spot. The soldiers were then ordered to board the trucks and be driven off to the front. I was not issued a rifle and was ordered to drive a CWT hundred-weight semi-truck and join the convoy to the besieged city of Jerusalem.

Without experience in driving a hundred-weight half-truck, I knew I would be as clumsy as soldiers carrying new rifles. But an order was an order, so I jumped in and started the engine. The truck jumped straight ahead because it was in gear and I had forgotten to shift it into neutral. I followed the convoy with my precious cargo onto a new road through the mountains. This road, nicknamed Burma Road, later became the main highway between Tel Aviv and Jerusalem until Bab El Wad. Before reaching Har Tov at the midway point of the journey, I was ordered to hand over the truck to another driver and return back to the camp with a jeep at the back of the convoy.

In Jerusalem, the Arabs intensified their attacks on the Jewish quarters. As usual, they declared a strike, which led to the burning and looting (*ghazoo*) of the shopping center. The British Palestine police stepped aside and did nothing to stop the riot. The fighting in the mixed cities and neighborhoods also intensified. There was shooting, sniping and car bombing — the Arabs' favorite method of terrorism. Many ordinary men, women, and children in the streets of Tel Aviv were killed or wounded by snipers.

Once, I was returning on the road from the Tiqvah Quarters near Tel Aviv with my uncle. We were in a direct line of fire from Salame, the neighboring Arab quarters. Walking along the street unsuspecting, I heard two shots — surely aimed at us — that buzzed over our heads. The same thing happened to me on Allenby Street across from the Carmel: shots were fired from the Hassan Bey Mosque's minaret, which was used as a sniping base.

Car bombs were used in the central bus station in Haifa and the offices of the *Jerusalem Post* newspaper, completely demolishing the buildings while killing and injuring several. With the help of a few British police and military deserters, the Arabs car bombed a residential apartment building on Ben Yehuda Street in Jerusalem, killing 50 people of all ages, including several families. Similar attacks in other places were taking place almost every day. We did remain passive; we settled accounts with the Arabs in similar attacks aimed only at guerrilla targets and personnel.

When the Czech rifles arrived in our camp, we were desperately short of arms and ammunition. But now we had rifles, submachine guns, Bren guns, and mortars. The Arab armies were well stocked with modern weapons, planes, artillery, and every type of gun.

Most of the Israeli heads of intelligence served in heavy-demanding situations and received few rewards. The Arabs had and still have the advantage in manpower and arms. In 1948, we were disproportionately inferior to them and our ultimate victory was rather miraculous.

*Rekhesh* (purchase of arms) was a department of the Intelligence Service (*Mossad*) under Shaul Avigdor. Ehud Avriel, representing the Jewish agency, was trying to buy arms from Czechoslovakia, but so was the Arab country of Syria. The Syrians succeeded in purchasing over 7,000 rifles and a million rounds of ammunition. Israeli Intelligence members managed to board the boat carrying these arms and ammunition. On the way to Syria it was held up by a Haganah ship and transferred to an Israeli flag corvette. The arms boat was sunk and its owners and crew were brought to Haifa and fairly compensated. Since everyone thought that the rifles were purchased from Czechoslovakia, we erroneously thanked the Czechs.

The Israeli Secret Service officially came into being in June 1948. At the headquarters for transport and freight of Israel defence forces, I was made a driver. As a matter of fact, I was not a good driver. The very first day, I drove my half-truck into the camp barrier at the gate. I was not satisfied with my job as driver and thought that my experience and qualifications could be better used in our efforts for survival.

Back in camp, I was told that two gentlemen would speak with me the next day at a certain café in Tel Aviv near the railway station. I was handed a slip containing all the information I needed to meet and recognize them. The next day, I was invited to a table in a corner of the café, away from other customers. The first man, who had green eyes and a fair complexion, introduced himself as Mordechai Werzman; the second man, who had dark eyes and fair skin, was Abraham Aloni. During the course of our brief conversation, Mordechai asked me if I were willing to join his intelligence unit, adding, rather diplomatically, that I came recommended by some *Shai* members. He said that now I would have a chance to exercise my qualifications, especially in Arabic. Abraham just listened and approved what Mordechai was telling me. Mordechai explained the terms of my service as a soldier and the deal was concluded then and there on the spot. Without knowing it yet, I became an official member of what was then called Intelligence No. 2, which became the most important intelligence unit in the State of Israel.

I went back to camp and waited for my transfer to the new unit, which came a few days later. I was transferred to a place in the middle of Tel Aviv on Shederoth Rothchild Boulevard, in the famous High House building which later became the residence of the first Russian Embassy in Israel. We occupied two or three rooms on the terrace of the building and there I was introduced to three Iraqi Jews — A. Sharoni (Shashowa), Ezra Mani, and Isaac Amber — and six Ashkenazim — the late Manis Weisman, Eliezer Carni, Michael Plosker, Reuven Ronkovski, Yosi Kapulnik and Yona Gofsayof. They were morse code operators, receiving Arabic messages in English characters.

Avraham Sharoni was a veteran who had served the *Shai* long before I joined in. Ezra Mani was an ex-teacher who lately had succeeded in completing, together with Sharoni, a special kind of Arabic-Hebrew and Hebrew-Arabic dictionary. It was actually an extraordinary one because it contained military and diplomatic expressions and idioms translated for diplomats and military personnel of Israel. Avraham Sharoni was an expert in deciphering dual conversation codes, especially of the Eastern and Northern Arab states bordering Israel and Jordan. The Ashkenazi men, mostly from Russia and Poland, were expert Morse operators who had perfected their experience, including Mordechai Werzman (later Almog), in the British army and police during World War II. Avraham Aloni was not only an expert Morse operator but also a reliable radio and electronic technician. Including myself, this was the nucleus of what was to become the most important intelligence unit in Israel.

At the beginning, my job was generally the same as at the Mikve Yisrael settlement — to search for and listen to Arabic transmissions and radio communications that might be of interest to the army and other departments of the new State of Israel. We used old-fashioned receiver sets and we scanned the bands by turning the knobs relentlessly all the time from one side to the other, stopping when a wave was in use to determine its origin and type of transmission. While the telephones at the bunker had been continuously busy, here it was different. We had to keep watch for anything and, once detected, the band was assigned to one person to fully investigate and report upon. If interesting, it became a permanent source for important information that might help our struggle to defend ourselves and our country. We registered everything at the beginning in long-hand writing and those who were experienced took important notes for further transmission.

The same was true with the Morse section of the unit. Everything was passed immediately to our translators while the highlights were explained either on the phone, using coded language, or in person via a meeting within the hour.

We were very crowded and Mordechai Werzman (Almog), who was more qualified to be a diplomat rather than head of an intelligence unit, managed to secure larger quarters for us. We moved somewhere near the seashore to a house that was nicknamed *Habayit Haadom* (the Red House) simply because it was painted red. Being near the seashore, radio reception become clearer; furthermore, our headquarters were located nearby on Ben Yehuda Street. The new place was more spacious, and we started to grow as a result. Reinforcements were added to our personnel, and better equipment was issued to the unit.

Moshe Sharet once made a diplomatic accusation against the British, claiming that they were selling army equipment to the Egyptians. The original information came from our unit; actually, the equipment was only spare parts for cars and radio sets. We were heavily attacked by the Arab Legion, who were advancing into a vulnerable place, pounding our poorly-fortified posts. A message with proper code names and cipher was transmitted through our unit as if from the Legion headquarters. The order telling them to stop fighting until further notice, was sent in Arabic, imitating the pulse of the transmitting officer's mode of Morse-tapping with proper call signs and procedures in radio communications. Actual fighting was stopped long enough for us to fortify our positions and was resumed a few hours later. Apparently, the Arab Legion was not fooled for very long.

This scheme was also carried out with better equipment and more sophistication at the start of the Six-Day War when King Hussein was hesitant in joining. The Israeli Intelligence was sure that Israel would win the battle but, wanting more than anything else to put an end to the attacks from the West Bank and East Jerusalem, not as sure that Hussein could be dealt with if he joined the forces. A message was sent from Cairo asking him to engage the Israelis because the Egyptian forces were retreating with heavy losses all along the southern front. Hussein would relieve the pressure on the Egyptians only if he knew they were winning. This message was blocked, quickly doctored by the intercepting unit and then retransmitted to Amman with the opposite meaning—that their forces were breaking through in Sinai and Israeli (non–Egyptian) formations were inflicted with heavy losses. The altered message also asked Hussein to join the successful Egyptian army and share the spoils of victory. Israeli Intelligence predicted that Hussein now would join before it was too late. His fateful decision to attack Israel resulted in the ousting of his armies from the West Bank, a retreat behind the international borders into Trans-Jordan and the evacuation of the city of Jerusalem.

International telephone communications were our task, too. We tapped scrambled conversations between Arab leaders (which I also supervised mostly during my reserve duties in our unit) and then unscrambled them. One such conversation was between Egyptian President Gamal Abdel Nasser and King Hussein of Jordan after the Six-Day War. This taped conversation was later played back to journalists to expose Nasser's lies.

In 1948, a few Jewish tragedies (actually political upheavals) were taking place among various fighting factions after the establishment of the State of Israel. Altelena was one such tragedy, and the other involved Isser Beeri, who assumed command of military intelligence (*Aman*) upon termination of the *Shai* after Israel became a state. There were many commanders better than Isser Beeri. There were two Issers: one was chief of military intelligence and the other was chief of the *Mossad* (department of security), previously called *Shin Bet*, or *Sherut Bitachon*.

I was there when Menachem Begin, leader of the *Irgun* (national military organization) emerged from hiding. Thousands of people gathered in the streets of Tel Aviv for a glimpse of the leader who forced the British to leave Palestine before they could prepare the land for only Arabs. It was very difficult to get a closer look at the man who was considered a myth, but he really existed. He smiled, meeting the crowd of the newly liberated nation in his rabbi concealment outfit. He declared that his organization would fully support the new government of Israel in the war with the Arabs and would integrate its troops into the Israeli Army.

During the first truce it was agreed with the United Nations that no war materials were to be imported into the new state, which was detrimental to our survival. The Irgun (Menachem Begin's organization) knew the Arab enemies better than the other political groups. In defiance of the agreement, the Irgun bought a boat from the U.S. Marines and registered it under the name Altalena, the pen name of party founder Meir Jabotinsky. The boat set sail towards Israel loaded with rifles, machine guns, hand grenades, cartridges and more than 1,000 volunteers from America and Europe ready to fight the Arabs. The boat arrived at the time of the cease fire in June 1948.

According to Ben-Gurion, Arab states and Israel agreed not to bring new arms into their countries. They both, of course, covertly violated this agreement. The Irgun decided to bring the shipment, openly, on the *Altalena*. Ben-Gurion viewed this act as a defiance of government authority and he decided to vigorously deal with it. Also, the Irgun disagreed with Ben-Gurion's imminent sellout and the Israeli provisional government's alleged peace mission with the Arabs. These arms were considered detrimental to the new state. In fact, the old rivalry and enmity between him and Menachem Begin was more likely the reason for the alleged disagreement. Because of this nightmare, an armed Jew versus Jew rebellion was feared. The situation is not much different even now with regard to the two ruling parties in Israel, the Likud and the Maarach.

Ben-Gurion's party was determined to exercise its leadership. When the boat arrived and was being unloaded by the Irgun people, soldiers of the Alexandroni Brigade from the Labour movement in Israel opened fire, and the Irgun fighters surrendered. Mr. Begin boarded the ship and ordered it to sail to Tel Aviv. A young officer, Yitzhak Rabin, who graduated with General Moshe Dayan, led the battle on the beach. Rabin, a Palmach commander and later Prime Minister, turned a cannon on the *Altalena* and fired.

In Tel Aviv, I happened to be in the Red House, in the crossfire of the cannon and the *Altalena*. We all fell on our faces so we wouldn't be hit by a bullet from the barrage of fire over our heads. When things quieted down, I went out on the streets of Ben Yehuda and met young girls and boys from France and the United States who were crying and screaming, "How could this happen? We are Jews who came to help the new state of Israel and we are fired upon." Several were killed by Jewish guns. "Oh my God!" one girl screamed hysterically in French and pulled her beautiful blonde hair almost to shreds.

The second tragedy touched me indirectly while I was under the general command of the ex–Shai chief of intelligence officer and then chief of Aman (military intelligence), Isser Beeri. Beeri, who had been a member of the Haganah since the beginning of World War II, was head of a privately owned construction company. At the time, corruption and protectionism flourished because they were not discouraged by the Labour politicians. Not long ago, the head of Solel Boneh (a giant government construction enterprise) boasted to the news media that during the British rule in the last war, he used to illegally appropriate materials from the British Army for various uses at Labour Party and Haganah sites. Isser Beeri abhorred corruption and was a zealot. Ben-Gurion once said that Israel needed to have its own burglars and prostitutes to be considered a nation like the others. Big Beeri did not agree; he believed, like many others, that Israel must represent the highest of values. Those who could not adhere to such standards should be ousted, he thought.

In spite of all this, to me he represented a dark chapter in the history of Israel and the intelligence service. His appointment to the job was a mistake. I remember when our unit became valued after our successes, he visited us with his second-in-command Chaim Herzog (president of the State of Israel from 1983–1993). Everyone in his entourage interested in the working of the unit asked many questions, but he remained completely silent. He just stared as if in a vacuum while Mr. Herzog conducted the whole show.

Before independence, Ali Kassem played an ambiguous role in the affairs of Palestine; nevertheless, the wealthy Arab helped the Haganah. After suddenly disappearing, his bullet-riddled body was found at the foot of Mount Carmel. The police discovered that he had been apparently killed by the Israeli Secret Service. When Big Beeri was confronted with the execution and asked whether it could have been justified as state policy, he said, "Kassem was a traitor, so we killed him." Ben-Gurion was informed, but it was too late.

Jewish frogmen had planned an operation to mine the Coast Guard vessels, intercepting illegal immigrants. On the evening of the raid, eavesdropping on the telephones intercepted British messages warning of the impending sabotage by the Jewish frogmen. British troops were instructed to move to the Haifa harbor to ambush the frogmen who were already there. One Shai officer managed to call off the operation in time by risking his own life, and the frogmen were saved. Thanks to the work of the interception, no damage was done and no one was injured.

There was no doubt that the planned operation had been betrayed. Big Beeri suspected the mayor of Haifa, Aba Hushi, who was a personal friend of Ben-Gurion and a Labour power member. One of Aba Hushi's friends was seized and beaten in an attempt to obtain a confession about Aba Hushi's guilt. He was returned half-dead and driven to the limit of his sanity from torture. He tried to kill himself. He could not give such a confession because it was not true. Big Beeri tried to prove to Ben-Gurion by means of top secret documents, allegedly found in the Haifa telegraph office, that Aba Hushi was a prime British informant. Later, the Haganah's top forger, the man who had constructed so many identities, admitted he was ordered by Big Beeri to forge the alleged British police cables. Before Isser Beeri ended his career, this appalling illegality committed by him came to light.

The new era was stained by a terrible crime committed on behalf of the new State. During the siege of Jerusalem, it was clear that the Arab Legion, commanded by British officers, bombarded an Israeli munitions plant, damaging the factory. In the secrecy of night, the equipment was moved to a new place. Within a few hours, the new place was also bombarded. The officer in charge of Shai in Jerusalem, Colonel Benyamin Gibli (who later became chief officer of military intelligence after Mr. Herzog), began inquiries that led him to the Jerusalem Electric Company, which was run by Arabs and British officials in the Arab sector of Jerusalem. The power was still shared by the Jewish and Arab sectors. The liaison officer who regulated the supply of electricity was Captain Meir Toubianski, an ex–Major with the Royal Engineers. Captain Toubianski was requested to arrange the supply of electric power to an address in the Jewish sector as a test. Colonel Gibli, without thorough investigation, was convinced that his traitor was an Israeli informer, and he suspected Captain Toubianski. In actuality, the new surge of electricity convinced the British Arab Legion intelligence officers that the new supply of power was for another arms factory like the one they bombarded before.

Gibli arrested Captain Toubianski, who was court marshaled by Isser Beeri, the head of the *Shai* (Intelligence), Benjamin Gibli, David Karon, and Avraham Kidron (who later became the Israeli ambassador to London). He was found guilty and executed by a *Palmach* firing squad.

The house where the author was billeted after the occupation of Jaffa (author's collection).

His wife, Lena Toubianski, left no stone unturned until she had her husband exonerated. The government restored, posthumously, his rank of captain and he was reburied in a military cemetery with full honors. She was also paid appropriate damages. Isser Beeri was dismissed, arrested, demoted to private and charged with the murder. He was found guilty and received a token jail sentence of one day from sunrise to sunset. David Ben-Gurion once called him a "rascal without a shred of conscience."

As soon as the State of Israel was declared, Ben-Gurion's people and the left-wing parties concentrated on consolidating their positions and grabbing the key influential positions in the government.

We again moved to a new place because the Red House became inadequate for the added work and personnel. Our new location was a villa in Jaffa abandoned by one of the wealthiest Arabs who fled the country. It was near Dajoni Hospital on the main street, now called Jerusalem Boulevard. Refugees from Europe and other displaced Jews from the Arab countries and Palestine began to populate Jaffa. The new deputy commander in chief of military intelligence, Colonel Chaim Herzog (who later became president of Israel) lived with his family next to us. We transferred all our listening equipment and began to intercept messages of the various Arab armies attacking the new State. Some were in code or cipher, others in plain language. First, whether code or cipher, we diligently listed the call signs of the sending unit separately. We constantly waited for a slip of a name of a place or an officer or anything to identify the origin of the transmission. Direction finders and radar were not in use then so we had to figure out for ourselves whether a call sign belonged to a division of the army, brigade, battalion, regiment, armored, artillery, foot soldiers, or others. It always paid us to construct the whole unit and also identify it logistically. The coded messages remained enigmatic. At the beginning they were tackled by various professors, none of whom could read or write Arabic. For some time their work resulted in no discoveries.

Military intelligence was not able to help much while various battles inside Palestine were raging and our losses were enormous. The internal fighting among those who grabbed high positions in the new State was selfish and egotistical. Only the foot soldier sacrificed himself for the State while most of the higher-ups struggled for positions.

Ben-Gurion was literally struggling against the LEHI extreme right-wing faction, which was headed by Yitzhak Shamir (later the prime minister of Israel), who was rumored to be responsible for his faction seeking Germany's help against the British before knowing of the extreme anti–Semitic doctrines of Nazi Germany. The Palmach and its leaders of the extreme left supported communism and Stalin, whose hands were already stained by the blood of two million Russians killed by direct orders.

Our commanding officer, Mordechai Almog (Werzman), served with the British police on behalf of the Haganah. After an explosion was set off near his workplace, he was arrested, roughed up and finally jailed in a room next to his office at the police station. The arresting officers beat and kicked him when he pled innocence. Later, he resigned his post and continued his skill with the Haganah, this time against the British Police and administration of Palestine networks. All intercepted information was passed on to the Haganah, especially about the coast guard blockade of illegal refugees from Europe.

Another Jewish police officer helped by passing the daily key code to Mordechai in a hollow pen. At their meetings at cafés or such, one of them would ask for a pen to write something. The other would oblige and, upon returning the borrowed pen, the replica was replaced and the one with the information would remain with Almog. The next day, all orders, instructions, and so on by the Palestine police would be decoded and made known to the people in charge of the struggle for independence. This was done almost daily until the end.

# CHAPTER 12

# Breaking Military Codes

Before the start of World War II and the German invasion of Poland, three British Secret Service men met with their Polish counterparts in an underground room deep in the Molokov Pyry forest outside Warsaw. There the Poles offered the British the Third Reich's most precious secret — the phenomenally complicated "Enigma" machine that encoded and decoded all German military messages. It was a gift that would change the course of the impending war.

The next day, this machine was in England, together with everything the Poles had discovered about its operation. The British immediately established a special center and gave the operation the code name ULTRA. Soon it became apparent just how complex the machine really was. Battery-powered for complete mobility on the battlefield, it resembled an electric typewriter. But when a key was pressed on the keyboard, a complex system of three parallel rotating wheels went into action. Each wheel displayed a full alphabet. The accompanying plugboard, similar to a telephone switchboard, ensured that a different letter would light up on a panel containing 26 bulbs — one for each letter of the alphabet. The devious way in which the different letters could be conjured up made Enigma fiendishly difficult for an outsider to crack, even if he had a machine.

The message sender and the recipient organized the machine in a different way each time that a message was sent. Both followed instructions in an operating manual. Before the war, the instructions were changed monthly. Toward the end of the war, this was done three times daily. A message could be garbled into a staggering number of different codes. To crack it would require exceptional ingenuity.

I lived and worked at the center with some of the foremost code-breaking brains in the world, including Alan Turing, one of the greatest mathematicians of his time. He invented a ten foot high electro-mechanical device that could test combinations of coded letters from Enigma at high speeds. The device contained more than 30 sets of rotating wheels; each set could simultaneously sift through 17,576 combinations.

Unknowingly, the Germans helped the British by repeating in their messages certain phrases such as "by order of the Führer," or, "with reference to," or "commanding officer." Once deciphered in one code, the message offered vital clues to the structure of other codes using the same phrases. Consistently, German operators would also align the three rotating wheels with the same three letters — such obvious combinations as ABC or XYZ — over and over again. This knowledge reduced the number of possibilities the code breakers had to consider.

The machine itself also had some limitations. For example, it was incapable of encoding any letter of the alphabet as itself. The British used this knowledge to their advantage. Occasionally they would send an aircraft out to bomb an insignificant target. Experts could then find the name of the place in the coded Enigma traffic that reported the incident. They searched for groups of letters that did not contain any of the letters of the real name in the same position. This was a way into the balance of the code.

Soon the British were reading Enigma messages and the center at Bletchley Park was able to relay enemy bombing plans. Fighter squadrons could concentrate around British cities well before a known German attack started. In the Atlantic, convoys carrying vital supplies to Britain were able to avoid packs of U-boats as Royal Air Force bombers destroyed the vessels supplying the U-boats. In 1940, Enigma revealed that Hitler had abandoned Operation SeaLion, his planned invasion of Britain. The next year, Enigma helped British warships destroy the battleship *Bismarck*. When British and American commanders discovered Rommel's plans, Allied bombers were able to destroy some of the ships carrying Rommel's troops to North Africa. In 1944, thanks to Enigma, the Allies knew that the Germans expected the main D-Day invasion forces to land at Calais, not Normandy, and learned exactly what opposition would be waiting for them.

Because Allied Intelligence was so proficient, the greatest fear at the center was that the Nazi high command would realize that their code had been cracked. Instead, however, the Germans believed they were the victims of an informer or, with the U-boat war, that tracking techniques had improved. So closely was the secret of Enigma guarded that many of the Allied commanders were unaware of the source of the uncannily accurate information they received. Indeed, no intelligence was ever released that could not plausibly be attributed to some alternate source. The breaking of the Enigma code remained a secret until the late 1960s, and even to this day, many details of the equipment and techniques used are not known.

One day I was shocked to learn that our unit was to be dismantled and reassigned to other units. By then we had two professors working with us in code breaking, Professor Gills and Professor Zvi. Also we had added to our staff more Iraqi Jews: the two cousins Zecharia and Ezra Sofer, and later Ihud

Kedouri. In spite of this impressive cast, it seemed that our chief Big Isser (Isser Beeri) or someone else was not impressed and gave orders to close it down. Perhaps that person was right; perhaps not.

I immediately approached Mordechai Almog, who was with Aloni talking things over in their station wagon. I asked them straight out whether it was true that the unit was being dispersed and why. Mordechai was very candid and said that those higher up believed that we were not furnishing adequate intelligence to justify keeping the unit going. We were given ten days to pack and go. He then added, "Batches of coded messages are piling up, picked up by our Morse operators, but no one can crack their codes." With concealed anger I retorted, "How do you expect any of the professors, acting alone, to crack a code while they don't even know a single word of Arabic?" I added: "Mordechai! You have ten days to wrap up and only eight or seven left. Why don't you let me try? Maybe I could do something. You have nothing to lose now!" Hesitantly, he looked at Abraham Aloni, who said, "He is right. We have nothing to lose." Mordechai rather reluctantly said, "Okay, we will let you try."

Soon after this conversation, I asked them to show me the riddle and explain its puzzles, or what might be the puzzle. I was introduced to Professor Zvi, who was in a room all by himself. He lectured me for a full day about the various ways to crack a code and showed me examples of a few different systems in English. I studied them all carefully and immediately started with the assumption that this batch of messages was Arabic while the characters were English. I tried one or two systems but nothing happened. We worked hard for two days to crack something with the respected professor; but still nothing.

Then we decided to concentrate on one system at a time. We picked one and concentrated all our energy on it to spot a word or half a word in order to construct some meaning out of it. In one of the tens of messages lying on our desk, I decided to pick one single letter and join it with every other letter in the message, and so on. It was like the ten foot high device which could test combinations of coded letters in the Enigma machine but it was only a few inches of paper and the letters were originals.

I noticed a glimmer of light in all this. If on one line I could make sure that at least one other such combination existed, then there would be hope to construct more and perhaps decipher a word or two, and the rest would be easier. I knew that in Arabic the most-used letters were "a" with "l" placed right after to form "al" which is the equivalent of "the" in English and "le" in French. We drew columns containing the scrambled text of the message. I started moving these columns one against the other, side by side. After many hours of trial and error we hit on two combinations of "al" that matched the distance between each other. All we had to do now was to match a third letter so that one of them would make some sort of sense in the Arabic language.

Already three days had passed and Professor Zvi had to undergo an operation at the hospital and could not stay with me anymore. He made his arrangements to leave the next day, no matter what happened. I was left alone tackling this hard problem. I kept playing with the letters, composing words or even sentences. If I succeeded to make out one word that was probably irrelevant to the hidden text, I lost others in the process and would have to begin again. The word-play was unlimited and one could figure thousands of them at a time, but would they fit the general puzzle and give meaning to the coded message? It was extremely hard to tell.

Working alone, I had no alternative now but to try and try again until some light was shed. In my mind, I was solely determined to crack this code and with God's help be able to save a lot of young lives fighting at the front. The complicated encoded military message would be a great gift to the Jewish people and change the course of the war already upon us, provided we could crack it and read its plain language.

What was doubly disastrous at the time was that no one knew what language the Egyptian military used. Later, we discovered that they used English, too, but at other departments. I kept on searching for a clue in a military Arabic word which would combine with the "al," because once such a word was deciphered in one code, it would offer a vital lead in breaking the whole key code.

Needless to say, I felt like an expert in the field because of my ardent desire to crack this code and assist in the establishment of the State of Israel. I slept for only an hour or two at night; otherwise, I kept playing, searching and mostly guessing at words and expressions which might fit the jigsaw puzzle. Twice that night, unknown to anyone else, I threw up from excitement and intensive concentration on this work. I kept thinking that if nothing came out of this most crucial endeavor that was laid in my hands rather late, we would have to pack up and leave. If we won the war, God willing, it would come with many more casualties.

A few hours before Professor Zvi was to leave for the hospital, I hit upon a different idea. Assuming that the message was in Arabic and contained repetition of words, why not compose the message most appropriate to the known alphabets using whatever known military expressions could be encoded there? By thoroughly studying plain messages, I found a pattern when they began replies with "Your message... [*Isharatekom*]." I concentrated on this exclusively at the beginning of the coded message and also "*washukran* [thanks]" at the end. After a hundred or more trials, I noticed a definite pattern emerging.

I called Professor Zvi, who was about to leave, and showed him my discovery. We dropped everything and worked feverishly to complete the meaning. Slowly but surely, I made some sense of the key to that day's message. The elusive words sat in place.

Professor Zvi acted like a little boy, happily shouting, laughing and jubilantly telling everyone of my success. He went into Mordechai's office and showed him our first triumph eight days after he issued the ultimatum to disperse the unit. It was indeed a miracle.

I sat still, entranced in silent prayer while waiting in the room. When he came back, we tried to apply the key to other messages but nothing came out. I had to work it out again to decipher the rest of the daily codes, sometimes twice a day. Professor Zvi left immediately for the hospital and I never heard from him again. I was left alone, working furiously to keep the southern commanders informed of the movements, logistics, and dispositions of the enemy waging war against us. The system was cracked but not the daily keys to the codes.

Mordechai took a few deciphered messages that same day to his inhibitive boss, telling him the news, and he got a reprieve to the closing down order. When he came back, everyone was happy and joking about the whole thing. When I asked Mordechai whether he fully understood and could explain the possibilities of our discovery, he smiled and said, "Don't worry. I told him exactly as you people explained it to me." When Mordechai, who did not understand what was going on, explained our discovery to his boss, he probably did not understand either.

I sat at my table working on cracking more messages — old as well as new ones. The reception of messages was intensified and more operators were brought in. Working alone, I had to effectively learn the system in order to master the flow of military coded messages onto my table. It took me another day or two to find the key to the coded messages of the last days. By doing so, it became clear to me that the code key was changed every day and sometimes twice a day. It could be anything from just numbers to Arabic sayings or verses. I resolved to crack it every day and even two or three times a day just to keep the Army informed of the attacking forces in the south. It was not an easy job, and in many cases it took me a whole day to crack one single key. I would always thank God for my success. History was in the making, and I was most honored and glad to have been a part of it. My colleagues were ecstatic every time I finally found the key and broke the code. They clapped hands or shouted excitedly, "He did it again. He did it!" They deserved to be happy, not only because every one of them contributed to this job, but they also realized what the result would be — a shortening of the war and the safe return home of their loved ones and friends.

Orders, attacks and movements of troops were sent often by coded messages, and most if not all of them were received in our general headquarters before they were decoded by the Egyptian commanders in the field. As a result, we were always prepared for any action taken by the Egyptian Army.

Every night, I worked until the waning hours of the morning and had little food or sleep. A week or more later, I was helped by a Jew from northern Iraq who caught on quickly and excelled in taking care of the never-ending stream of coded messages which we dealt with. We expanded our work to cover the whole spectrum of the radio band.

When Mordechai Almog, our commander, took our product to his superiors, great attention and interest was bestowed upon our unit. The interest was so high that Prime Minister David Ben-Gurion waited on the phone for our information before making vital decisions during crucial times. On many occasions, high-ranking officials watched us work and expressed candidly, like Professor Zvi did, that victory in the Battle of the South was sealed on my table. Most of the techniques we used and developed remain a secret to this day.

To us, the Egyptian army was an open book. All we had to do was to refer to certain messages and know exactly the strength of a certain battalion and its movement as well as other posts and personnel in the area. I thanked God many times for helping me reveal the structure and strength of our enemy, which saved a lot of lives — not only Jewish lives but also Egyptian lives. Thousands of Israelis are still living today thanks to the cracking of the Egyptian military code, and they surely still remember the 1948-1949 victories that Israel achieved as King David did against Goliath.

CHAPTER 13

# Master Intelligence from the Nonexistent Informer

Egyptian forces commenced their advancing attacks on May 15, 1948, and moved in two columns from El-Arish. One column moved along the coastal road, the second from Abu Ageila toward Beersheba, Hebron, and Jerusalem. They were confident in quickly reaching Tel Aviv and Jerusalem, neutralizing all other resistance on the way. The Egyptians reasoned that once Jerusalem and Tel Aviv had fallen, the war would end with the same tactics Hitler used against Poland in World War II.

Their advance was glorified by the Egyptian and the Arab media. Daily headlines announced the army's progress in capturing (so they claimed) Gaza, Mijdal and Beersheba, but these were already Arab villages. They were sure they could take Tel Aviv next, but they did not take into consideration the settlements lying in their way, somewhat distant from the main roads. They scorned the Nirim, Kfar Darom, Beerot Yitzhak, Saad, Yad Mordekhay, and Nitzamim, believing they would automatically fall into their hands after the capture of Tel Aviv. First they attacked Kfar Darom. We suffered a lot of casualties and, because of the fierce defensive fighting by our settlers, the Egyptian Army besieged the settlement. At the same time, they attacked Nirim (now Nir Yizhaq).

The attacking columns of tanks and soldiers stopped some distance from their target because of signs written in English: "Caution — Mines." They withdrew under cover of fire from their artillery, leaving behind over 40 dead soldiers. They tried again the next day with the help of their air force, but reinforcements arrived too late. The Egyptians, satisfied to just bombard the settlement, decided to bypass it on their way and concentrate on reaching Tel Aviv at the earliest possible time.

During their advance northward, they had to deal with Yad Mordekhay. The defenders fought heroically, but no reinforcements were sent in. After five days of fierce hand-to-hand fighting, they evacuated during the night through enemy lines, arriving at Gvaram. The capture of Yad Mordekhay boosted the

Egyptian morale and temporarily slackened the Jewish fighting spirit. Our forces reorganized and began attacking the Egyptian communication lines and military posts behind the lines. Bridges were destroyed and all types of light guns were taken from the enemy.

Fighters of the Moslem Brotherhood who were part of the invading Egyptian Army were positioned from Oja (Aslouj, now Nitzana) to Beersheba. The Moslem Brotherhood fighters who had already fought at Kfar Darom took charge of the Beersheba area. Following the same strategy as the main Egyptian army, the Moslem Brotherhood fighters disregarded the settlements on their way, passing Hebron Hill and reaching Bethlehem, a few miles from Jerusalem. The Jordanian monarch disapproved of this because of the strife and quarrels between the Arab Legion and the Brotherhood fighters. The Brotherhood attacked Ramat Rachel from Bethlehem. The forces that were fighting in the corridor were brought down to Sarafand camp, which had been handed over to the Arabs by the British. The camp was taken with few casualties but, unfortunately, one of them was my future brother-in-law, Moshi Sharabani.

Our forces moved toward Ramle to help the Etzel. All non-combatant adults as well as all children from Nitzanim, Negba, Gat, Galaon and Kfar Menahem (all southern settlements) were evacuated. When the fight for Yad Mordekhay was at its peak, Israeli forces directly confronted the Egyptian forces for the first time. In the beginning, we took prisoners in an attempt to gain vital information about the enemy. After we attacked Iraq Sweidan Police Station, the Egyptians attacked Negba. There its commander, Yitshak Dovno (nicknamed Yoab), was killed. The camp of Julis, behind Negba, was taken by our forces.

As a result of these attacks and counterattacks, the Egyptians changed their strategy. Their column of 500 various vehicles at Migdal started moving northward along the Shore Road. This brigade of artillery and tanks advanced to within 30 kilometers of Tel Aviv.

These were fateful days for Israel: the most powerful army of the Arab world was within reach of Tel Aviv and Jerusalem. Our forces were minimal and the Egyptian column was still advancing. Just a few kilometers from Ashdot, they stopped at a bridge which had been demolished the night before by our forces. Our Air Force flew into action as four Messerschmidts attacked. But the Egyptian Air Force bombarded most of the settlements in the south, as well as Rehovot and Tel Aviv, which received about 15 to 20 sorties until a truce was declared. The first truce imposed by the United Nations was desperately needed to reorganize and rest.

During that brief cease-fire, soldiers from both sides came out of their bunkers and posts. Egyptians and Israelis from nearby posts met and exchanged views and conversation. Most of the Egyptians asked questions about the Zionist gangs they had been fighting for the last month. They were surprised to learn that these gangs were falsely portrayed by their newspapers: they were also fighting men, defending their right to live.

The truce, which began July 9, 1948, was violated and fighting resumed on July 18. In the north, our forces fought Kawoukji, whose army assumed the name of the rescuing forces. Mishmar Hayarden was taken from the Syrians. The Iraqis stayed put at Ramat Jenin. Kawoukji's attack on Sejara (Elanit) was repulsed, but we attacked him from the rear. Lod and Ramla were taken. The Burma Road east of Latrun was completed and the siege on Jerusalem was removed. The road from Tel Aviv to Jerusalem opened through the New Burma Road. Israeli forces did their best on the central and northern fronts but nothing in the south against the Egyptian forces. However, the Egyptian forces succeeded in capturing Huleikat — a clear victory. They captured other strongholds, and when the situation worsened, strongholds near the Negba settlement also fell into their hands. They were fired upon relentlessly. When our units got the information that strong forces were about to attack these places, they successfully evacuated the area. When the Egyptian forces reached the evacuated settlements, they suffered heavy casualties from minefields placed throughout the area.

It was revealed that a second Egyptian column was moving to occupy the triangle presently known as the West Bank. A Sudanese unit attacked and occupied Beit Daras but was expelled later as more information about the movements of the Egyptians was received. After this attack failed, the Israelis counter-attacked, foiling the Egyptians' plan to capture the triangle.

Our units' attempt to capture Iraq Sweidan Post failed again. However, Beit Afa and Abdis were taken. Much arms and ammunition was also taken in capturing Abdis, including Bren gun carriers and anti-tank guns. Also, taking Abdis and defending Beit Daras foiled a plan to cut Julis and Negba from the reach of Israeli forces, leaving an open corridor to those places. Iraq Sweidan was evacuated because the police station was still in Egyptian hands. They retreated again, but we fiercely defended and held Abdis till the end of the war, inflicting many casualties upon the invading Egyptian armies. Julis remained in our hands despite many Egyptian attacks. Miraculously, no one was hurt thanks to the anticipated action of the enemy.

The Egyptian Army commanders were very surprised to learn that in Negba there were only about 100 to 150 fighters. They pounded it with over 4,000 cannon shells, predicting a fatality rate of at least 50 percent with another 25 percent wounded. Wave after wave, they attacked with tanks and foot soldiers. At the last moment in the nearest place to Negba, Israelis fired at near point-blank range, killing most of the attackers who didn't flee. About 40 wounded were taken to underground shelters in Negba for treatment. It was a fight-or-die situation for us, and we made our point. The spirit was very high and this is what counted for our survival. Our Intelligence played an important role in the fighting around Negba.

The Egyptians fortified their positions at a hill not far from the settlement, in hopes of capturing the settlement in due time. When our Intelligence learned of their intentions, it was decided to capture the hill before a Sudanese column could dig in there for the projected attack on Negba. Our forces were quick to attack, and the Sudanese escaped, leaving behind a lot of materials. This came about because the Israeli forces knew the strength and the logistics of the Sudanese intentions beforehand.

Galwan was continuously pounded for over four hours. When they moved on it, the prepared Israeli forces repulsed them. They tried again, but they were repelled again when their cannons hit their own attacking forces by mistake.

At this point, I was working hand-in-hand with many people, day and night, to intercept, decode and translate all messages in the southern theater. Our unit, after its preliminary successes in small operations by the Egyptians, began to gain importance in the eyes of the military planners on that front, namely General Yigal Yadin (the Archaeologist of Massada). Our unit became one of the most important in Intelligence and continued to grow and expand in later years to become the most significant (and jealously rivaled) Intelligence Unit in the Israel Defense Forces.

Operation Yoab was the code name for the recovery of the Negev region from its severance from mainland Israel. We did not plan to open and hold onto another corridor; we wanted to control that part of Israel by incapacitating all Egyptian forces. Before commencing the above operation, the chief intelligence officer sent Arye — a deputy serving as his personal envoy. He sat with me to check for himself how things were going and also to make sure that, as he put it, there were no tricks by anyone, especially the Egyptian command feeding us false information, that would lure our forces into an unescapable trap. I understood his reasoning because the results of my work were too good to be true, and my superiors still doubted the authenticity of information flowing to headquarters. They eventually made checks in the field to reassure themselves that every thing was genuine and ethical. Finally satisfied, he gave his superiors the green light.

For reasons which were unknown to us, Isser Beeri apparently was slipping and his deputy, Chaim Herzog, was becoming more responsible and active in this business. I had one or more encounters with the new chief, which made me feel better. Mr. Herzog (later the president of the State of Israel) was fully aware of the importance of our work, unlike Isser Beeri. It did not matter much to me who exactly was the boss. All that mattered was to give this most important service to the State of Israel. I just wanted Israel to get rid of its enemies.

Yigal Alon (of the Mapam leftist party) became the commander of the southern front, and his main objective was to clean up once and for all the way to the Negev. There was some hesitation early on for fear of intervention and assistance to the Egyptians from other Arab states. Our information made it clear that the friction among Arab nations was increasing, especially when there was failure on the battlefield. It was felt that the Arab nations would stand still and do nothing. By knowing in advance the logistics, manpower, arms, and equipment of the Egyptian Army from our intercepted and decoded messages, the Israel defense forces were able to design exactly the adequate number of troops and materials, not only for the whole operation, but for every front in the south, without endangering other fronts.

The objective of the initial attack was to cut the Egyptian forces in Majdal (now Ashqelon). Part of the attacking forces continued southward to disrupt traffic and communications at Ghaza-El-Arish, thus hitting the Egyptian Air Force in that sector. Thanks to our decoded messages, the Israeli commanders in the south knew exactly what to expect in terms of the strength and number of troops and materials, which were rather heavy, of the enemy in Yad Mordekhay. They also knew that in the vicinity of Beit Hanon, near Yad Mordekhay, the Egyptian strength was minimal. Therefore, it was decided to cut off the Egyptian forces at Beit Hanon near Nir Am, which was used as a jumping point for this action. In order to reach the Negev, it was decided to capture Kawkaba, Houlaikat, Falouja, and Iraq el Manshiya on the main shore road. We knew there were sizable Egyptian forces on the western road near the seashore and the breakthrough there could be very costly. The story was different on the eastern Sandy Road, so it was decided to break through the eastern road Gat-Rouhama. This plan necessitated capturing Falouja and Iraq el Manshiya first.

On October 15, all the forces were ready to go. Our convoy was attacked in the corridor at the crossroad, precipitating Operation Yoab. In the evening, the El Arish Air Base was attacked. Railway lines on the borders of Egypt were demolished and the line Khan Yunis-Rafih was mined. Egyptian camps, guards, and watchtowers were attacked and demolished in the rear of the Egyptian Army, which damaged their rear communication lines. At night, demolition squads worked on bridges that were attacked and destroyed.

Kherbat Massar was captured without a fight and the road to Beit Jibrin was cut. When our unit learned that one regiment's battalions were dispersed along the main road, they attacked from the rear. The Mijdal-Faloujah road was cut off. A diversion attack was successfully launched to draw the fire of the regiment toward the rear. The Egyptians were forced to shorten their supply lines. The diversionary attack made the Egyptians withdraw from Ashdod and Mijdal in order to concentrate on Rafih and Gaza. During their retreat southward, they left behind about 5,000 Egyptian soldiers and officers (along with their materials and equipment) who were unable to join the retreating force. As usual, the Israeli forces were immediately informed about the retreat. The retreating convoy was attacked, leaving many dead or wounded, but the rest eventually escaped under the cover of night. We also learned from our decoded messages that the Egyptians eluded our blockade and withdrew along the main road. The main road itself was then cut off, severing all possible withdrawal. The area command headquarters slipped away from Ashdod to Falouja, which later became the Falouja Pocket.

The United Nations Security Council was assembled to impose, as usual, a truce. Israel, sure that no other country in the north would act or interfere, added another Jewish Brigade drawn from the northern borders of the country. Despite the Security Council's decision to save the Egyptians when we began winning, the objective of our forces was always to clean up the way to the Negev.

Therefore, on July 20, 1949, Houligat was captured after our unit informed our forces that it had only three battalions. The way to the Negev was now wide open.

# CHAPTER 14

# The Capture of Beersheba

Mordechai Almog, our commander, told me after the capture of Beersheba that I would be decorated. He claimed to have already filed such a request because I was instrumental in the capture of this historical village.

The retreating Egyptian command instructed the commander of the Falouja, just before the truce was obtained, to break through and reach Beersheba. At the same time, this message was received by our unit and on my desk.

An hour or two before the truce was announced, David Ben-Gurion was immediately informed of the importance of my decoded message. He specifically instructed his commanders in the south that, truce or no truce, the Israel forces must not allow the Egyptians to take Beersheba and that Beersheba was to be taken immediately. All this happened between 9 P.M. and the early morning hours of July 20. Our forces moved from Mishmar Hanegev on the Gaza–Beersheba main road to a hill three kilometers from the village. The bridge at the entrance to the village was demolished. Beersheba was a small village behind the British World War I cemetery and the railway station. There were a few brick houses along the main road, and at the end was a square with a police station and school. Across from them stood a mosque where nearly a thousand worshipers gathered every day to pray.

Few Egyptian soldiers were stationed in the police station and, together with the local Arabs who numbered about 500 fighting men, the resistance was insignificant. At around 9 A.M., the 60 Israeli soldiers announced to Ben-Gurion that Beersheba was in their hands. I felt glad to be a part of this achievement through my work. Ben-Gurion wrote later, "The capture of Beersheba was an exclusive example of quick victory during the War of Independence."

The acting Egyptian commander of the area said that he was not informed by his superiors that the way to the Negev was opened by the Israelis and, therefore, he did not make any preparations to defend it. My contributions to the cleanup of the south and the capture of Beersheba was well known by my peers at that time, but they chose to ignore me entirely.

The author (right) with his wife and brother-in-law in a bark on the Yarkon River in Tel Aviv, 1949 (author's collection).

The Faluja pocket, besieged by our forces, is still being debated in Egypt between those who support or oppose the commander of the pocket, Sayed Taha, a Sudanese who was nicknamed "the Black Panther." He succeeded the commander of the Egyptian forces who left him behind after retreating from Ashdod to Gaza. The supreme commander's friends insist that orders were given to him to retreat to Beersheba as long as it was possible establish a firm line on the Gaza–Beersheba road. The deciphered message was passed to Ben-Gurion, who ordered the capture of Beersheba before anyone else did.

The supreme commander claimed that the "Black Panther" did nothing to capture the village. We knew this was impossible because we were seemingly attacking them from the rear, and Beersheba's fate was already sealed by Ben-Gurion.

The state of the besieged troops was very poor. On many occasions, the Egyptian command in Gaza tried in vain to relieve them with food, supplies, arms and ammunition. Our Arabic-speaking commandos, armed with the deciphered password code, overpowered the soldiers disguised as Bedouins who were accompanying the camel caravans.

Among the commanders besieged in Faluja with the Taha was officer Gamal Abdel Nasser, who later became the president of Egypt and Israel's opponent during the Six-Day War of June 1967.

Several meetings were arranged between Taha and the Israeli officers headed by Yigal Alon. Nasser also participated in those meetings. Taha categorically refused to discuss surrender ("only if ordered by my government," he said) and only requested that the Red Cross arrange to take out the wounded. He said this was the only reason he met with the Israeli officers. I read all his messages and communications with his superiors prior to the meetings.

Despite our physical and psychological assaults, it was clear that the Egyptian troops would never negotiate or surrender. Yigal Alon lavishly praised the Egyptians' courage. He also admitted that the capture of Iraq Sweidan and almost half of the besieged pocket was made possible through great effort and resulted in few casualties. He did not add, however, that our decoding and deciphering of the Egyptian Army's messages also saved lives and made victory possible. Alon was a diplomat rather than a military person.

I admired Sayed Taha from what I knew of him through the decoded messages and the reactions he made during these meetings. He expressed his personal admiration of the Jewish fighters who threw out the British. He hoped to do the same for Egypt. Taha repeatedly emphasized that, being an officer, he had no other option but to obey his government orders and, therefore, refuse to surrender. He admired the planning and courage of the Israeli fighting men. If not ordered to surrender, he would uphold the Egyptian Army's honor and fight to the end. His only promise was to inform his government in Cairo of his negotiations with the Israelis.

Fighting around the pocket continued, and because of a mistake made by our forces (the commander of Alexandroni), the Egyptians broke open into the rear. They first mistook the breaking column for Israelis; even the air force failed to recognize them as theirs. It was already late before it became known that the column was Egyptian and not Israeli. This mistake cost us one company that was annihilated, and the Egyptians gained some ground that they held till the signing of the armistice. The Faluja Pocket was not attacked anymore after that. We had many victories in other fronts in the south, which actually brought the Egyptians to the armistice table. After the armistice, the Pocket was relieved and the besieged Egyptian forces returned to Egypt with due honors.

Before the signing of the armistice, there was a U.N. decision on October 19, 1948, to cease hostilities in the south. Dr. Ralph J. Bunche, the U.N.'s American diplomat, made great efforts to bring the two parties to the table to sign a peace treaty. Regretfully, the mediations failed. In order to bring the Egyptians to the negotiating table along with the rest of the Arab nations, it became necessary to strike with military force to ensure our freedom of movement in the Negev.

Operation Horeb began on October 22, 1948. Our forces crossed the borders into Egypt, and their troops fled. Our deep penetration into Egypt greatly influenced the Egyptian command to start a political war against Israel. Egypt tried intensively to get some military assistance from other Arab nations, but these nations were afraid to interfere.

Ironically, the British offered to help without being asked by Egypt. They acted in accordance with a 1936 treaty that obligated them to defend Egypt. This treaty was rejected by the government of Egypt, which did not want to recognize it anymore. A strong ultimatum was sent by them to Israel through the United States. Our forces obliged and retreated to the Palestine international borders. The British RAF (Royal Air Force) was, however, active in the air. On January 7, 1949, the day a cease fire was signed, our pilots downed five RAF planes.

Soon after Operation Horeb, the Egyptians were left in Gaza and the Falouja Pocket. As a result of pressure by world foreign powers, many of the Israeli demands at the armistice agreements with our Arab neighbors were reduced. Nevertheless, Egypt was compelled to negotiate and sign an armistice with Israel in Rhodes on February 24, 1949. With the Falouja Pocket evacuated, all but Gaza, Khan Yunis, and the Rafih strip of the Negev remained in our hands.

During the entire eight-month campaign, I didn't relax at all because I knew that if I made a mistake or missed any information, it could cost lives. All of my co-workers were exceptionally dedicated and served our people and new State irrespective of political affiliation, origin, or creed. I have never again witnessed such dedication and faithfulness. I salute them and wish God's blessings upon them and their families.

During the last days of the campaign, I was reinforced by more worthy helpers who did impressive work and excelled in becoming part of the history of the State of Israel.

# CHAPTER 15

# Armistice in Rhodes

It was announced that the armistice with the Arab nations, especially Egypt, would be signed on the island of Rhodes off the coast of Turkey. I was included with Israel's technical delegation as undercover telecommunications operator. I deciphered the Egyptian delegation's messages and served them to our negotiators to mitigate their accomplishments. Essentially, it was the same job I did before.

I was issued a clean new uniform, the rank of Sergeant, and a diplomatic passport (probably one of the first issued in the name of Israel). We were taken by truck to Dov Airport in Tel Aviv, where we boarded a United Nations Dakota plane together with other delegation members and security agents. Among the higher ranks was David Saltiel, a former Intelligence service chief.

It was the first time in my life that I flew, and the seating on the U.N. transport plane was not comfortable. It was no wonder that, after nearly two hours of turbulence, I threw up. Upon arrival at Rhodes Airport, we were met by Greek officials who provided us with a hundred-weight half-truck to carry our equipment. At the Albergo del Rose Hotel, site of the negotiations, we were met by one of many photojournalists.

Our special unit was headed by Abraham Alony, deputy to commander Mordechai Werzman (Almog). Before we left Israel for Rhodes, our people, unbeknownst to me, met with the boss about the low ranks given to my colleagues and myself in the old tradition of proletarian advocacy. It seems that my friends were rather alarmed that I was only given the rank of Sergeant, so they brought the matter up with the chief. Mordechai called me before I left and rather angrily asked why was I complaining for not being given the rank of an officer. Instead of officership, he said, what I really deserved was a special medal for my achievement. He then showed me a letter to general headquarters that recommended me for such a medal. He added, "You surely deserve special commendation for the capture of Beersheba because, thanks to your work, we got there before the Egyptians."

Until now, I had not received any medals or proper rank. Mordechai himself did not fare well in this regard, and only after I was discharged from the Army did he begin a new career with the Mossad. At that time, the power

The author (far left) in Rhodes with his underground unit just before the 1949 armistice between Israel and the Arab nations (author's collection).

struggle in Israel began and Ben-Gurion decided to issue a medal to everyone who served, irrespective of achievements, much like other communist states of Europe were doing. I cannot blame our commanding officer because I am sure he did his best, but the higher echelon had it its way.

As soon as I reached the door to the Hotel Albergo del Rose, a Greek soldier stationed there jumped in front of me and asked with great admiration, "How on earth did you down five British Spitfires without any damage to your planes?" I smiled and said, "I am sorry. I belong to the ground forces and this can be answered by our air force only." After we were taken to our rooms and had our equipment installed in a nearby house specially provided for our work, I was determined to explore my surroundings on foot, as customary.

The hotel (which is now demolished) was an old structure of four floors. The ground floor served, like most hotels in the world, as the lobby and the restaurant, together with a large conference room with decorated walls and paintings. It was situated not far from Rodi, which is visited by tourists from all over the world. Legend has it that a 100-foot-high bronze statue of the sun god Helios once straddled Rodi's harbor, allowing vessels to sail underneath. It was built around 280 B.C. but was destroyed in 224 B.C. by an earthquake. It was considered one of the seven wonders of the world. The island is not far from the Turkish shore, and a beautiful, castle-like residence was built for the governor at the top of a tall mountain near the center of the island. The view from there is breathtaking.

I shared a room with my colleague Reuben Ronkovski (later Reem), a Morse operator in our unit. With us, from the communications and signals unit, were two girl *kibutznikiots*. Present were General Yigal Yadin, who commanded the Southern front with Yigal Alon during the war; Reuben Shiloah, the then-head of the Mossad who served in Baghdad under the cover of a teacher; Dr. Walter Eytan, director general of the foreign office and later ambassador to France; Eliahoo Sasson, who later became the first ambassador to Turkey; and Mr. Rosen, our legal adviser for international foreign affairs. The army was also represented by Lieutenant Colonel Yitzhak Rabin, who later became commander-in-chief of the Israel defense forces, Prime Minister and Defense Minister.

In the restaurant, just like in Israel, we had our meals at the same table with generals and high-ranking officials. The Egyptians, who were only civilian diplomats and probably less important than the Israelis, sent their officers and NCOs (non-commissioned officers) to eat in the kitchen. The high-ranking officials of the Egyptian delegation sitting across from our table continued to scrutinize me and the other Israeli privates and NCOs, as if questioning, "How could it be that they are casually and freely sitting at the same table with high-ranking officers?"

We didn't talk directly to the Egyptians except during official business. We were ignored every time we made an attempt to converse with the Egyptians.

Our joy and contentment of those days arose from the comradery and fair treatment of one Jew to another. I cherished every moment and looked forward to better living and understanding among future generations of the State of Israel, irrespective of political beliefs. A rather naïve thought, but I could not help but believe it at that time. However, I am convinced that should the generals and high-ranking officials of the State of Israel have been from the Irgun (Begin's party) or Lehy (Shamir's faction) the same equality would have existed.

When the Greek Governor of the island paid a visit to the Egyptian delegation at the Hotel Albergo del Rose, he stepped by mistake into the identical suite of the Israelis. Not realizing his mistake, he greeted General Yadin with a short speech intended for the Egyptians. While he was thanked for Egypt's good treatment of the Greeks in their country, General Yadin listened without interruption. After the Governor finished his speech, General Yadin stood up and saluted him and remarked that his excellency meant to address the Egyptian delegation that occupied an identical suite one floor above. Embarrassed, the Governor said that he would have meant it for the Israelis, too, and immediately invited the delegation to his mountaintop mansion for dinner the next day. General Yadin accepted.

General Yadin selected his entourage for the upcoming party, including the girls from the *kibbutz* and other laymen in the service. At the table at the Governor's mansion, the delegation was seated together as in the Hotel Albergo del Rose restaurant. The lavish table was set with gold plates, vases, mugs and all types of Middle Age drinking vessels never before seen by any of us.

The main course of the dinner was fried chicken with vegetables. Since we were all hungry, we were anxious to start eating, but we could not because of the toasts and speeches made for the occasion. Our food was served by elegantly dressed waiters — a special occasion for those who came from the *kibbutz*.

As soon as we were seated, everyone noticed that there were two almost identical vessels filled with plain water. But, we didn't know which one was for drinking, and we could only ask in English while in the presence of the Governor. General Yadin, who could speak fluently in languages such as English, French, German, Yiddish, and naturally Hebrew, noticed our puzzlement and started conversing with the Governor about languages. Fascinated by the Hebrew language, the Governor asked General Yadin to say a few words in Hebrew so that he could hear it for the first time and appreciate its sound. Unhesitatingly, General Yadin said loudly in Hebrew that the water vessel on the right was for drinking and the one on the left was to dip one's fingers in to wash after eating the chicken with the bare hand, which was permissible.

He turned to the Governor and asked, "How does it sound?" The Governor replied, "Very nice. Oh! Very nice." We could barely hold in our laughter.

Yitzhak Rabin, the long time Minister of Defense, Israel's Prime Minister and head of the general staff, spoke only Hebrew, so he demanded that I translate every conversation and discussion taking place at the hotel and outside in my spare time. I became, like it or not, his more-or-less personal interpreter the entire time he was there. Frankly speaking, I did not like it at the time because I had enough to do, but I did it out of Middle Eastern compassion, and because he was a Jewish officer. I later learned from him that this was his first trip outside the country.

Back in the hotel lobby, a Greek colonel in charge of security for the delegations suddenly got interested in Rabin, who was sitting not far away from us on another sofa. The Greek colonel first asked what rank Mr. Rabin wore. I looked at the Greek colonel and hesitated for a while because I knew that this question would lead to many others since Rabin was a colonel, too. Rabin was at that time the youngest Israeli officer with the delegation and what made him more interesting to the Greek colonel, who was probably in his fifties or

The author (fifth from left) in Rhodes during the 1949 signing of Israel's armistice with the Arab countries except for Iraq (author's collection).

sixties, was that Rabin looked no more than 18 or 19 years old. I did not know his exact age but I believed that he was probably 20 to 24.

When I answered, the Greek officer looked at me in bewilderment. I knew what he was thinking. His next question was, "How come so young a person is promoted to colonel? How old is he?"

I hesitated, not wanting to hurt his feelings, and said, "Oh! He is over twenty-five, probably, but looks younger." He did not wait to ask what military school or academy he graduated from. He added, "But, you don't have any military academy in Israel, as yet?"

He put me on the spot and I impolitely blurted out that we did not need military academies to get capable persons in proper positions when they had proven themselves on the battlefield, which Rabin had now done. Of course, I did not inform him of my low rank or of Rabin's association with the Mapam Party, which was all-powerful at that time.

The Greek looked at me intensely and said, "You are lying. I don't believe a word of what you are saying, and if all this is true, this colonel is destined to occupy the highest post in the country because he is chosen for such position at this very young age." (The Greek's prediction was very correct.) We parted with the unconvinced Greek colonel, who kept shaking his head in disbelief of what I had said. He was probably lamenting the 50 years or more it took him to reach his rank. When Yitzhak Rabin became the head of the general staff, the Maariv newspaper ran the story under the headline "The Greek Officer Did Not Believe."

My colleagues and I were sent to Rhodes to break the code of the Egyptian delegation, which was, like the Israelis, sent through their transmitter direct to the Foreign Ministry in Cairo. Supposedly, the officer in charge also commanded the communications and ciphers team from the Ministry of Foreign Affairs in Tel Aviv. He was also an expert in ciphers, coding, and decoding.

After an intensive work on my part to find the key, I discovered that their diplomatic messages were different from their military ones. In employing the statistic of alphabet arrangements in the coded messages, it became clear that unlike an Arabic message that usually contained an "a" and "l" to form the equivalent of "the," the count was entirely different. After many trials, I passed it to my commanding officer — a Jew from South Africa and a veteran of World War II. After a few days, he was convinced that the language was Arabic and not English. After another failed attempt, I was very sure that the language was English. I was clearly told not to continue if the language was not Arabic, to avoid trespassing on another department. When it became clear that no one would take the authority to decide this issue, I asked to be sent back to discuss this matter with a competent person who could settle it.

Ultimately, a charming girl by the name of Hanna was dispatched. She had experience with English ciphers and with the help of my analysis she cracked the code, which was indeed in English. As far as I know, she did not profit from this, neither in rank nor citation. She received great satisfaction, though, from rendering a great service to the new State of Israel in building a stronger foundation for the future.

An armistice was signed, except by Iraq and Saudi Arabia, and the North African and Gulf States except Egypt. Some of my colleagues signed up as regulars but I sought discharge, erroneously believing that as soon as I was out of the army, I would be able to return back to my previous occupation in the import-export business and start a new life. I discovered how wrong my expectations were. In order to keep me in, I was quickly promoted to Lieutenant with possible Captainship soon. I signed up for one year and continued to work with our unit as before.

All officers were invited to meet with the chief, who was by then Chaim Herzog (future president of the State of Israel). He had two purposes: to convince many of us who thought of leaving the army to stay and sign up for at least another year (which I did); and to warn us of the dangers still ahead despite the armistice that only a few Arab states signed. Mr. Herzog warned emphatically that the Arab countries were re-arming themselves for another round, and we could not allow ourselves to be unprepared for such an eventuality. He made it known, though, that the Arabs were prepared to sign a peace treaty and that the British government had worked hard against such an idea because of sales of British war materials to the Arabs and the fear that Israel would take Britain's place in that part of the world. That was confirmed 40 years later when British intelligence documents were released and published even by the Arab press. This so-called international intrigue cost thousands of lives.

CHAPTER 16

# Power Struggle
# in the New State

The power struggle in Israel still affects all Israelis, young and old. It is fierce, dominating, selfish and continuous. Unlike the Arab countries, it is non-violent (no assassinations or eliminations but only intrigues and inner morality fights in a certain few cases), and extremely persuasive and argumentative.

The Israeli Army lacked tradition and seemed to be nothing more than a disorganized mob. As a matter of fact, I personally liked the dealings and comradery among everyone. Everything was done nonchalantly and without commands or orders from higher ranks, even if people had to follow strict instructions from higher-ups. Everyone knew in his heart what had to be done. The main object was to realize a 2,000 year-dream for the Jewish people, especially after what happened during the Holocaust and its aftermath. We were like members of a big family taking care of their own home.

This situation changed after the Altalena affair (the cargo ship full of arms and ammunition appropriated by the Irgun Zvai Leumi, a right-wing faction that fought the British and brought about their withdrawal from Palestine). On the other hand, the Palmach, which represented the left and played a pivotal role before the establishment of the State, gave the newly born State many senior officers during the War of Independence. In 1948, the Altalena affair almost caused a civil war. The fears that the Etzel and LEHI (right-wing factions) would refuse to disband were unfounded. They later merged with the Israel Defense Force and were swallowed up by the new army. Some of Ben-Gurion's associates tried to maintain units loyal to the Histadrut (Israel labor union) and the left-in-general Palmach, the finest in the new army, was disbanded at the end of the war. Yigal Alon resigned and was replaced by Moshe Dayan.

Because I did not belong to any political party and was not a veteran, I was denied promotion and my deserved rank for a long time. There were many others like me who achieved plenty. The minority of Iraqi Jews were aware of the political struggles and tumult taking place, but most of us remained rather neutral. We were prepared though, to make the supreme sacrifice without reward because of our love of Israel.

It was also feared that the leftists would turn to Russia and form an alliance after the war. I remember one day when high-ranking officers and functionaries were sent to all Intelligence Units, including ours, to instruct us to take the path toward our sealed destiny in the United States of America and not the U.S.S.R.

By then, the struggle for positions and recognitions had begun. The assault on ranks became wild by most of the veterans who, irrespective of their achievements, completely disregarded the ones who had achieved much. They took all the credit to secure a high position in the newly-formed army and government. They sculptured the laws and regulations in their irrevocable image.

Personally, I remained adamant about all this because I found it disgusting. I became rather touchy about the subject because I was working at my best, not for a rank or position, but for Israel itself, which was sacred in my eyes. I made known these feelings to many of my colleagues and friends who looked at me in bewilderment as if I came from another world. What could I do? I was a modest person, I said.

Our common Iraqi Jewish modesty and sensitivity did not help us then and later contributed to prejudice and discrimination. Once preference is given to one group of people because of their long-time service and the real achievers are overlooked, it would be interpreted as discrimination, especially by those who are not accustomed to the kind of political struggle Israel is still going through.

It is amazing to what lengths politicians, accompanied by well-known journalists, would go to achieve their political goals and objectives. For instance, the late prime minister of Israel, Golda Meir, went so far as to describe the newcomers from the Middle East countries as primitives who could not read or write or eat with a fork or spoon or use modern toilets. Her objective was to raise money by selling Israel bonds. She told Jewish people everywhere how Israel desperately needed money and financial assistance, which was true. Although there were other acceptable means to do this, she chose the most dramatic theme, repeating it again and again in spite of protests. Worse yet, prominent journalists repeated these statements in books and newspapers, knowing perfectly well that such statements were inaccurate. Jews from the Middle East were literate and had more education than others there. This fact was constantly mentioned in reports from non–Jewish visitors who made a distinction among Jews. In most cases, the Jewish populations of the Middle Eastern countries were praised for their knowledge of many languages and in the running of big businesses and government administration in the Arab world.

How on earth could a prominent journalist write that immediately following the War of Independence there was a period of decline for the Israeli army, primarily because of the great immigration of Jews from underdeveloped North African and Middle Eastern countries. The army absorbed, it is alleged, thousands of illiterate recruits who had to be taught basic grooming, reading, and writing, in addition to soldiering. Further, it was stated that they lacked motivation and regarded army service as punishment. They reduced the Israel Defense Force's operational level and the commanders became concerned about the low level of the average Israeli soldier. I have never read or witnessed worse nonsense than that.

At Latrun, most of the fresh recruits were from Europe, the United States, and the United Kingdom. Eighty percent of them were killed because the leaders failed to see the danger in entering Latrun on the way to Jerusalem. Besides, nearly all of the newcomers then from Europe and the United States did not know Hebrew. Were they to be called illiterates, too?

Most of the Middle Eastern newcomers did read and write Arabic and those who came from the colonies knew French and Italian. Surely the Falashi Jews from Ethiopia knew Amharic or Tigrini. I am sure they were different from their European or Sabra coreligionists, but they could hardly be called primitive because of their different backgrounds. This way of thinking towards others, including our Arab neighbors, could lead to disasters in the future. The Jews of the Middle East are related and should not be downgraded or looked down on.

Israel at its creation faced many dilemmas. At the end of the war in the south, Ben-Gurion maneuvered to get General Yegal Alon out of the army. Most of the Palmach officers resigned, refusing to serve in the regular army because of lost influence in the future structure of the State and government of Israel. They were mostly pro–Russia. Upon forming of the regular army, there was strong debate whether to create an army from selected Jews who resided in the country before the War of Independence and treat the others as second class or to conceive the Israel Defense Force as part of the problems of a state that was absorbing immigration.

Later the Hebrew newspapers tackled a similar civilian problem about the government and the social position of Israel — whether it should become a Levantine or European nation. They failed to ask themselves if Israel should be a Jewish state. The leftist sociologists claimed that newcomers from the Middle East and North Africa reduced the Israel Defense Force's operational level and filled its ranks with manpower of the lowest standard. The army tried to produce good commanders but failed because it indoctrinated them with socialist thinking and little military training. Added to all this, the new immigrants worried most about their family and parents who were left in camps without sources of income for their welfare. Many people, including my father, lived in leaking tents and degrading deprivation. While immigrants from European countries were treated differently, it was no surprise that the new immigrants from the Middle East lacked the enthusiasm and will for combat. The feeble economy of the State also contributed enormously to this situation. At the time, I was also a victim of this pattern of behavior despite all I did for the State of Israel.

The influence of the left was enormous. At long last our unit became the most important in the Intelligence community. It still is today, with modern equipment and dedicated personnel. New recruits tried desperately to join this elite unit. When army ranks were allotted to us for the first time in the history of the unit, the highest ones were given to three veterans. The others got lesser ranks.

I kept dreaming that very soon I would be discharged and become an ordinary citizen, enjoying ordinary things and businesses as I did when the British were there, when our firm enjoyed the trust of our Arab compatriots and made few businesses together. Soon I would find out that such a dream was much further from reality than I expected.

Because I was an outsider, someone who did not belong to any party, I was ignored by those who were in charge in the military intelligence community. The argument supporting this attitude pivoted on the Socialist Communist maxim that no individual can be laureated for what he did because such deeds and achievements are and remain the property of either the Party or the State ruled by such Party.

It was proposed that I be sent for indoctrination, but I turned it down. It is still argued today that for the people from the Middle East and the Third World countries to be able to advance and gain respectable positions in the government, they must be educated. The others are exempt. This attitude for governing is negative but it has been present, probably less today, for the last 40 years. As a result of my refusal, I became the man who "never was." Reviewing the achievements of the Iraqi and other Middle Eastern Jews who operated in various fields within the Haganah, Etzel, and LEHI and ultimately during and after the War of Independence, I cannot help but think of the famous words of Winston Churchill: "Never in the history of Jewish people was so much owed, to so few, by so many."

I was determined to be demobilized and return to normal civilian life. I hoped that someday I would be remembered for my work just as Paul Revere is remembered for his midnight ride during the American War of Independence, shouting the warning "The British are coming!"

Restrictions for advancement in the Army made me seek another occupation in civilian life. The restrictions were also mainly directed towards the extreme parties and those who did not belong to any party, like myself. On the other hand, even within the middle Mapai party members, promotions were given mainly to veterans who came to Israel with the first, second and third waves of immigrants. The Middle Eastern and Sephardic Jews were not candidates for high-ranking posts in general, neither in the government nor in the Israeli Defense Force. The maximum rank given at that time was captain. (This was later changed, gradually, to major and lieutenant colonel.)

Although this attitude was not discriminatory against ethnic or factional groups, our people considered it as such, not realizing that it was very political. It was almost impossible to make any type of progress in Israel unless one was a veteran of the Mapai Party; party discipline was extremely strict to the extent that the party mattered more than its philosophy. (One occasionally heard of suicides that stemmed from indoctrination by some of the party members who were either disgraced or who had nowhere to turn.)

Of course, none of this was officially known and the others rightly mistook it for ethnic discrimination. As for the other officers and men from the left or right, they were encouraged to resign by the Mapai (Labour Party). The majority of resigners refused to sign up in lesser positions; a few enlisted in the regular Army. Hundreds of efficient and brilliant officers who made the creation of Israel possible were among those who resigned.

Isser Beeri's deputy, Colonel Chaim Herzog, senior Intelligence officer with the British Army during World War II, was chosen to head the Military Intelligence. Ben-Gurion preferred this appointment because he feared a political challenge from the Palmach (left-wing units) commanders. He increased his reliance on those commanders and officers who had acquired their experience in the British Army during World War II and he appointed more graduates of the British forces to senior positions.

Until then the military Intelligence did not function properly. As soon as Mr. Herzog took over, it was organized into a smooth working machine. He persuaded the new leaders of Israel to allot more funds to the army. Then, military intelligence was taken very seriously, especially after my unit's achievements. Since our Intelligence was constructed after the British model, our ranks were much lower than the regular army. A chief could not be ranked higher than colonel. As far as my rank was concerned, nothing much had changed and the prospects of being promoted to my deserved rank were as bleak as before.

I became somewhat famous among the community of our unit. Some of them became friendly; others were jealous and developed some kind of hostility towards me. I did my best to avoid any confrontation and, in the meantime, nursed the idea that I would demobilize shortly and return to the mainstream of regular civilian activities.

In Israel, the army that emerged from the War of Independence victorious now faced many problems. For instance, it was less prepared for war. In fact, this should never happen to the Jews or Israelis as long as they want to survive. It is known that the Arabs would rage war again as soon as a new demagogue emerges to arouse their *razzia* (plundering and slave hunting) instinct. Many Arab people are decent and unique, but they would be helpless in stopping such a leader from again taking control of their country.

CHAPTER 17

# Walk Gate Tour of Israel

The demobilization and return of thousands of soldiers to civilian life without interruption is a problem still facing the State of Israel.

In fact, it was more difficult on the outside than in the army. Because of all these difficulties, I decided to sign up in the regular army until things changed and normalcy was returned. Taking advantage of the transition I had just made, I decided to tour Israel because so far I had been only to Gaza, Tel Aviv, Jerusalem, and Haifa. It is still very common for almost all Israeli girls and boys to tour the land. My target then was the northern part of the new-old country, and I set out to visit every place on foot.

I began hiking on the main old road towards Haifa. For the next three or four weeks, I became a real tramp. On a few occasions, I was picked up by a passing military or civilian vehicle. I was soon joined by another soldier out hiking on the highway like me and we went together to places where I had not been before.

At night, we sought shelter in military camps or settlements (*kibbutzes*). It was easier for us because we proudly wore the new State's military uniform. We were always well-treated during our trip to the north. The Galilee is cooler in the summer than the rest of the country and thus is a great vacationing resort. Elat is a perfect place with a mild climate and virtually no rain. One can camp and sleep in the open. Also, one can swim in the Red Sea in the winter or go scuba diving and watch the multicolored fish swimming by. In the north, one could ski almost year round on Mount Hermon, provided there was peace between Israel and Syria and the Syrian borders were open. The size of Israel at the time was 600 kilometers long and 12 kilometers wide. A very small state — the approximate size of New Jersey. It could be covered by car from north to south in about ten hours.

The only snow which fell on the shores and lowlands of Israel came in January 1950. The snowfall covered most parts of the country, including the coastal plains. During the summer, the heat wears people down and it is the best time to travel north where the climate is somewhat cooler. The nights, even in June and August in the center of the country, are as cool as any other place in the land, especially during the morning breeze. Summertime makes

The author (second from left) enjoys Israel's first snowfall in 50 years with members of his unit in January 1950 (author's collection).

one become slow and easygoing, undemanding and contemplative. The mountains are rather somnolent and the days wash away like castles of sand until the more pleasant climate of autumn arrives.

My first stop was Nathanya, a very pleasant summer resort in the middle of Israel about 10 to 12 miles from the Jordan border. The high cliffs at the seashore were an inspiring place to contemplate the wide azure waters of the Mediterranean as they form a cupola with the cloudless blue sky, making a halo with the silver rays of the sun. The beach under the cliff was one of the best in the world. It was wide, long, and very clean throughout the length of the shore of Nathanya. The town did not differ much from any other in the United States of America. The people there were hospitable and accommodating. Little did I know then that my future wife would come from such a captivating place in Israel.

Leaving Nathanya for Haifa was a short trip. The historic port of Haifa is well-known throughout the world. Mount Carmel stood guard over the Mediterranean shore overlooking the bay of Haifa underneath — a scene to remember for a very long time. The houses in the lower part of the city looked like toys. The wooded valley and mountains on the right made Haifa look like a small city lying at the bay across from the ancient town of Akko, the old Crusaders' fortress, on the other side of the bay.

Following the seashore road further north was Nahariyya. This town was inhabited mostly by Jews from Germany who fled after the rise of Nazism there, and they still speak German. Nahariyya was a model in cleanliness and leisure hotels and motels. It was a relaxing summer resort for the city inhabitants to escape the heat. A little stream which runs through the middle of the town made it a romantic place for lovers and newlyweds. I myself spent my honeymoon there.

On the way up the mountains toward Zefat (Safad) up on the Galilee hills, one could see a mixture of woodland and pastures, hills covered with olive trees and groves. In the middle of May, both Lake Tiberias and the Mediterranean in the west could be observed simultaneously. Lake Tiberias showed its glorious beauty surrounded by mountains that on a clear day were reflected in its calm clear waters. The lake appeared majestically like a scene from paradise.

Arriving in Safad, it felt like walking back in time. It was a place of pilgrimage in the Middle Ages where the *kabala* (a mystical Jewish cult) was studied and practiced. The scenery around the town of Safad was breathtaking. The main street, which surrounded the town on the top of the hill, also led to other side streets which could only be reached by stairs especially built for pedestrians. Most of the inhabitants were religious and most studied the *kabala*.

Moving down toward Lake Tiberia, I passed Rosh Pina, the earliest town settled by immigrants who worked on the land and cultivated it by draining many swamps, including Lake Hula. Going downhill, I reached Lake Tiberias (*Yam Kinneret*) and moved south toward the town of Tiberias itself. Tiberias was famous for its hot springs and the fish which were plentiful in the lake and made a delicious year-round gourmet food. Tiberias was a winter resort because of its low altitude and mild climate. Tourists from all over crowd the hotels and other places in town.

The road down to Tiberias from Safad was tough. It was steep and twisting just as it was from the south coming from Tel Aviv or Haifa. My fellow soldier companion and I drew strength from the clean fresh air of the mountains surrounding us, savoring every moment as we pushed forward to catch another scenic place still undiscovered by us. The soil in the morning was always covered with dew and there were green grass and wild flowers of all kinds all around us. The slight breeze was like music and we felt intoxicated by the beauty of the surrounding vast stretches of landscapes that nature had molded into the space and time of that period.

Nazareth, situated on the hills southwest of Tiberias, was inhabited by Christian Arabs who became an integral part of Israel, choosing to become Israeli citizens. The alleys and ancient buildings in town were maintained as they were 2,000 years ago. The town was well protected by the surrounding hills and the antiquity of Christian and Jewish culture was abundant all around. South of Lake Tiberias and Nazareth was the plain of Esdraelon ('*Emeq Yizre'el*), which was mentioned in Biblical times as the land of milk and honey. Mount Tabor lay in the heart of a unique scenic setting. Built on its top is a Medieval church and around the hill is a vast green plateau. Into the far distance stretches the Plain of Esdraelon and its greenery which covers the land. The town of Afula lay at the tip of Kvish Hasargel, named "the ruler road," because it was built like a straight ruler crossing the Plain of Esdraelon to Wadi ha-Arava in the south. To the north of Afula on the hills of Galilee, the little village of Nazareth swept upward, tinted a delicate blue from a distance. Far to the right was the somber summit of Mount Tabor, which bars the view with the deep cleft of the Jordan Valley. This was for many thousands of years the scene of mighty battles and momentous and decisive history.

Continuing south through Wadi ha-Arava, we reached Hadera and were back again on the seashore road south to Tel Aviv. On the way lies Caesarea, the ancient city on the Mediterranean seashore where Roman rulers lived during the occupation of Israel. It is also where Bishop Eusebius of Caesarea discovered the writings of Philo of Byblos, which said that at the head of the many Beals Gods of Canaan was the god El. His wife was Asherah (Astarte), referred to in the Bible as Ashtaroth. El killed his brother, his own son, cut off his daughters' heads, castrated his father, castrated himself, and compelled his confederates to do the same. Also, it was said that at that time men and women prostitutes were considered "sacred" to the followers of the religion of El. The records of their services went into the temple treasury as offerings for the god.

I continued my exploration of Israel and visited the south, the Negev, and Elat. It was without suitable roads, and thus extremely dangerous. The barren hills around looked sinister, like the ones on the moon landscape. There were small rifts, valleys covered with dust, and volcanic craters with colors alternating from sandy gray to green and burgundy. There were many standing rocks in various shapes and figures as if carved on purpose. The successive layers of deposited sand in various colors depicted a stratum which looked like cumulus clouds at sunset.

The sea below, the Dead Sea, is really dead. Not a living thing exists in its very salty and mineral-thick waters where nothing could sink except, perhaps, heavy metals. These waters have a healing effect on certain skin infections or diseases. Bedouin nomads were everywhere with their tents and animals but they were like a phantasmagoria—first you would see them and then you would not. Nothing grows there and the Israelis, driven by the inspiration of the late David Ben-Gurion, were determined to make it bloom and become a habitable land. This dream is now being realized.

CHAPTER 18

# Dawning of
# a New Existence

The employment market in the civilian sector was in its worst state. Everything became rationed and the word *tzenaa* (austerity) took root in our lexicon. It was commemorated by the famous Hebrew song which is still played today, "Tzenaa-Tzenaa." Some time before the creation of the State of Israel, I had applied for immigration to the United States. I did not give much thought to immigration because I never expected such a visa would be forthcoming. Surprisingly enough, in 1952 I was asked by the U.S. Embassy in Tel Aviv if I was still interested to immigrating to the United States. I was also told that my application would perhaps be considered favorably because of the new rules on immigration coming into effect at that time. I politely declined and my application was canceled. Immigration to the United States became secondary to being an Israeli.

My search for decent work in civilian life was not fruitful and I therefore decided to sign up for a year with the regular army, hoping that things would get better by then. In the meantime, I started looking for my lost girlfriend whom I had not seen for the duration. To my surprise, I learned that she had married a wealthy person, something she had wanted all the time. Suddenly, and with some anxiety, I found myself alone in facing my new life after the war. All borders were sealed off and we lived as if in a prison, surrounded by enemies who stubbornly refused to sign any peace treaty that might enable me and many others to visit relatives and friends after such a long separation. We gradually became aware that such a dream was still far from our reach because of the poisoning politics of the Middle East.

Looking back at other wars in my lifetime, most all of the warring parties of the world signed peace treaties and became friends. Most, if not all, of the belligerent nations made peace with each other, whether victors or vanquished, and prospered afterwards.

Looking at the Arab nations' stubbornness for half a century, one cannot understand why such proud and basically decent people refused to consider even elementary humanitarian contact with the State of Israel. I wonder what makes them behave like that and nurse an uncontrollable hatred?

A friend of mine from Ben Yehuda Street in Tel Aviv introduced me to a girl named Juliet, and we sat together in a nearby café to chat. Juliet was to meet another fellow who did not show up, so the three of us decided to go out for a while. I was attracted to Juliet and asked her if we could go somewhere to dance. My friend had to leave and she accepted my invitation, and we went to a dance café somewhere near the Yarkon River north of Tel Aviv. We had a wonderful time. After accompanying her home, I asked her if she would go out with me again the next day or perhaps later. She graciously agreed and we set out on our next date sooner than I expected.

So far, I had lived and felt very much alone. All of a sudden, I had the feeling that it would be different from now on and drew comfort that, at long last, I had found what I was looking for all my life. The visual fragment of that first night has returned to me many times.

The thought that I had just passed another birthday and was not getting any younger culminated into the decisive idea that it was time to settle down. I kept on wondering why Juliet did not vacillate or seem unreachable, like other girls, but she agreed to see me again. Perhaps it was my lieutenant's uniform, which usually attracted girls in those days because it was a most impressive and proud thing to wear.

She did not know that I was just a soldier with a meager income that could not even cover my next date with her. However, all I could think about was her and I did not really think much about financial problems.

As a result of our short past and what had happened to our Jewish people, I began to think that what we had went beyond romance, dancing, or dreams. Suddenly, I realized that the same thoughts might have crossed Juliet's mind. She was like me, Iraqi-Basra Jewish born, and had come to Palestine at a young age. I also learned later that she served in the new army for a short time and was afflicted with the tragic death of her brother Maurice (Moshe), who was killed in action on the battlefield of Sarafand. In spite of everything, we were still romantic young people who longed for love and aspired for social respectability. We could only think that, no matter what, we were the sum of all the lives we once lived, perhaps. After having lived alone all this time, Juliet and I went dancing for the second time with a purpose.

After that I was in a trance-like state: walking and working in a dream world and unable to take my mind off Juliet. I became more entangled with her, especially after many of my friends and colleagues complimented the beautiful and sweet girl I was dating.

My fears of losing her were baseless because there was nothing that could separate us anymore. She continuously hid the grief brought about by the death of her brother, and only on a few occasions would she hide her face and shed a tear from when we encountered someone or something which reminded her of him. Every time this happened, I thought about my many friends and acquaintances who lost their lives in the War of Independence, which claimed the heaviest toll in the whole history of the State of Israel. I wondered what they would say to us from their graves about their sacrifice and whether it was made in vain or not.

Our attachment to each other turned into a preliminary love affair and after a few months we decided to get married. There was some hesitation on the part of her family because another contender was seeking her hand, but soon it became clear that I finally was the chosen one. It made me very happy because by then I had discovered that she was the one I was looking for. She would definitely be a great mother for my future children and an exceptional equal partner in my life. Amazingly, she believed the same thing too, which was perhaps why we were attracted to each other. I was 28 and she was 23 years old. It was the hand of fate perhaps that brought us together because we later discovered a group photo taken during a party a long time before the war in which she, a stranger at the time, was standing right behind me.

The army took care of everything for our wedding and my commander, Major Mordechai (Almog), in appreciation for what I did in his unit, worked hard to secure the military restaurant in Jebelia in Jaffa for the ceremony. He also ordered soft drinks and food for hundreds of people. I was delighted and grateful to him because it proved to be the best wedding, considering the then prevailing circumstances, ever given to a soldier in the Intelligence community. We invited lots of friends, many colleagues and fellow officers, including Colonel Herzog, our chief Intelligence officer (later the President of the State of Israel).

Four soldiers held the *chupa*, the canopy for the ceremonial wedding, with four rifles, one in each corner, in the tradition of military weddings. Few photos were taken because of austerity prevailing at the time, but the spirit was high in the tradition of a Babylonian wedding ceremony.

Mordechai Almog authorized us to occupy a suitable room on the second floor in the building where our unit used to be before expansion. His efforts to keep us in the room failed because some Labour Commissar girl lieutenant whisked it away to a newcomer from Belgium who recently joined the Israeli Army. Of course, I was indignant and felt cheated because I had the right to stay in our room because we were there first.

There were many pleas from high-ranking officers of the unit, including Mordechai Almog. Whether true or not, I was told even our Chief Intelligence officer, Mr. Herzog, tried to help. But nothing could make the lieutenant change her mind. I visited her and pled for her to let us stay until we could

The author's wedding was celebrated under a *chupa* (canopy) raised by four rifles and held by four soldiers with a traditional reading of the marriage contract (author's collection).

find another suitable place to live. After those pleas fell on deaf ears, I went to the military legal adviser, but he could do absolutely nothing because there were no laws governing such cases, as yet, and it seemed that everyone was on his own.

Deciding to resist, I wrote to every newspaper in Israel, a weapon which I considered very democratic. But instead of getting help I was summoned to a court martial because I wrote to the left-wing *Al Hamishmar* newspaper. When I tried to explain that it was only a copy of the original letter sent to all other newspapers, I was rudely silenced and sentenced to be rebuked. The sentence went on my military record book and any further promotion thus became impossible. I left the court when I found out that my belongings were being taken out of our room by force. The door had been forced open and they transferred us downstairs to a small place previously intended for servants. This became our new home.

A friend of mine of Iraqi-Jewish origin, who faithfully served in the Intelligence, was promoted to a suitable rank. One day, whether or not precalculated, a provocation was staged against him. After a fistfight, he was stripped of his rank in a similar court martial. Being the type who does not give up easily, he struggled again and got to the rank of colonel. When he realized that he could push no more, he resigned and tried his luck with the civil administration. Only a few years ago he became a special advisor for Arab affairs to the Prime Minister of Israel. He was again apparently cheated out of his post and he fought back through the due process of the law, but the outcome was not as he expected. His only mistake was that he did not belong to any of the Israeli parties; but, he was a faithful lover of Israel and a fighter who risked his life many times for the State of Israel.

The Mapai (Labour Party), which was in power, began to promulgate regulations and by-laws using the old Ottoman codes of Palestine. They restricted everything under the pretext of economic squeeze and security. Their rank and file enjoyed all the luxuries of a ruling party, while the others lived in austerity. Virtually all the administration was filled with their cronies. All others struggled to serve the State of Israel, whether in the army, settlements or other Labour ventures directed and managed by the ruling party.

Most of the new immigrants who were raised as Jews did not bother about Labour laws and, as free enterprise people, carried on their practice as they knew best. Despite the many economic restrictions of the laws, they thrived on their own self-reliance. Others like myself who respected the laws found themselves unable to cope with their economic positions and make ends meet. The situation went from bad to worse while those who made the rules used them to fortify their positions as well as that of the ruling party, which made democratic governing impractical. After they consolidated their power, they succeeded in ruling the country in a semi-democratic system of voting that assured them of remaining in power. The laws of Israel were forged in the image of their lords. The common people, who helped them achieve this, were usually preferred for jobs and housing; even bribes were taken on days of elections. The ruling parties treated them like children who were doing their best to become heroes by supporting and blindly joining the party in power.

Out of the hodgepodge, Israel grew in population, development, and relative advancement due to the contributions made from abroad, especially from the United States, which were prodigiously spent on such government-sponsored projects. A portion of the contributions went to the parties themselves.

After our wedding, the value of our currency (the lira), which was based on one pound sterling, went down to 2.80 per U.S. dollar instead of 4.03 U.S. dollars, which indicated that the financial support from the United States would be worthless. The Israeli leaders falsely told the public that this would not affect the Israeli position because our imports came mostly from the United States. All prices would remain the same, they said. The financial wizards of the Labour Party added that because our lira was already devalued to a third of one U.S. dollar, the new rate would be of 20 *agurot* (percent) difference, a margin which could not harm the Israeli economy.

After the State was established, our boys when abroad would sell the new Israeli pound for more than its official value. A friend called on one particular money changer in Rome for the second time, and when he gave him more new liras to exchange, he was refused because the money exchanger had lost so much on his first lira transaction and could not possibly accept any more losses. When asked why he bought the new liras the first time, he said that since Jews were so smart in financial matters, he was sure it would go up in value in the future. The true value of our new liras was rapidly declining every day in September 1949.

Today, that same lira has been changed to the shekel. The value of the lira, before it expired, reached millions to one dollar, but we survived thanks to our wizardly manipulation of things.

At that time, the government even interfered in the baking of a loaf of bread for the public. This interference eventually led to the strike of bakers, which also led to scarcity of a necessary dietary commodity. Dov Joseph ordered the bread to be baked in a round shape instead of a long shape which, according to him, would cost less and cause the dismissal of 15–30 percent of the labor force.

Labor was, and still is, strong and protected by the Histadrut (Israel State Union) Mapai. Right or wrong, it was an attempt to dominate one of the two largest parties (both Labour) by the other because the populace must have the rationed bread in times of austerity. At the time, the world media were focusing on the fate of the displaced Arab people. Husni Zaim, the ruler of Syria, agreed to accept half a million refugees, but he was met with strong opposition from his government and foreign Arab countries and, therefore, the idea was abandoned. Husni Zaim wanted peace with Israel but was overthrown and executed on August 14, 1949. Arab refugees were also denied settlement in other Arab lands. In the meantime, Israel was absorbing its displaced persons and refugees from Arab countries as well as Europe and was somewhat successful in taking care of them until they were properly settled.

The rationing of food for the holidays sold against proper coupons was meager. Each person in Tel Aviv could buy 10 grams of hot dogs, 200 grams of fresh meat, 1,570 grams of sugar, 200 grams of margarine, 6 eggs per child, 3 eggs per adult, 1 cake of soap, 50 grams of hard cheese, 250 grams of carrots, 250 grams of onions, 1 kilo of potato, and so on.

In spite of all the mentioned difficulties, very few left the country. On the contrary, many new immigrants kept on pouring in and settling there. There was still continuous strife between the many parties trying to seize as much power as possible. We were all content and happy and the songs and lyrics of that period expressed fully such peaceful feelings towards Israel. We all looked forward to a bright future for all the people of the Middle East.

# CHAPTER 19

# A Changing of the Guard

Chaim Herzog's deputy commander was Major (later Colonel) Benjamin Gibli, who took over Military Intelligence when Herzog was sent to Washington as a military attaché—an apparent demotion. The new commander was mistrusted by both Isser Beeri's friends and foes. Beeri's friends mistrusted him because he testified against Beeri in Toubianski's rehabilitation trial. His foes mistrusted him because he was one of Toubianski's judges who ordered him executed on the spot. Nevertheless, Benjamin Gibli packed much glamour and charisma with his superiors despite his youth. He was also intelligent, shrewd and popular, but he portrayed himself differently to our unit.

While our commander Mordechai Almog was doing his best along with his deputy Abraham Aloni to elevate the unit and introduce higher ranks and positions long overdue for everyone, their efforts were played down by their superiors. Gibli gave Mordechai the *coup de grâce* when he ordered all officers and men of the unit, who were mostly of Iraqi-Jewish origin, to attend a meeting at the Jebalia restaurant where my wedding took place. With Mordechi and me sitting next to him, Gibli started to praise us lavishly for our achievements to a point that we felt that he was overdoing it. As is our tradition, we kept listening silently, attentively.

He began to mention that it was not Mordechai who made all this possible, it was us—the rank and file—who succeeded to turn around the status of the whole Intelligence work. I could scarcely believe what I was hearing because we were always told that we were nothing but a small cog in a big machine. Then he announced that our commander was being transferred to another unit and a new officer would take over. The new commander was there, too, but we could not have known that he was to take over Mordechai's place.

It was rather a shock to all of us. In an extravagant speech, he repeated that it was not just Mordechai who brought this unit to the present high standard, but it was us who made this possible. I noticed that Mordechai was sitting there rather stunned, and we were dumbfounded. I realized that there was some truth in what he was saying, but no one could deny Mordechai's major role in coordinating, forming, and running the unit successfully.

Mordechai Almog was transferred to the Mossad (Foreign Intelligence), similar to the CIA of the United States. He loved our unit. It was his creation, so to speak, and sending him to another post was like a demotion for him. However, there was a consensus that Intelligence officers from the army could be loaned or transferred to this service, and vice versa.

I continued my work at headquarters and sometimes in the field and was able to contribute my share in postwar Israel for over a year. My wife was expecting our first child in our humble room. A shortage of money for a down payment in an army project for houses, and the resentment I had because of the way I was treated, made me decide against joining up any further.

# CHAPTER 20

# Landsmen's Exodus

The *aliya* (immigration) of the Iraqi Jewish population from Iraq was in full swing, and my brother Naim arrived in Israel. My brother was given a job in Elat, the remote southern port of the Negev on the Red Sea across from Jordan's port of Acaba. There were very few pioneers with him. His job was to erect, operate, and maintain a communications station with the mainland. He succeeded in realizing his objective and remained there for many years, meeting many famous tourists including the late comedian Danny Kaye.

My father and stepmother arrived soon after Naim, as did many of my relatives, friends and classmates from school in Baghdad.

At first, I was very happy about it, but soon my happiness turned to sadness merely because there was no way to house them all. Like the Arab refugees, we created displaced persons of our own, but ours had a different ending than our cousins in Arab countries. All the Iraqi Jews left everything behind and came to Israel almost penniless. Back in Iraq, all their properties were confiscated, including bank accounts.

After demobilization, I was under the impression that I would be able to extend more assistance to my parents and brother, but such thoughts grew further and further from realization.

Just a few weeks after becoming a civilian, I was called for reserve duties. When I came back, I sought employment with El Al, where many Iraqi Jews were accepted, but I was turned down. On my application I had to mention my previous employer, my intelligence unit, and it appeared that word was sent to defer me from being employed so I would be forced to come back and ask them for a job. I could not vouch that this was the case with me, but the fact was that less qualified and less experienced people were accepted for that job, and more were being accepted after I was turned down by them.

Among the newcomers from Iraq were many distant relatives, especially from my mother's side. One day I crossed Shederoth Rothchild at Allenby's corner and heard a lady calling my native name, "Shoua." I turned and met one of my cousins accompanied by another female. After the usual greetings, she took me by the hand and said, "I would like you to meet my niece, Dee."

Confused, I gathered my strength and with mixed feelings shook Dee's hand and greeted her rather clumsily.

Looking back at my first love, I must have recovered because I acted naturally when I saw her again after more than a decade. The actual sight of her was a shock. She was different. She looked much older than she actually was — there were wrinkles on her face and she was unattractive. When back at home I looked at myself in the mirror and saw a middle-aged man in Israeli reserve officer's uniform, one not as handsome or lively as he had been during the time of his first love.

Continuing to reflect upon her, I recalled that she was at the age of puberty while I was only 17. It was virtually impossible for a young man of 17 to marry and support a family at that age. War and world events were major factors not to realize my dream, and her family's not permitting me to see her again contributed to my leaving Iraq for good. Abroad, I managed somehow to sneak a letter to her, but I do not know if she read it or not. I last heard in 1949 that she was forced to marry and had children.

In 1952, most other people were doing very well in the black market and in dealing in foreign currencies. These kinds of businesses were hotly investigated and those caught were severely punished or jailed for breaking the law.

Nobody cared, though, and such businesses continued to flourish, forcing the authorities to engage more policemen, especially economic agents, and to spend more money than the laws were saving. Later the Labour government also lost the battle with income tax laws and other taxes.

I struggled because I did not wish to break the law in spite of the fact that the law, according to my principles, was crooked. I tried extremely hard to earn my living the old fashioned way. Soon I realized that the old fashioned way in Israel became the fight against socialist rule that touched almost every life. I did my best to fit into the new way of life, but I failed. I also tried to join the group but it was too late for me. I distrusted the dictum that the Israeli government was an equal opportunity employer. Despite remaining faithful to Israel, I kept wondering why my people, whom I served so faithfully and well, would allow this to happen.

The answer came much later on when I learned that the same tactics were employed against our famous master spy "Elie Cohen." Forced to rejoin, he was ultimately captured, arrested and hanged because of some silly perseverance in sending him back despite the sensed danger. His story could have ended better if it were not for his employers who ignored the sense of danger because of their lust for power.

I could hardly believe that Ben-Gurion's generation of Mapai (the left wing party) brought with them from Czarist Russia an authoritarian view of life and politics. Party discipline was (and still is) very strict and nothing was possible unless one was of Mapai.

There is a proverb which says, "If you can't bite the hand of your adversary, shake it." Clinging to remain in business, I came into agreement for a new venture with three newcomers from Baghdad. We all went into partnership with a friendly land-owning Arab from Ramla who was on good relations with the Jewish people and the government. The land was properly cultivated and the products were marketed through Tnuva, the dairy product consortium controlled by the government union Histadrut. We were somewhat successful but because of our dependence on Tnuva we decided to sell out and split whatever we had invested. Everything was legal and official accountants controlled, audited and signed the liquidation. All dues for government tax were correctly paid. Later I received a note from the tax authorities my army service owed me a sum of about eight liras and was asked to call on the tax officials to collect the amount, which was an appreciable sum in those days when I needed the money badly.

However, the tax officials in Jaffa ruled that I had to pay an additional eight liras as tax on the agricultural project we labored on and lost. According to the tax officials, we made a profit in spite of the official statements by their people that we lost money on that project. I then realized that the Labour Party was really in power. I paid the cashier and left feeling as if I'd just been robbed.

This system established with the State of Israel is still being applied by the Labour Party today. It has been said that if you trace a circle 500 miles in diameter around Kiev in Russia, you would find that more than 80 percent of Israel's leaders until the late 1970s or their descendants came from one of the towns or villages located within that circle.

While the Jews from the Middle East, North Africa and the Sephardic community contributed much to Israel in various fields, it was said that the Sephardic Jew did not like to engage himself in matters or works done by the Jews from Europe. Maybe it was true because they were not allowed to ply their skill in the new State. Their contribution to the peace process would have been, for obvious reasons, much greater than those who Arabicized themselves rather clumsily to deal with the Arab world. The lust for power went to a ridiculous level in teaching Polish, Russian and other European Jews to speak Arabic in a short time for filling even low-skill positions, which more likely could be filled by Arabic-speaking Jews who were taught the language since birth. Israel is still suffering from this mistake.

One day in the company of a well-educated Arab from Jerusalem, the subject of conversation turned to the status of Middle Eastern Jews in Israel. I did my best to convince him that we enjoyed equal rights. He contradicted what I was saying and concluded that he would never accept Israeli rule because it never treated them as equals. He added that since the Middle Eastern Jews were treated as second-class citizens, he could not accept a third-class status for any reason.

There must be a sense of sharing with those who contributed to the State, whether old-timers or newcomers, because all deserve their share in building, holding, and maintaining their home.

# CHAPTER 21

# Struggling in a Socialist State

Jews who realized what form of government Israel was heading to ignored most of the restrictions and laws which limited them to a few activities and carried on their business in the Black Market. They prospered in spite of continual harassment by the economic police or income tax authorities who were unsuccessfully trying to enforce the left wing rules and policies. I felt that breaking the laws of the government of Israel was like committing a sin. Many others like me were brainwashed into believing that the government policies were the right ones in spite of the fact that the parties allowed deviations from what they preached and promulgated in rules and laws. Still, we believed that we could prosper within the law.

I created a corporation in which I was given shares to export goods to Africa. As an independent firm I chose to export to Eritrea (Ethiopia) where I spent more than one year during World War II. This venture did not yield fruitfully — except for a few import orders for Israeli articles — because a Jewish merchant from Aden who loved Israel decided to make an exception and to import from his beloved land, realizing that he might sell it either at cost or at a loss. I realized that free business with Israel was out of the question and decided to pack up and return home as early as possible. I knew that other firms connected with the government of Israel were doing fine because their losses were covered with substantial subsidies which rendered their exports competitive.

I was feeling frustrated and homesick when an Israeli acquaintance bared his real identity as a Mossad agent and presented me with my ex-commander's handwritten letter which asked me to assist and follow him. This was the first time that the Mossad proved that I was worth something. Due to my past experience, I was not surprised at all and reacted with mixed feelings of anger and love toward the State of Israel.

They approached me probably due to my achievements and loyalty to the State. They knew that I did not need a course of brainwashing and molding.

Also, because I was part of the academy and versed already in the business, I could pass to others the experience which I had gained through trial and error. Besides, they relied on us because we would never do an immoral thing while in the service.

I cooperated with the agent for a while and when he put to me his real intention of becoming a Mossad agent to cover Aden, Kuwait and Saudi Arabia, I asked him to forward my mixed demands for security and future, as that I would work for Israel without becoming a pawn to the ruling party. I was not at all surprised that the Mossad gave a negative reply to my conditions, which I watched being transmitted by means of the agent's secret transmitter. Since I was an ordinary citizen, no one pressed me to accept and I was left alone.

While at my friend's secret place sending my conditions, I noticed that messages transmitted and received in Asmara were especially clear and loud. Outside, I befriended a United States GI stationed there and learned that a unit similar to ours was being operated in the city by the CIA because almost all Middle Eastern states' transmissions could be covered and perfectly intercepted due to our location being 10,000 feet above sea level.

I booked a flight with Cyprus Airways — the only one operating out of the Middle East — and my journey back took me from Asmara in Eritrea, Agordat, Khartoum (the capital of Sudan), Port Sudan, Nicosia and finally Tel Aviv. On the day of my departure, authority over Sudan was passed to the Egyptian government, and Anglo-Egyptian Sudan became Egyptian Sudan only. The Egyptian consul general in Asmara became the only authority to issue visas and transit visas through that country. I had little hope that such a transit visa would be issued to me because of my Israeli passport.

The only way left for me would be to go on a passenger boat through the Suez either to Cyprus or Napoli and then to Tel Aviv. The passage through the Suez would also be risky even though I could stay on board under the protection of the captain of the boat. I figured that traveling through the Suez could be more complicated and I discussed the situation with the Mossad agent, who suggested that I squarely confront the Egyptian consul for a transit visa. It was time that an Israeli passport be respected in international matters, he said.

On November 1, 1955, I went to the Egyptian Consulate and was politely greeted at the entrance by a beautiful Italian secretary. She listened attentively to my request and proud reply that I was Israeli. She smiled and said that she could not promise that a transit visa could be granted on my Israeli passport, because new guidelines were being applied. She requested that I fill out my application and sign it, and she would let me know what could done. When I handed back my completed papers and Israeli passport, which she put into the newly opened file for me, the Egyptian ambassador or consul came out of his room. Noticing me near the secretary, he approached me and asked if I spoke Arabic. I enthusiastically confirmed that I did. He looked at me from head to toe and then invited me to his room. I am sure that he was convinced that, because of my Middle Eastern appearance, I was a Moslem Arab of one of the Middle Eastern countries, but he did not ask. He ordered coffee for me and we talked and joked about a lot of things in Egyptian Arabic, which I had mastered while in Cairo during World War II.

While I was having a good time, the secretary knocked at the door inquiring whether she could issue me the visa, without telling him my actual nationality. He approved and later she came back and politely asked me to pay the fee, which I did, and handed me back my passport which I quickly slipped into my pocket. When I got up to take leave, he asked what Arab nationality I belonged to. I turned around and told him that I was an Israeli. He laughed his head off and said in Egyptian, *"Bardoo maaleish"* which means "It is also O.K." I thanked him and was on my way to fly to the Sudan with an official visa and ultimately back home to Israel.

Not long before, I had met with Israeli sailors in Asmara who were about to board a ship in defiance of the Egyptian blockade against Israeli shipping through the Suez Canal. Their objective was either to break the blockade or draw the attention of the whole world to the behavior of the Egyptian government, because access to the canal was supposed to be free to all nations. This was in conformity with the advice I had from a friend of the Mossad.

In September 1954 the Israeli ship *Bat Galim* was seized in the Suez Canal and the sailors were imprisoned. They were released in January 1955 after making Israel's point to the entire world.

It was naive to believe that, because of the kind of work I achieved in the military intelligence, I was not watched or surveyed by Mossad agents during my sojourn abroad, despite the Mossad residing agent baring himself to me. Some of the watchers were hard to detect; others kept wheeling and dealing to no end.

Before leaving Asmara, I had made the acquaintance of a young Jewish agent who was born in Haifa but claimed to be living in London. At the airport I found out that he was taking the same flight as me, with a British passport. Naturally, we spoke Hebrew. To my surprise, before boarding the plane he took me aside and demanded that I speak only English with him until we reached Tel Aviv. I reluctantly agreed to do so. We conducted our conversations in fluent English until Khartoum, the capital of Sudan, where we landed to spend a night or two until the connecting planes arrived to fly us to Nicosia, Cyprus.

In Khartoum we went to the only decent hotel in the city, the "Grand

Hotel", and to our bad luck there were two or three other passenger airlines that day whose connecting planes had also failed to arrive, and the hotels were filled to capacity. My Israeli-British friend insisted that he go see the manager and convince him to make room for us for at least one night. He requested that I wait outside until he fixed everything using his British passport and English accent to win over the manager.

When I woke up from my recollections in Khartoum, I noticed that over an hour had passed since my friend had went in. When I went into the manager's room, my friend was sitting in a chair across from the manager. Because of my anger, I forgot our agreement about the spoken language and yelled at him in Hebrew, asking what he was doing all this time and why he did not tell me what was happening while I was outside suffering in the heat. Before he had time to react, the manager looked at me and asked him whether we were Jewish. He had no alternative but to say we were. In that case, the manager said, I have a room for you, actually my room, on the second floor. We profusely thanked the manager, who was happy to extend a helping hand to a fellow Jew. That night we slept in the manager's room while he went home. Later I refused to abide by our agreement and spoke Hebrew during the remainder of the trip.

At the Cyprus Airways offices in Khartoum, I discovered that my luggage was booked direct to Cairo instead of Nicosia. I did not fear, though, because in it I had nothing but clothes. I approached the Egyptian Airlines office in Khartoum and explained the mix-up to the responsible agent in Asmara who was also the agent for Cyprus Airways. He politely took down all the details and promised to see to it that my luggage be redirected to Tel Aviv. While I was doubtful of this because Egypt and Israel were still at war, he said that I could count on him.

I had no choice but to fly to Nicosia without my luggage and on to Tel Aviv. A few days later I was notified that my luggage arrived from Cairo. This prompted much investigation by custom officials and Mossad agents, but they released the luggage after they were satisfied that it was an "honest mistake." There were no indications that the luggage actually went to Cairo, and my claim for compensation and information from Asmara again remained unanswered.

# CHAPTER 22

# Intelligence Comeback

While in Asmara, Eritrea, another Mossad agent contacted me without identifying his real name. Posing as a businessman from Israel, he apparently wanted to study my reaction to the proposal from the first agent. The businessman was well known to me in Tel Aviv but I was surprised to see him in Asmara because his work had nothing to do with Africa. When I returned to Israel, this same businessman unexpectedly approached me in Tel Aviv at least once a week and bugged me with impractical and unrealistic business proposals, which made me wonder whether the Mossad had anything in mind for me.

Upon arrival in Tel Aviv, as a loyal Israeli, I reported my conversation with a United States GI stationed in a unit like ours in Asmara. Since the city was situated high on a plateau, virtually all Arab and Middle Eastern communications could be perfectly intercepted.

This kind of intelligence was already so advanced that planes loaded with sophisticated instruments could land in enemy territories just long enough to intercept vital military or diplomatic communications impossible to detect at base, and fly out before enemy planes or ground forces could detect them. Even simple call signs could be of great importance.

Back in Israel I met with military commander Abraham Aloni, in charge of technical equipments, and convinced him that Asmara was an ideal place for a branch of our unit. An Iraqi-born Jew was dispatched there to investigate and soon after a small unit of Iraqi Jew operators left for Asmara.

While I was in Eritrea from May 1954 to November 1955, many things were happening back in Israel. There were border clashes with Jordan and a three-day exchange of fire with the Jordanian legion at Jerusalem and other border cities which continued until September. Acts of sabotage by infiltrators from the Gaza Strip were taking place. In December 1954, 11 Jews were put on trial in Cairo, Egypt, charged with sabotage and spying. Later known as the Lavon Affair, it was the most controversial affair about intrigues and plotting in Israeli history. On January 31, 1955, Egypt hanged Dr. Marzouk and Samuel Azar, two Egyptian Jews who lost their lives needlessly for fire bombing the United States Cultural Center in Cairo and making believe it was an Egyptian plot.

The author (standing, second from right) in 1955 among the first Falashis (Ethiopian) nucleus pioneers for training and return to their country to prepare and train others for immigration to Israel (author's collection).

Lt. Colonel Motke Ben Zur, who was in charge of our Beersheba unit and operated as an undercover agent back in Baghdad, Iraq, was married to an Iraqi-born girl who worked with us. He was drawn into the Lavon Affair by no other than our Chief of Intelligence, Mr. Gibli. Ben Zur was a career officer who most of his friends and his colleagues predicted would have a bright future in Israel's military institutions. Pinhas Lavon resigned as minister of defense in February 1955 and Ben-Gurion returned to power.

In April and May 1955, during border clashes with Egypt, the Egyptians shelled the *kibbutz* (settlement) in the Negev. In July Bulgarian fighter planes shot down an El-Al passenger plane, killing 51 passengers and three crew members. Egyptian units penetrated deeply into Israeli territory and the Israelis raided the Egyptian base at Khan Yunis. Fedayeen (sacrificial death squad) terrorists attacked the Israeli borders. Egypt signed an arms agreement with Czechoslovakia. A joint Egyptian-Syrian government was established between the two states. There were continued clashes in the Negev (Nitzana) in Israel and Kuneitra in Egypt. In November a new cabinet was formed and Ben-Gurion was again selected as prime minister.

The late comedian Danny Kaye (center) calling home to Hollywood, California, with the help of Naim Horesh (left). This photo was taken in 1956 (author's collection).

All this made me feel sad because what was going on in Israel was a sheer game for power, in disregard for those who gave their lives so that a strong Jewish State could stand up in the future for their descendants and the rest of the Jewish people. It became more clear that there would be no peace with our neighbors nor an end of anti–Semitism in the world.

We had a brief respite after the Holocaust but never an end to persecution or undermining of freedom. Our only remaining home was the State of Israel. I always hoped that the memory of those who died in the Holocaust would remain sacred and never used for political gain. In spite of everything, I remained sober and my feeling towards Israel did not diminish at all, no matter what was happening there between the ruling groups.

Two months before the 1956 campaign, I received orders to serve in the reserve. I also had to face new responsibilities toward our first son Moshe, who was born on March 6, 1952. On many occasions my wife and I sought the help of others to keep our small family afloat. I was often away and I was very sorry to hear that Moshe was teased by the other boys who said he did not have a father. In spite of all the obstacles, nothing deterred my belief and determination to serve Israel. I never tried to run away from reserve duties and always gave my best in the same spirit and zest that I had shown before.

Sometime before the Sinai Campaign (Kadesh) I was ordered to evaluate a new base for our unit in the Jerusalem Hills (Bayit Ve Gan) and to report the possibilities of interception of the Egyptian Force which was being reinforced by Russian MiGs. We wanted to keep an eye on them and follow up the new situation thus created vis-à-vis the Egyptian power. I was able to confirm that the new base was best for this purpose. An Egyptian pilot of a MiG unknowingly helped by reporting to his ground control in the Canal Zone that he was 500 feet over the Bitter Lake and descending. His clear transmission was recorded for my confirmation. Conversations in Russian were also recorded and submitted to the proper people for translation and evaluation. My superiors, thus encouraged, decided to establish a branch base in the Jerusalem hills, which was later manned by elite operators and personnel.

When it was secretly decided to attack Gamal Abdel Nasser's Egypt, I was called again to serve in the reserve as the officer in charge of the new base in the Jerusalem hills. We were ostensibly told that the upcoming operation was against Jordan and Syria, but we were specialists on the Egyptian front. When Nasser decided to act against Israel, reserve manpower was called up for the Jordanian front. It did not take me long to realize that the target was Egypt, not Jordan. Meanwhile, all the newspapers obediently followed government instructions to make believe that the preparations were intended for Jordan and Syria.

In October 1956, we were told that Gamel Abdel Nasser, the president of Egypt who had enraged many by nationalizing the Suez Canal, was to be dealt with. Israel, taking advantage of the new situation, created an unholy secret pact with Great Britain and France to strike the Sinai Peninsula and return the Suez to their control. Egypt's continuous supplying of arms to French Algerian rebels made the French government eager to join hands with Israel, while the British were seeking to gain back their lost prestige. Thence, the unholy tripartite pact was arranged by Shimon Peres, a protected official in the foreign office by prime minister David Ben-Gurion. Ben-Gurion himself did not like the troika arrangement very much and was skeptical of the British, but Peres convinced him to give the green light. Egypt had received a recent shipment of over 500 guns, 150 MiG-15 fighter planes, 50 Ilyushin-28 bombers, submarines, and hundreds of transport vehicles from Russia. The balance of power with Israel was already upset.

As far as I was concerned, my given target was President Abdel Nasser. The trackers at headquarters reported that he was visiting Jordan and Syria to convince or force its rulers to sign a tripartite military treaty and to establish a joint Arab command. We were told by headquarters that Nasser was traveling with most of his high commanding officers on an Ilyushin-28 plane specially equipped and furnished for his own personal use by the Russians. Our orders

Fellow officers pay a visit to the author (seated, second from right) after the birth of his first-born son, Moshe (author's collection).

were to keep track of this plane and report its whereabouts all the time. In the meantime, the whole Arab world was hailing Nasser's new activities and their broadcast stations were greeting the president with enthusiasm, loyalty and new fervor. The emotions ran high and the future for Israel looked bleak.

After all the ostentatious ceremonies in Syria and Jordan, the entire Egyptian military group and the president were supposedly returning to Egypt on the same plane. From a short Ilyushin transmission, we were able to learn that the plane had left Syria and was on its way to Cairo. We learned from another transmission that steps were to be taken to welcome the arrival of the president, which made our people believe that Nasser was on that plane.

At about 9 P.M. on October 27, an Israeli Hunter Night Fighter equipped with radar took off from an Israeli military field. As soon as the Hunter plane spotted the Ilyushin and reported the contact, orders were given to shoot it down. The last we heard from the Ilyushin was an SOS over the Mediterranean Sea; then, complete silence.

General Harkavi (Fati) the commanding officer of Israeli military intelligence, wanted assurance from me that Nasser was on that plane. I could only tell him that as far as I knew, Nasser was on the plane. General Moshe Dayan also asked the same question, and I gave him the same answer.

We continued our lookout and caught a brief message by the Egyptians that Nasser's plane was landing. Amazingly, the signal came from a United States-made Dakota. Then it became clear that the Egyptian president preferred a Dakota for his travel. It might have been a precautionary procedure to mislead the Israeli Intelligence and risk the lives of his entire military general staff of high ranking commanders as a protection shield for his own safety.

Nonetheless, the loss of high-ranking military officers severely diminished the capabilities of Egypt's air command. The Egyptians contended that the Israeli Air Force downed this plane, but this was never admitted to by the Israelis. I personally think that Nasser was tipped off by a Russian Jew spy close to Ben-Gurion, who probably knew about the plot against Nasser. About 18 officers and men perished with the plane.

The world press did not know about the downing of the Egyptian plane, erroneously reporting that British war planes were sent from Cyprus to stop Israel from attacking Jordan. In fact, the British planes were trying to pick up survivors, if any, from the downed Egyptian plane. Thus the troika pact between Israel, France, and Britain was doomed from the start despite the painstaking efforts of Shimon Peres, Moshe Dayan, Ben-Gurion, and General Harkavi, commanding officer of Israeli military intelligence.

The Sinai campaign began on October 29, 1956, and lasted seven days, on the Egyptian front only. Other Arab states bordering Israel did not raise a finger despite the military treaties signed with Egypt. Again the excellent Israeli soldiers gave the state a clear-cut victory thanks to their field commanders like Eric Sharon, General Rafael Etan, and Abraham Yoffe. Britain did not uphold their end of the troika deal, but Israel nevertheless emerged triumphant. During the next eight peaceful years, *fedayeen* (terrorist) activities were virtually unknown, and the Israel defense force was developed and strengthened for future encounters with the Arab nations.

After the Sinai campaign, I was ordered to remain in the service to keep surveillance, especially on the Egyptian Air Force. Later, Israel was forced by the United Nations, after objections from the United States and the Soviet Union, to return the Sinai back to Egypt.

CHAPTER 23

# Intelligence Foul Play

The section of our unit operating in Ashqelon, just a few miles near the Mediterranean Sea, specialized in Egyptian Air Force operations. I was called in 1958 to watch and investigate the training and operational exercises of the Egyptian pilots in the Russian MiGs. During that period I was also told that a very high-ranking officer of the Israel Air Force would photograph air bases behind the enemy lines by himself.

A pilot with the rank of major was attached to me for the first time, and I was threatened with a court-martial if I deviated from my instructions. All information was to be passed first to the Air Force Major and under no circumstances was I to contact the Air Force Control like I used to. I eventually let the Major do this direct reporting himself. I was under the impression that the Major was demoted to Intelligence busywork.

I was responsible for defending the advanced base against infiltrators from Gaza. One night after we were warned that Arab infiltrators were in our vicinity, I began the routine of posting my men in strategic points for any eventuality. Most of my people were Iraqi Jews who knew what to do, but our Major went up the terrace, laid down on his belly like a bombardier, and held a grenade with the pin off in his hand over the wall of the building, waiting. When I asked what he was doing, he said he was waiting for the infiltrators to approach the wall of the building and was ready to let the grenade go. He did not take into consideration that he might tumble over the wall he was on and let the roof come down with him. I pulled him away from there and posted him in some other place.

After receiving word that the high-ranking Air Force officer planned a photography mission behind Egyptian lines, I set up all personnel at his post, watching, listening and scanning the skies for any suspicious sign which might indicate danger to our most precious photographer pilot. After a while, I picked the word "bogey" from one of the Egyptian planes patrolling the sector. The Egyptian pilot told his ground control that he spotted a bogey (enemy aircraft) and asked for instructions. Our Major was informed and I kept following the dialogue between the Egyptian pilot and his ground control.

When Major Zvi said that he was going to the bathroom, I objected. But, he left anyway. The next message from the ground control to the patrolling pilot was "Shoot down the bogey." This order was confirmed by the Egyptian pilot who proceeded to dive down on our photography aircraft. These were crucial moments because in a minute or less our plane would be downed without being able to alert our Air Force of the danger. Our high-ranking officer, completely unaware of the Egyptian plane zooming down over him, continued his mission as planned. I frantically went out to where the bathrooms were and called for Zvi, but he did not answer.

I realized that the officer had only a few seconds to live. After once more getting no reply from Zvi, I did what I knew best. I picked up the red emergency telephone and warned our Bakara (Ground Control) of the imminent danger. In a few seconds, two Israeli jet fighters were sent up to protect our pilot, who took evasive action after being warned of the danger around him. When I put my earphones on, I heard the Egyptian pilot telling his control that he lost his bogey. After reviewing the tapes, I understood that the controlling Egyptian pilot hesitated in fear for few seconds when he had him in his sights and our pilot flew low and headed back to base.

Everyone jumped for joy for saving a life and congratulated me for what I had done. A few minutes later, Zvi came in. I was nervous and screamed at him as to where he had been. He claimed he was in the bathroom, which was a lie. Zvi picked up the phone and talked with someone on the other end and then handed me the receiver to speak with his commanding Air Force officer. What I was told on that phone was unbelievable. He accused me of breaking orders and I was to be court-martialed in two days. I tried in vain to explain what was going on.

Curiously enough, the next day I was told to forget about the court-martial and consider the matter closed. Many high-ranking Israeli Air Force officers visited our unit in Ashqelon and listened to the full taped record of what had happened, which conveniently had been voice registered and translated. I kept Zvi's bizarre conduct from the panel, because I would have been subjected to more trouble than I had seen so far.

Later we learned that the high-ranking officer was Ezer Weizman, commander in chief of the Israeli Air Force from 1958 to 1966.

Years later, Weizman was interviewed in New York by Mike Wallace of *60 Minutes*. I wrote a letter to Wallace telling him that I saved Weizman's life once and that Weizman did not know who his savior actually was. On Wallace's own initiative, he forwarded my letter without my knowledge to Weizman, who sent me a letter of thanks.

I later learned that the Mossad did not trust Weizman, father of the Israeli Air Force. Many believe that he was a traitor. Of course, even as defense minister no top secrets were shared with him.

The author (head of table) commanded the unit in Ashqelon that intercepted Egyptian air force communications, including air training and patrol or air attack (author's collection).

On September 29, 1959, another boy was born unto us and we named him Ouri after my wife's father, Kedouri Sharabani. It was another joyous moment in our lives and again we hoped that, as the Psalm says, the deliverer would come and let it be a good sign for all of us.

For some time, the Israeli Air Force and the United States CIA, were completely in the dark about the MiGs that Egypt and other Arab countries were receiving from the Russians. After Israel returned the Sinai to Egypt under pressure from the United States and the Soviet Union, it became clear that Russia was eagerly building up its influence in this part of the world and lavishly supplying arms, ammunition and planes to the Middle Eastern Arab states.

I was ordered to go up in an Israeli Dakota Bomber that was specially equipped with all the necessary gear for our particular work. Actually, the Dakota became a flying part of our unit, and the mission was to gather as much information as possible about the MiGs throughout Egypt. We had to fly over their bases and register every communication for analysis back at home. At the designated date I went to the military airfield where the Dakota plane was ready to take us on our mission.

In last-minute briefing, we were told that, in case we were downed and captured, we should not give our military ranks and insist, as our clothing suggested, that we were lost civilians. We were unarmed as was the Dakota, which in a short time could be transformed into a military cargo plane. I doubted that the Egyptians would accept such a story, so I thought of alternative ways to deal with the Arabs in case anything did happen.

After taking off we flew about 100 miles west toward the blue horizon of the Mediterranean Sea, then back northwest toward the Suez Canal, where most of the newly acquired MiGs were stationed. Part of my duty was to detect any suspicious movement in the sky through communications between Egyptian ground forces and airborne planes in the area. Soon after entering the Canal Zone, one of the Egyptian Air Force ground controllers reported a Dakota flying toward their base. Once informed, our pilot immediately escaped toward the sea and international waters. As everyone took the necessary precautions of battle, I and an Egyptian Jew colleague kept dissecting every word or code uttered to enable our pilot to maneuver accordingly.

After a few minutes of tension and fear, we heard the ground controller telling the other MiG planes to clear all runways for the President's Dakota plane that was landing. We then realized that President Abdel Nasser was landing in a Dakota plane like ours in the same airfield we were surveying. Unwillingly, we became part of the Egyptian president's escort party.

As soon as Nasser's Dakota and its MiG escort landed, we resumed our work uninterrupted for over an hour. The Egyptians, absorbed by the arrival of their president, failed to notice or detect the second Dakota which was flying right over their president's. Once our mission was accomplished, we returned home safely. Our work was brought back to base for analysis.

The MiGs remained an enigma and, unless one was captured and studied well, there would be much work to do to solve the problem. The solution came later in the 1960s when two Iraqi-born Jews dissected and scrutinized a MiG made available by both the Israelis and the Americans.

The Mossad always took all the credit for important achievements, sometimes twisting the facts to suit its purpose. For instance, they claimed credit in bringing the first MiG to Israel for the United States, but carefully eliminated one important fact.

When the Americans offered a million dollars for a Russian MiG, it was an Iraqi-born Jew who had the initiative to bring them one. This Iraqi Jew whom I will call Abraham sent a note via a friend of his to the Israeli Embassy in Paris which contained his telephone number in Baghdad. Taken as a hoax and forgotten for a year, General Aharon Yariv decided to give it a try.

Another Iraqi Jew from Petah Tiqwa called Mansour was assigned to go to Baghdad to check on the authenticity of the offer. He checked with and talked to the godfather of the pilot, who was a squadron leader. Abraham was instrumental in influencing the pilot to defect with the MiG. Mansour returned to Israel and confirmed his genuine suggestion or offer. The Mossad planned and executed the operation with the help of the CIA and the FBI.

After the evacuation of Sinai was completed, the flow of oil in the Eilat pipeline and the tankers reaching Eilat after Israel's seaway was opened to Africa and Asia, which supplied the new state with precious oil. Other ships took exported goods to various countries abroad. For the first time, Israeli jet planes in 1957 were shown on Independence Day and the Huleh Lake drainage project was completed.

There was a renewed flare-up on the southern and northern borders and Prime Minister Ben-Gurion resigned in a dispute over reparations.

A great journalist once wrote that the moral foundations of any state (especially the Jewish State) were the first guarantee to its existence. At the minute that its leaders undermine these foundations, everything would be undermined and blurred in society, finance, politics, and defense. In 1958, a new government was constituted as before and Ben-Gurion headed it again. For the first time, there was a controversial debate in the Knesset (Israeli Parliament) about Jewish identity. In December an air battle with the Egyptian Air Force over the Negev took place and the first referendum on change in the electoral system was turned down by the Knesset as detrimental to its members and the ruling party or parties.

In the meantime I was doing my best to readjust to civilian life. I did odd jobs without keeping any because none were sufficiently adequate to support my growing family. In 1959 ten years of food rationing was finally abolished. Infiltrators killed Jews in Ramat Rachel near Jerusalem.

Already over a decade had passed and my father and his wife, as well as most of those who came from Iraq, were still lingering in a *maabarot* (refugee camp) with no solution yet in sight except for the privileged who were whisked away during the night to homes specially prepared for them. The others suffered from the cold and rain in the winter and heat during the summer in tents and tin-roofed cubicles. I felt desperate for my father and the rest of the family, but there was nothing that I could do to help. Others, because of their origins, had more influence, protection and rights than my family.

A distinguished writer born in Iraq who immigrated in 1952 with the rest of my people to Israel, wrote several books in Hebrew about the plight of the Iraqi Jews in refugee camps in Israel. Two of his books describe the suffering and humiliation of a proud people who have chosen the love of Israel over anything else, and in spite of the fact that they accepted their fate, they were deliberately neglected while those in power protected their own.

In 1960 an anti–Semitic outbreak in West Germany and Europe flared up again. In April, American and Canadian ports imposed a counter-boycott on Arab ships in reaction to the detention of Israeli ships in the Suez Canal. Adolph Eichman was caught, brought to Israel and tried for his World War II crimes against the Jews. The first Israeli-made Fuga Jet was handed over to the Israeli Air Force and the Eilat pipeline was completed. Also Israel's first atomic reactor started functioning at Nahal Sureq. A special committee was formed to investigate the Lavon mishap of 1955.

I took pride in Israel's achievements and felt rather secure for the future in spite of the fact that I did not identify myself with the ruling party. What really upset my thoughts were the overzealous procedures applied to execute the socialistic reforms and laws imposed by the government on the people of Israel. We had more economic police agents than regular policemen arresting, searching, and confiscating anything connected with foreign exchange funds or currencies.

The ruling parties were possessed by the socialist vision of eliminating differences between cities and settlements, between workers and businessmen or doctors and scientists who must study six to seven years to achieve their objectives. When employed, their salary did not exceed that of a sanitary worker by much, as regulated by the socialistic laws. There was also no difference between bankers and farmers, except if one was shrewd enough to make his banking knowledge his own personal business without being caught.

Because of the destruction of the economy through excess in spending and social engineering, thousands fled the country for Europe and the United States. The houses built by the Labour government–sponsored firms were typically built as "systematized" villages or neighborhoods called *shikunim*. The insides usually crumbled in after a season or two. They were so small that many families could not raise their children in human conditions. In industry, things were visibly deteriorating. One might be looked down upon if he dared, as I had, to write to newspapers against the government.

In spite of all this, thousands of Israelis, especially the religious groups, continued their business as usual without allowing themselves to be harassed or caught as a result of those unjustified laws. It was almost impossible to achieve anything on a freelance basis without the protection of the ruling party.

My alleged Israeli businessman Mossad agent made it his business to meet me, whether accidently or on purpose, almost every second week; probing, asking about my affairs. Great pressure was exercised upon me by the Mossad through a relative of my wife who was employed by them.

Finally, I succumbed and decided to wait until things changed to do it on my own, probably after the next election, or the one after that, and I might as well accept a job for the duration. This sounded naive and very simplistic but what else could one do under the circumstances? A good father has to support a family with children and no help or assistance was forthcoming from anywhere.

It was routine for a military intelligence officer to be transferred and accepted by the Mossad. Like the others, I would be doubly paid: one meager salary abroad plus controlled expenses and my wife would get the same amount at home. I agreed to meet with the boss for an interview. To my surprise, my new boss was none other than Mordechai Almog, my previous intelligence commander during the War of Independence. It was under the same conditions when we met before joining his military unit, in a café in the center of Tel Aviv. It was rather a pleasant surprise and it seemed that everything was already prepared beforehand, as far as security, scrutiny and personal investigation were concerned. I realized my Mossad alleged businessman had been checking on me.

# CHAPTER 24

# Mossad Training

During my meeting with my "new" boss, we talked about the old days and both of our families. At the end, he asked me to see someone at the Ministry of Defense and get acquainted for further contacts and instructions. We cordially departed until our next appointment at his office.

Back at home I informed my wife and explained to her without going into details my new work and that I would be traveling alone at first but perhaps later she could join me. She did not like my new job but we had no choice to keep the family afloat.

I did not realize at the time what I was getting into. Upon meeting the fellow at the Ministry of Defense, I was told that I was already assigned to attend a course the following day which would last a few months or weeks because I was a veteran. It was around the same time as Elie Cohen (the famous spy who was later hanged in Damascus) and Mr. Lotz took the course. Nobody was supposed to know who was who and we were referred to by our code names — mine was Robus. We were trained together without any of us divulging his real identity.

I was in training for many arduous months. At the beginning, those who were destined to deal with Arab activities were taught how to act like Moslem Arabs. The others who were heading for Christian lands to act as Christians were taught the Christian religion. I had an unpleasant feeling as if I was about to change my religion. The trainees were completely familiar with the language and traditions of the country where they were assigned. They were all recruited as Israelis on a patriotic background rather than professional or amateurish reasons. There were some protectionists but they were, with few exceptions, never in the field. This powerful and sophisticated Intelligence made Israel one of the greatest in the field.

My instructor in Moslem doctrine was also an Iraqi-born Jew by the name of Sami who was with the Mossad immigration group in Baghdad before the War of Independence. He asked me to be familiar with the Moslem religion to a point that I could practice it flawlessly if needed. I clashed with him on many occasions. Once he called me stupid, to which I said I would rather be stupid than to change my religion. However, we continued with the

Islamic religious rituals until he was somewhat satisfied that I had learned enough.

Sami insisted that I learn the Moslem prayers well and also memorize excerpts from the Koran (the Moslem Bible) and learn perfectly the steps for the cleansing absolution before prayers. The subject of Islam and their various sects were unnecessary for me because I was well acquainted with the subject.

One day we were assembled on Gordon Street in Tel Aviv and told for the next few days we were not supposed to know Hebrew at all. There would be no approach or contact or knowledge when we were being tested. There was one condition — to stay out and roam the streets of Tel Aviv from 9 A.M. until 6 P.M. every day until it was called off. We were allowed to walk through the streets, ride buses, go to the movies, etcetera, but never to stay at home during these hours.

The second day, I went out early in the morning to the Tel Aviv seashore, my favorite place, and spent most of the day there. Nothing happened. The third day, while I was comfortably riding the bus from Ramat Gan to Tel Aviv, I overheard two fellows telling spicy jokes to each other. They were telling their funny stories in such a loud voice that all within hearing range could not help but laugh. I was about to laugh, too, but remembered the test and refrained with some difficulty from even smiling.

Later that day, someone stopped me innocently on the street and asked for the time. I was so concerned that this might be a part of the test that I pled ignorance, until he picked up my hand and looked at my wristwatch himself. The next day when it was over, I was informed that I passed the test but I was never told how, or when and where.

The next training was about being followed and how to detect someone who was following you. We were taught that no matter how suspicious you are that you are being followed, never abruptly turn around and let your follower know that you suspect him. There are several methods to find out, such as bending down as if you are buckling your shoes or tying your laces. Or, stand in front of a show window and without looking back, move further away and then make an about turn as if to have a second look, and then glance sharply at the people behind you to find out whether any of them was hesitating or stopping at the same time. Also try to pick up a familiar or recognizable face that you might have seen or suspected before or remember a person's dress, hat, shoes, or tie.

In some cases, small tiny cameras are used. Using this sophisticated gadget, you can photograph the people behind you on every street. Such cameras can be positioned in a flower button hole, back jacket or shirt collar and triggered by a mechanism operated by a special button on the handle of a suitcase or a tiny wire in your pocket for button hole cameras.

In Prague, Czechoslovakia, our instructor, who was a Yemanite Jew, suspected someone of being an Arab and took pictures of him using this device. When he developed his film, his superiors told him that the man he was photographing was one of the Mossad agents sent there for the same purpose. They showed him pictures of himself taken by the other agents while he was pointing his suitcase at the other photographer. The same story happened with the other photographed agent who was photographing our instructor. Our instructor was surprised to learn that while he was photographing someone in enemy territories, he was being photographed himself.

In order to shake off a follower, one must be very familiar with his surroundings. Whether followed or not, an agent is always wise to apply the shake-off methods before meeting a contact or receiving orders at a cache. If followed, an agent can also discreetly enter a narrow alley and quickly emerge in the opposite direction, seemingly disappearing into thin air. It is also important to draw a follower to your pre-arranged point of escape in order to shake him off.

When we practiced this training, our group had a lot of fun. We were divided into followers and those being followed, on the streets of Tel Aviv, Jerusalem, and Haifa. This training brought back memories of when we were kids at school playing hide-and-seek or touch-and-run or cops-and-robbers.

We were then trained to crack open doors, safes, windows, and other locked-up units. We were also trained to steal or photograph documents (which was nothing new to me).

We learned to operate a tiny transmitter-receiver and use the Morse system, which was not new to me either. There was an exercise in invisible writing and how, with simple lemon juice and a clean instrument, a letter could be written between the lines of already-written text and, with the use of a little heat, the secret writing would come out early. Various invisible inks were famous for this purpose and every intelligence agency specialized in some aspect of its use. In brief, it was all right to steal from your enemies but you had to remain extremely faithful to your country's laws and your own law-abiding officials.

Many people believe that this kind of job is glamorous with fulfilling adventures. This is very wrong and could be disappointing when such an undertaking is begun. An agent cannot tell his friends or family what his job really encompasses. Such a job also leads to a sense of isolation. The agent withdraws into himself and his only trustworthy friends are other professionals like himself. Any glamour the job may have wears off very quickly because it is a closed, almost claustrophobic, world in which the agent lives. When I was on my first assignment in Turkey, I wrote my wife through my control and told her she could never imagine how lonesome I was.

I barely passed firing training because I was convinced that intelligence did not need guns; the only weapon I would need was my brain. Besides, our operations were not cloak-and-dagger; therefore, physical combat and fire-arms training were unnecessary, except in rare and exceptional cases.

I was perfectly aware that any operation I was ordered to carry out would be unique and executed beyond the laws of the countries in which I had to serve. I was also well indoctrinated with the best principles of morality, decency and honesty. A Mossad or intelligence agent must have had those traits before he was accepted to serve. In no other department in the State of Israel was such rigorous scrutiny applied.

Mossad chief Isser Harel was an absolute monarch in his field, loved and respected by his subordinates. He was very loyal to Israel and Ben-Gurion. Advancement for those from the right wing or those unaffiliated with any party was unlikely.

Everyone in Israel knew about the Mossad, but officially it did not exist. Local security made sure that all our phones were bugged and we learned not to talk about our training or future work with anyone because the walls had "ears."

Preparing myself to go abroad and assume a new identity, I had to make sure that my luggage did not include anything Israeli-made or relating to any-thing connected with Israel. Israeli brand names or Hebrew letters were not admitted. If something could be identified with Israel, I had to leave it behind and buy a new one made abroad. This included underwear, pajamas, shirts, ties, toothpaste, brushes, shaving articles and many other items.

I was given a new name, Said Hareth, which means "ploughman." I also had a code name for identification within the Mossad, because Mossad oper-ations were less important than ones concerning military intelligence that could involve the life or death of the State of Israel.

After my field training, I was told to report to the ministry of defense and be prepared to fly to Zurich, Switzerland, the next morning. Each member of our group was instructed to go to his assigned destination. I was issued a diplo-matic passport (the second in my line of duty), and an El-Al one-way ticket. At the Lod airport, I was bade "Godspeed" by an official of the ministry of defense and security who accompanied me to the plane. At the last moment I was given a telephone number to call as soon as I arrived in Zurich.

# CHAPTER 25

# Recruiting Agents in Turkey

It was my first time in Europe. When we landed, I had no difficulty clearing out of immigration and customs with my diplomatic passport. I was ushered through a separate exit to escape souvenir photographers who were likely employed by some spy or security agency. As soon as I was out of the airport I approached one of the public phones nearby and called the number I was given before boarding the plane.

After I gave my code name a female voice asked where I was. After I gave her my exact position, I was told to stay right there; a car would pick me up in a matter of 10 to 15 minutes. She described to me the car and its driver.

Exactly 15 minutes later, a car matching her description stopped. The driver opened the door, motioned to me to put my luggage in the back seat and hop in beside him. In Hebrew, he told me of my past activities before I left the State of Israel, which made me feel more at ease. He stopped at a place known in Zurich as a tea house, which to me looked like a café or restaurant. After identifying himself as the Mossad representative, he asked me to hand over my diplomatic passport. In return, he gave me a genuine Lebanese one with the name Said Hareth and my photo on it. He also gave me a few hundred dollars for my immediate expenses — airway and railway tickets to Milano, Italy, and Rome. I then hailed a taxi to take me to a predesignated old fashioned hotel called Albergo d'Italia, where I would spend two or three days until I could obtain visas for Italy. From that moment, I was entirely on my own except for one single call either before I left Switzerland or in an emergency. He also provided me with another number to call as soon as I arrived in Rome. Emotionally drained, I went straight up to my room and slept till the next morning.

The next day I woke up around ten still thinking that I was Yehoshoua Horesh. The weather outside and the noise on the street brought me back to the reality of my new identity. Dressing warmly, I went out to tour the city of Zurich, as usual, on foot. While strolling the streets of Zurich I began to

The author in front of the Piazza del Uono, Milan, Italy, during service abroad with the Mossad, circa 1961 (author's collection).

admire the behavior of its people. No hot tempers, like we have in Israel, or coarse attitudes toward others. My visits and encounters with people in restaurants, movies, or on the streets were as smooth as if I were at home. No one really got interested in me and my past, unlike in Israel where one was confronted with many questions when meeting new people. I walked around the lake and rode the cable car over it, filling my lungs with the fresh and clean air as the city itself was astonishingly clean all over.

I was not permitted to write directly home, but postcards to my wife could be delivered by my contact via a diplomatic pouch and a special messenger to our house. I already missed my two sons very much. My messages were short and dry for obvious reasons, but they relieved my tension and worry for a little while before I left for Milano, Italy.

On the third morning, after obtaining the necessary visa for Italy on my new passport, I was on my way to Milano. It was a journey full of thrills, especially when the train crossed the snow-covered Alps, passed through many long tunnels and crossed long bridges. I was awed and enchanted by the nature and scenery around which resembled a framed picture.

As soon as I arrived in Milan, I noticed a few Middle Eastern faces, especially in the railway station. In the elevator of my hotel, I noticed a fellow with a Middle Eastern complexion following me and also watching me all the time. I was a little scared but managed to avoid talking to him even when he went out at the same floor as mine. I was instructed to report any suspicious event or anything out of the ordinary such as this. When I did, I was told that this person was a Mossad agent watching me as instructed by a superior.

A few days later, my contact in Rome asked me to meet somewhere on Via Veneto. He would be carrying a red envelope under his right arm, and I was asked to describe the attaché case that I would be carrying. It was not difficult to recognize each other and we greeted as if we were old acquaintances. At a nearby café, he told me that I had been selected to serve in one of the neighboring Arab countries, but that a higher authority had decided at the last minute to temporarily station me in Istanbul, Turkey. After receiving more instructions and money, we decided to meet again before I left Rome.

Remaining in Rome to build up my cover story, my first aim was to find a hotel and rest. I registered in a respectable one, befitting my status as a movie dealer. After resting for awhile, I started calling movie producers in Rome whom I knew from my real work in Israel but had never met. Amongst those I called was the famous movie producer Dino De Laurentiis, who had started his career not long before I arrived in Rome. He was glad to receive me in his office and when we met we talked real business. After awhile Mr. De Laurentiis was convinced that I was a genuine movie dealer and knowledgeable in this business.

He offered to show me his two first films and to decide whether I would like to distribute them or not. We went to a large theater in Rome and he instructed the operator to roll the two films for me. I sat alone there watching his wonderful productions. When I finished I went back to his office and explained to him that I was on my way to Istanbul and would try to interest some buyers there. If not, I would surely contact him again when back in Beirut, Lebanon, after March 1961. De Laurentiis was skeptical about Istanbul, and I agreed. Consequently, I was furnished with every pamphlet and brochure I needed for my cover story as well as a draft for a proposed contract. I cordially departed with the promise to be in touch again in the near future.

For the next few days, I toured Rome and met other movie producers for the same purpose. Every day I had to pass by the famous stairs of Trinity del Debionti Church. I visited the Colosseum and Victor Emmanuel Plaza, which are tremendous structures. Then I visited the Vatican and went inside the Basilica de St. Peter. Once inside, I forgot about my role and stood reading some Hebrew writings on the wall. A priest came right up behind me and asked if I understood the line. Surprised at the question, I shook my head and told him I could not. When I asked what language it was, he said "Hebrew, my friend; Hebrew, the language of the Bible of our God." I thanked God that he did not try to carry the conversation further, for I would have probably failed myself and screamed loudly, "It is my language! My language!"

Once on the street, I bought an Arabic newspaper not only to read the news but to continue relating myself to my new identity. Suddenly an Egyptian approached me and asked in Arabic if I could lead him to a certain street. It was the first time in a long while that I had spoken with an Egyptian. I became scared, thinking the Arabs already knew about me.

Then I looked at my hands and understood that my Arabic newspaper drew him to me. I told him that I was also new here and could not furnish him with any information about the place. I immediately left in order not to give him a chance to continue the conversation. I was aware that an Arabicised Jew like myself was very likely to be subjected to security or Arab intelligence unless one was extremely efficient in being accepted as Arab.

From there I went to the Arch of Constantine and the Titus Arch. The latter is related to our sad Jewish history. It was built to commemorate the Roman victories and the destruction of the second temple in the year 70 A.D. and the victory over the Jews in Jerusalem. Passing under the Titus Arch was made a sin by the High Rabbinate at the time for every Jew. Being a Jew, I did not walk under it. I just went around it and noticed with sadness the reliefs of chained Jews being dragged to slavery.

When I concluded preparations for my cover story, I obtained a genuine

The author in Rome, Italy, near Titus Arch (Victory Arch), which was erected for sacking Jerusalem and destroying its temple (author's collection).

visa for Turkey and was issued a one-way ticket to Istanbul with Turkish Airlines. Arriving in Istanbul, I took a taxi to the city and went to the pre-designated hotel not far from Galata Bridge. I established contact and was told that my control agent would meet me in two days after I got acquainted with my new surroundings. The next day, I explored the town on foot.

At last I established contact with my control, Shmuel Gorden (Goren), and met him at the place he instructed. Later I wished I hadn't ever met him. It was a typical Middle Eastern café where Arabs and Turks with dark complexions sat and smoked water pipes (hubble-bubble). I would be okay there but my fair-haired controller was somewhat out of place, especially because Shmuel spoke no other language but Hebrew. When we sat down and ordered tea, everyone in the café examined our odd encounter, because he was out of context in the prevailing atmosphere. The next time we also met at the same café (a mistake in itself). Shmuel did not know much about me and he asked me about my previous work. I told him about my independent work in exporting and importing and suddenly he grimly asked why I did this kind of work. Since he was from the *kibbutz* (settlement) I thought it was useless to explain to him that his Labour government did not encourage independent or free enterprises and I that could not succeed in my work so I decided to accept the job offered to me by his superiors. Instead, I decided to ignore his question and just smile when he remarked that I was in it because it was like being in the movies.

In the late forties, Israeli agents in Europe were suspected as Russian spies and were reported to the police because they did not know how to behave or normally check into a hotel. Their table manners were appalling; good manners and education in fine dining were introduced later in the training programs.

I felt insecure but was unable to protest as a beginner in this field. I conducted my business as usual. Shmuel's instructions were that I frequent a certain café called Taqsim because most Iraqis, especially Iraqi military officers, call on this café when they are on their way from or back to Baghdad during their stay in Istanbul. Most of these officers traveled to Europe by the famous line known as the Orient Express. The main railway station of Istanbul was usually bustling with these travelers, as well as others who went to Yugoslavia, Greece, western Europe and England.

During moments of relaxation, Shmuel talked about his past experiences in the Haganah, the Palmach and the Army. Like me, he was an Army Intelligence officer lately transferred to the foreign section controlled by the Mossad. He admitted that he was listed as a deserter along with one of his friends. According to his version, they were lost during a battle and showed up a few days later for duty.

At the time when Shmuel Gordon (Goren) and I started our new job, already there were some problems with the organization. The Mossad became incapable of keeping pace with its extraordinary reputation. Computers were rejected and the head of the organization still relied on the human mind. Administration of the Intelligence organizations throughout the world became the order of the day in every country, especially in the West, but Israel still lagged behind until an Israeli-born Intelligence officer introduced the new watchdog in the fifties — the "computer." The computer was first rejected outright by the bureaucratic government that thought it was very expensive. It took the government a long time to confirm and make major use of this revolutionary device which proved extremely important for Israel.

For Intelligence personnel like ourselves who began to work for the Mossad, things began changing, too. Ever since the creation of the State of Israel, Ben-Gurion regarded the army as the deliverer of Israel. Then things began to change and many felt that corrupt politicians dragged the army down. Rumors of the imminent danger of a military coup circulated around, reaching their height before the Six-Day War.

My relations with Shmuel (Shmuel Goren-Gordon) were not solid enough. He was, like myself, still a novice in handling such kinds of jobs abroad. The difference between us was that he was protected by his peers and his superiors, and was safely operating from the Israel Embassy in Istanbul, while I was the foot soldier in the field operating under an assumed identity. Nevertheless, we were both eager to make it work at all costs.

The next time we met he mentioned that a transitional meeting would have to take place before I could replace my predecessor who was being transferred. When we met, I discovered that I sat and talked with my predecessor at the Taqsim Café without realizing that he was a Mossad agent. I found out that, like myself, he was an Iraqi-born Jew. After he handed over his duties to me, he continued to show up on many occasions at the same café, but we treated each other as Arabs who had just met in Istanbul (which was otherwise true).

One day, when I went in, I found him in the company of a few Iraqi officers in civilian clothes. That evening I learned from him that one of the officers he was sitting with and whom I joined later was none other than the military judge who was instrumental in the cruel hanging of Shafiq Adas, a wealthy Iraqi Jew. Adas was well placed in Iraq with high-ranking officials with whom he frequently visited and established strong friendships. When the War of Independence started, small functionaries in the district of Basra decided to harm the Jew who was not only close to high-ranking officials but also their friend and confidant. Adas had nothing to do with Palestine and Zionism. Every Iraqi Jew who was connected with him fled the country, but

Adas, knowing that he was completely innocent of the charges, decided to stay. That was a fatal decision. No one raised a finger to save him from hanging for the blood libel, Zionist, and arms shipments to Israel, which were completely false accusations brought against him.

My predecessor entertained the idea of administering justice and convinced us to eliminate the Jew-hanging Iraqi colonel. The proposal to Shmuel was, much to our regret, turned down by a superior and we continued our business as usual.

The principal activities in my new work were to track, befriend, scrutinize, and assess possible recruits among the Iraqis and other Arabs (whether military or civilians) to work for our Intelligence Services in their respective Arab countries. This was quite a difficult assignment; mere spying would have been much easier. For the next few weeks, Shmuel was pushing for results that would establish him as suitable for the job, but such results could not be achieved in a short period. Frank left for his new post and I was left alone in the field. I succeeded to gain over the confidence of some permanent Iraqi Arab residents in Istanbul and became a friendly fellow Moslem with shared roots.

The group that usually gathered at the café included an Iraqi Jew associating with them plainly with his actual Jewish identity. He claimed that he was in Istanbul awaiting his papers to emigrate to the United States where his relatives were living. He used to be an important employee for the Iraqi government in accounting before leaving his job because of what happened to the Jews there during and after the establishment of the State of Israel. Little did I know then that he voluntarily reported to Shmuel about the events that transpired in that café. Once he reported my arrival, my controller wanted to know more about me without telling him that I was one of his agents in Istanbul. I, of course, knew that he was a Jew from Baghdad. The first time we met, he gave me some sharp glances, but I felt safe because he could not have known me since I had left Iraq at a very young age and was much younger than he. He was unable to discover my real identity but he must have had a strong doubt in his mind about my acquired origin.

In one of my meetings with Shmuel, he inquired about a trivial matter that I had not yet reported to him. When I asked him how he could know that, he could not hide a sheepish smile. When I pushed him to tell me the name of his personal spy, he declined. Suddenly, the image of the Iraqi Jew flashed into my mind. I mentioned his name and he confirmed my guess. We agreed that I should continue to hide my real identity.

One day at the café, I was introduced to Mohammed El Qubanchi, a new arrival from Baghdad and a Makam singer like my father. I had heard a lot about him from my late father because he was well known, too. While we talked, I noticed that he stared fixedly at me most of the time. Immediately I felt that he was associating my features with my father's, but I was not sure.

Suddenly, he raised his hands and swore by Allah in front of everyone that he knew me. I just smiled and said nothing, but deep down in my bones I felt as if he was seeking to remember something which sank a long time ago into his subconscious.

Mohammed turned towards me again and swore to God that he knew me from somewhere. I smiled at him and said, "It can't be; I left Baghdad when I was little over ten years of age and you are almost double my age now." (He was over 65 and I was 39.) Then I added, "It seems that a lot of people make the same mistake because I greatly resemble an Egyptian movie actor and also Gamal Abdel Nasser. Because of this resemblance and how often you see them in the newspapers, it makes you believe that you know me." Everyone laughed in agreement, and everything quieted down after that.

Usually, I was left out in the cold for a while after I reported such an incident to Shmuel, but he decided to shift my activities to something else. I also argued with him again about us meeting in places that are usually frequented by Arabs and Middle Easterners. He promised to get someone of Middle Eastern descent to act as a liaison and avoid suspicion.

One night at the hotel, I noticed a group of Israelis staying there. What attracted my attention was that some spoke English with a cockney accent and others French or Italian. All, though, were registered as Israelis. Some spoke Hebrew like a native. The receptionist, with whom I had become friendly, told me that the same group visited Turkey at least once a year.

As usual, a report was submitted to Shmuel and a few days later I was instructed to get every possible bit of information about the reported group. While Shmuel dismissed my reporting as irrelevant, officials at Tel Aviv thought otherwise. After all their activities were reported to headquarters, he reluctantly congratulated me, which confirmed that the operation was important and successful. Apart from information and activities about the group, nothing else was disclosed. The request to follow their tracks remained an enigma. Later I learned from another source that they were big drug traffickers.

It is well known that the KGB (Russian Intelligence) was very active in Turkey. We also knew that the KGB assisted the Arab nations in their fight against us all over the world, including Turkey. Since the Turkish government was not democratic, anyone caught spying or trafficking was cruelly interrogated and given heavy sentences. Like other Middle Eastern Arab countries, because of pride and sometimes fear, no one would help bring real justice to those in jail. Once inside, it was almost impossible to be released even after your term was over, if someone decided to keep you there. The prisons were as bad as concentration camps. I was made aware of all this when I accepted the job, just like when I was drafted into the Army and when I joined the underground. It is only through sheer luck that I am still alive and I consider every enlisted Israeli that put his life on the line as lucky not to have been killed or wounded. In many countries, including Israel, a discharged soldier is looked upon as a slave who has completed his work and should go home and be forgotten.

I always had the feeling that the Turks would catch up with me someday whether assisted by the KGB, Arab Intelligence, and informers, or due to mistakes made by me or my controller. Usually, our operations were measured and executed within a certain timeframe that had to be strictly adhered to in order to prevent some kind of suspicion from creeping into our enemy's mind. There were exceptions to this rule, though.

Part of my job was to check suspected firms or businessmen, like myself, as well as our agents by drafting and writing business letters signed by fictitious names from outside Turkey. These replies would go straight to Mossad addresses in European or Arab countries. All this was carried out while meeting Shmuel during our scheduled meetings.

Fate always played a great part in our work. On my way to a meeting on Istiklal Jaddasi, I heard someone calling my Iraqi name, Shoua, from the other side of the street. I ignored it at first but I turned around to look after my name was repeated louder. One of my acquaintances from Tel Aviv was running toward me from the other side of the street. Thinking quickly, I realized it was impossible for me to convince him that it was not really me. I decided to tell him that I was in Istanbul for one day on my way to Europe and I was rushing to a business meeting that if missed would cost me plenty. Luckily, the truth worked very well and after the usual greetings he apologized for holding me out and asked when we could meet again. I said next week in Tel Aviv, and that was the end of it. The street was crowded with people and no one noticed our brief encounter. I breathed a deep sigh of relief because this meeting could have spelled disaster for me.

Frequent visits to the Taqsim Café in Istanbul did not produce anything worthy of following up. Shmuel, eager to prove that he was worthy of his assignment, began to pick on me for his imagined failure. I finally agreed to spend more time on arrivals from Europe at the Istanbul Railway Station.

Oded Shasha, an Israeli-born Jew, was sent to act as a liaison between me and Shmuel. When we met for the first time, Oded invited me to one of the best cafés in Istanbul.

For some reason, Shmuel again undermined my work when he planned an operation with another Iraqi-born Jew merchant residing in Istanbul, who apparently was being used with Shmuel's connections as a businessman dealing with Iraq. This businessman informed Shmuel that a school friend of his who became a high-ranking officer in the Iraqi Army would be passing through Istanbul on his way back to Baghdad and would see him upon his arrival at the Istanbul railway station at a certain time and date. It appeared that the officer, being friendly with the Jewish people of Baghdad, was a potential candidate for recruitment into the Israeli Intelligence.

Shmuel, without informing us of this plan, decided to let the Iraqi Jewish merchant deal with his friend himself. Oded, who was in on the planning, requested that I be informed so that no double work would ensue. But Shmuel dismissed this request, claiming that I was not good enough for this work. Shmuel ordered everyone that I should not be told, commenting that I would surely miss the opportunity of making contact with the officer in question. So, the operation began without my knowledge. This attitude was not unusual in Israeli Intelligence work because almost all of the old-timers and veterans sought to single themselves out for the glory and blame failure on someone else.

Going to work one day as usual, I had no idea that I was surrounded by our watchdogs from the Embassy. When the train from Europe arrived, I walked among the arrivals as if expecting to see someone before shifting to the single staircase leading to the café below. Pausing at a window mid-way down, I suddenly heard Iraqi Arabic being spoken; I turned my face to find out who it was. I was met with the same reaction by a couple who asked if I spoke Arabic. After replying in the affirmative, I was invited to join them in the café downstairs. I gladly accepted and then a lively conversation ensued.

While the three of us were sitting at the café, I noticed that one of them just smiled and threw sharp looks my way. After a while the silent person excused himself, saying that he had urgent business to attend to. We promised to meet again. It did occur to me that the person who left us was Jewish and perhaps knew that I was Jewish, too. I was left alone with the Moslem Iraqi person. He felt more comfortable with me because I pretended to be a Moslem. Later at his hotel, we promised to meet again the next day and visit Istanbul and other places in the evening. I already suspected that my new acquaintance was an important person in Iraq.

That same evening, I met Shmuel to give him my report. I was surprised to find Shmuel with my good friend Oded. I was pleased to report that I made the acquaintance of an Iraqi military colonel who could be of great interest to Israeli Intelligence and that I made an appointment with him early the next day and would like to have further instructions for my next action. Shmuel listened with annoyance before he said, "Yes. We already know." I felt dumbfounded when, after asking if this was a test or not, he added the complete details about the Iraqi colonel. When he complained that I ruined his plans for the colonel, Oded boldly intervened and asked how I could have ruined his plan when he ordered not to tell me about it. Apparently, the Jewish person who came to meet him at the station was supposed to take care of him and in due course introduce him to Shmuel for the final contact.

Many years after I left the service, I met the Jewish merchant from Istanbul in Tel Aviv. He told me that at the time he thought Shmuel sent me to take over and he knew that I was from Tel Aviv where he met me once before. After a long argument filled with accusations, we decided that I should continue with the task because there was no point in returning him to Shmuel for fear that we would lose him all together in the process. Reluctantly, I took over, or rather continued, my work according to my instructions on the next day when we met again.

According to the guidelines I received, it was my duty to check the colonel and make sure that everything he was telling was true and not a bluff or a trap. As usual in such activities, it was assumed that this was indeed a trap. Therefore, I had to make an on-the-spot assessment of the contact with the Iraqi colonel. We had several days to engage the officer in an entertaining activity in order to keep him away from the hotel room. That part of the plan was allotted to me for execution. Oded would go into his room while he was away and check his belongings — tickets, luggage, photos, letters, papers — for any indication that he was trying to purposely mislead us.

I made an appointment with the Iraqi colonel and promised to show him an eventful evening. I suggested that we go to a cabaret where beautiful Turkish belly dancers performed to Turkish music. During this time my friend Oded secretly entered the colonel's hotel room.

While with the colonel at the cabaret, an argument flared up between two Turks. The Iraqi colonel became nervous and threw a Jewish insult at one of the Turks arguing next to our table. The insult, which was not understood by the Turk, alarmed me because I began to suspect that he knew all along that I was Jewish and not a Moslem like him. At that moment I became worried and, suddenly mumbling my words, I had to go to the toilet to calm down. While there, I knew that my reaction to his Moslem expression caused some panic and I had to control myself to face whatever came next. What made me calm again was that I knew my life was not on the line, as yet, because that was our first meeting and his first odd remark in a strange atmosphere. We left the cabaret rather late and agreed to meet again the next afternoon.

After handing Oded a written report of my day's work, I also verbally detailed everything that took place, including the colonel's insult of the Turk. Oded calmed me down and said that it meant nothing but, to make sure, he would inquire from Tel Aviv about its implication when uttered by an Iraqi

Moslem. Because of the importance of this case, we agreed to meet again the next day instead of next week. The answer to our inquiry from Tel Aviv astonished us all. It was confirmed that Moslems, too, use this insult among themselves and toward others, which made it a kosher Moslem Arabic expression (or insult). I felt some relief and continued my task as usual.

During the ensuing days it was my duty to use all my talent to drag him into conversations against Israel and the Jews in order to register his deep feelings about us without revealing my real thoughts. I had to become especially friendly with him so that he would not hide the most intimate happenings in his life. When asked how many languages I knew, I said that because of my long time abroad I was fluent in Arabic, English and French. To my surprise, he said that he would see to it that I get a job with the foreign office in Baghdad, probably as consul or ambassador in one of the countries in Europe. He explained that not many Iraqis like me could be found in such posts. I respectfully declined and thanked him, claiming that I had bought and ordered many films that I could not dispose of for another two to three years. A lot of money was involved, I added.

All this was communicated to Shmuel, who dismissed it as insignificant. A few days later, I was ordered to disconnect. I don't know what happened next because the ultimate recruiting was done by another team, probably in Istanbul or perhaps even in Baghdad after he arrived.

Our work must have been successful because I was not transferred back to Israel. In coordination with Tel Aviv, Shmuel gave me a new assignment, which in itself proved that the previous one was a success.

Our next target was the local manager of the Middle East Airways (affiliated with BOAC) in Beirut. He was a Lebanese Christian and we knew that he would be a hard nut to crack. He could also be in the service of one of the Arab countries or perhaps used by the British Intelligence. Orders were orders, though, so I began my attempts to get acquainted with him, which was rather easy for anyone else except me. Adjacent to the MEA offices on Istiklal Jaddasi were El Al offices headed by an Iraqi-born Jew from Basra who knew my wife's family very well. Though I did not know him well at that time, I was sure that he knew me. Because of the wide glass windows at both premises, all customers and visitors could be easily seen at both the offices of MEA and El Al. But I was told to carry on with my mission, ignoring the El Al manager as if he did not exist.

My first step was to visit the MEA offices on some traveling pretext and try to bring my business to the manager himself. I succeeded to make his acquaintance and secured the possibility of seeing him again the next day. As the El Al manager was not in the adjacent offices, I felt some relief and hoped that my future visits to MEA would be limited or shifted to somewhere else.

Shmuel was pressing again for results, but the MEA manager was really a difficult customer. One morning when I was scheduled to be at the airline office, I came face to face with the Iraqi Jew from Basra. Miraculously, he ignored me and passed by without even looking at me at all. Later in Tel Aviv, I learned from him that he had recognized me but because of my rank and position with Israeli Intelligence, he decided to ignore me at that time and place.

That encounter was easy, but one day I and other Arabs visited a café not far from the El Al offices. I went in first and immediately noticed my wife's cousin who had come from Baghdad to see his daughter. I made an immediate about-turn, telling my Arab friends that we should go to some other nearby place instead.

Again, while walking on Istiklal Jaddasi, which was almost deserted, a girl to whom I taught French back in Baghdad was heading straight toward me to say hello. I still do not know whether this encounter was staged to test me or put me out of business with Shmuel because I knew that the girl was working for the Israeli Security Department. Since the street was almost deserted, and I didn't know if I was being followed, I pretended to give her directions as if she were lost. Explaining that I was lost and not her, I abruptly departed from her without letting her start some idle conversation on the street.

Later, another cousin of my wife approached me but was smart enough to notice through my gestures that he was not supposed to talk to me.

A few days later it was decided that our efforts with the Middle East Airways manager would be fruitless. It was a mistake to begin with.

My next assignment was more dangerous. A Syrian living in Istanbul with his mother became our target this time. After making contact, I discovered that he was a young man of 18 or 20, which made me (at almost twice his age) feel rather uncomfortable.

One day, the Syrian and I were invited to his Turkish friend's beautiful house in the suburb of Istanbul, which looked more like a palace than an ordinary house. I learned that he lived alone in this house and had no family, which caused me to be concerned.

For awhile I thought that I was trapped. I had made a mistake in agreeing to go to a place that I had not suggested. Not only had I accepted an invitation initiated by the Syrian, but I had allowed myself to meet with a third unknown person. This was a blunder. Instead of being the initiator, I became the game itself. I feared being targeted as a spy, but those fears proved to be unfounded.

Later we met many times and I did what I was supposed to do — evaluate him for possible recruitment into the Israeli service. I studied him carefully but got nothing out of the ordinary for an Arab youth at his age.

Six months after I first arrived in Istanbul, I began to detect some suspicion surrounding me with my constant contacts there. It was a fact that other nations were very active there in spying, intrigue, and all types of deceptions. The Turkish government, though not very effective, was vigilant enough to ruthlessly smash any underground activity by any country. On top of all this, the KGB became deeply committed to the Arabs and extended a helping hand to them. I was sure of this when Egyptian sports teams arrived to take part in games sponsored by the Turkish government in Istanbul.

I infiltrated the Egyptian camp at a certain hotel in the city and a foreigner who spoke broken English with some Russian dialect approached me and asked if I were an Arab. After I replied, "Certainly, what do you think?" an Egyptian who appeared to be in charge of security announced that all Arabs were welcome. When I noticed that the players were reluctant to talk with me, I realized that they were being watched carefully.

Something weird took place after that. For a few days, wherever I went, I noticed an Iraqi Jew, whom I had seen before in Israel, driving a Volkswagen through the streets of Istanbul. I tried to avoid any encounter with him as much as I could. I thought that he was probably vacationing in Turkey. On many occasions he popped up in places where I happened to be.

One morning, I went into a restaurant to have my favorite breakfast. To my surprise, I saw my Iraqi Jew entering the restaurant. I turned my face the other way, but he was not that naive to sit far from me. On the contrary, he chose the table right across from mine, in spite of the fact that the restaurant was half full at the time. For a while he kept silent, but when I was about to leave he asked my name and whether or not I spoke Arabic. He questioned me in Iraqi Arabic Yiddish, which led me to believe he either knew or felt that I was Jewish. I answered him in a Lebanese Arabic accent that I was from Lebanon. Making him realize that I was not a Jew, I stood up to leave. He insisted that I stay and even invited me to eat another course, for which I thanked him and left. A little shaken, I smelled something fishy in this encounter and wondered if Shmuel's hands were not in the planning of this incident.

One evening before retiring to my hotel, I went into a nearby café to have a cup of tea. On my way there I felt that I was being followed by two men whom I could not shake because of the short distance to the café. There was no danger that my residence at the hotel would be revealed by entering the café. Besides, I was not sure that I was their target. As usual, I sat at a spot where I could scan the entrance without being noticed, but this late at night the café was almost empty. After a while, the two men whom I suspected entered and approached the man in charge of the café. I watched them both talking to the café manager, probably asking him if he knew me. The manager, though, looked at me and shook his head. More questions were also greeted with a negative response. This made me sure that I alone was their target.

After they left, I casually (but riskily) asked the manager what these two gentlemen wanted. He said, "Oh, nothing, just directions." I knew he was not telling the truth, but I didn't want to arouse further suspicion.

After leaving the café I decided not to go to my hotel but to apply the training I had to shake off my real or imagined followers. I walked around without any particular destination or purpose.

I continued walking for about an hour until a man suddenly stopped me. I first suspected that he belonged with the two guys who were in the café. When he pulled out a cigarette and asked for a light, I was temporarily relieved. When he continued on his way without even looking at me, I became somewhat convinced that he stopped me for the light only because he did not even thank me for it. It is commonly known that Turkish men in many Arab countries do not bother to be polite even when offered something on the street. But, who could tell at this point if he were not one of the team keeping an eye on me?

I was not going home anyhow and decided, no matter what, not to fall into a trap. By then it became late, after midnight, and I discovered that I was heading towards Galata Bridge where a lot of people were still to be found.

Fearful thoughts which I would not wish upon anyone haunted me for the first time. It seemed to me that the two guys were always watching and waiting behind every street corner. I went so far as to think of what I might say if I were caught. I kept going through the alleys slipping from one corner to the next, trying to shake off anyone who might be following me.

Late into the night, the alleys became like shadows in the dark. When I started to go back, I realized that I was completely alone. When I looked at my watch, it was after four in the morning and almost dawn. When I was convinced that I was not followed by them, I went into my hotel room. Exhausted, I lay down with my clothes on and slept till noon.

Shmuel insisted that I leave the hotel and rent a room with a certain Turkish Moslem family of Iraqi descent. I noticed that my Moslem Iraqi friend avoided me every time I asked him to take me to the house that he rented out like a broker. Other Iraqi Moslem friends began to avoid me, too, whenever I met any of them. There was no doubt in my mind that I was (in undercover lexicon) about to be burnt.

At my next meeting with Shmuel, I reported the whole thing to him, seriously indicating that my task in Istanbul could be extremely dangerous. Shmuel angered me when, after I finished my report, he smiled and said again, "Just like in the movies! Yes?" I was dismayed that he made fun of my life being in danger. Maybe he did not realize, as yet, that I was becoming a burnt agent. He insisted that it was only suspicions and that I had nothing to fear. However, I insisted that my report this time be sent in its entirety to Tel Aviv, especially about the incident in the café and my contacts with other Moslem Arabs. He could not fail me this time because of my own request and did in fact transmit everything to the boss at headquarters in Israel.

Tel Aviv's decision was not delayed for long. I was to be sent as soon as possible to Zurich, Switzerland, for a new assignment. It was a shock to Shmuel because he did not agree with the assignment; he also knew that it would be a long time before a replacement was sent.

After somewhat hasty preparation, I safely left Istanbul for Zurich. After a couple of days in the capital of Switzerland, I was issued a railway ticket to Koln, Germany, where my new destination would be arranged. I left behind mixed feelings about the Turks, who are accused of murdering over one million Armenians during World War I. However, I would very soon be in another land whose inhabitants murdered over six million of my own people and where over 40 million others were killed or wounded during World War II. The idea of visiting or staying in the land where my people were herded for death to concentration camps made me sick. Before going there, I had been determined in my mind never to visit either Germany or Austria. I simply could not bear the thought of living among people who, in my opinion, were as guilty as Hitler himself for the Holocaust. The extermination of innocent human beings and the cause of the death of over 50 million people were too much to bear. What made me feel worse was that, while in Koln, I was told that I would be posted in Vienna, Austria, the crossroad country between east and west where most of the spying and intrigue was concentrated.

# CHAPTER 26

# Unmasking an
# Egyptian Double Agent

I had to abide by my agreement and take the train to Koln. I stayed there for a couple of days because there were no clear instructions yet for me. I went out to look around in the city and do some sight-seeing, too. I saw many destroyed sites still uncleared from the bombing of thousands of Allied aircraft during World War II. Thoroughfares and streets were built anew after being completely destroyed by these bombings. There were some historic structures left untouched by the war, mostly religious sites and cathedrals.

Also I had a chance to spend a few hours in the nearby city of Düsseldorf. This city could serve as an example for the entire world in its cleanliness and beautiful landscapes.

When my papers arrived with our people in Koln, I was issued a train ticket to Passau. I reached Passau on the Austrian border and had ample time to board the train again to Vienna.

Arriving in Vienna at the new *bahn* (railway station) I called my control and soon after had a brief meeting with him. My first impression of him was that I would be dealing with a typical semi-autocratic employee of the government with some eccentric attitudes attributed to committee members in the diaspora. He was just like all the others who were running Israel and did not change their thinking and behavior to fit state officials who held the fate and future of Israel. My controller behaved and acted like a true functionary. He seemed to be of German background but, nevertheless, I hated when he enthusiastically spoke German, even when it was unnecessary to do so.

I could not help but think that here again were a fair-skinned person and someone of Middle Eastern extraction with a dark complexion, meeting at the same café almost daily. With few foreigners around, we were an odd couple among the Viennese people.

After a week in a hotel, I rented a room in a boarding house run by a Viennese lady who took care of visitors from Middle Eastern countries, mostly Arabs. As usual, I toured Vienna to be familiar with its surroundings, mostly on foot, until I settled in my rented room of Maria Hilder Strasse in the center of the city.

As an Arab, I was told many times of hatred to the Jews in a much stronger manner than any other Arab could say to me. This brought me once to erupt and rebuke one of my Viennese conversationalists when anti–Semitism became the subject. I said, "I as an Arab do not hate the Jews as much as you people do. Our enmity is strictly political and Arabs don't massacre innocent people simply because they are Jews," which is close to the truth. After that I was left in peace and nothing of the sort happened again.

There were two main places to operate — the new railway station and the Café Arondo under the crossroads of four main streets in the heart of Vienna. The former was utilized to watch Arabs arriving in the city and the latter was a well-known place to meet new visitors from the Middle East, including Israel and other nations.

I first chose the café at the Arondo Circle, which I found rather pleasant. It is a round café with chairs all around and four access points to streets in all directions. The place is also where pedestrians cross the street because aboveground crossing is lengthy with many traffic lights and also risky in negotiating the wide boulevards. At the underground center there is also a wide round bar, kitchen and other fast food displays. There is enough space for customers to enjoy some pleasant time watching passersby of all nations looking at the tourist merchandise in the windows.

Each store within is also usually full of customers. The place was a strategic spot to execute my work without even being suspected. It seemed that other intelligence agents of other nations, including the Arabs, thought likewise and made it the spot for their purposes, too. Besides, it was also an ideal place for me to have breakfast, lunch or dinner sometimes, or simply late snacks before retiring to my room. It was open 24 hours a day and was continuously crowded with people from all over the world.

After a few uneventful visits, I noticed a Middle Eastern gentleman sitting by himself. I recalled that I had seen him alone here having his dinner. He probably came here every day, I thought. I figured if I sat near him and listened to his conversation with a friend, I would be able to determine his nationality. I could have just approached him and asked him, but this kind of planned contact was not the rule in our work. Besides, he never showed any interest in me even though I looked and behaved like an Arab.

It did not take long to find out — the second evening he was there at his usual place with another person. I waited for the right time to catch a table next to him, which was rather difficult to do at a time when the place was full and all tables were taken. I sat with my back to them to listen with more ease. I identified the language as Egyptian Arabic. I secured a place near to him for several evenings without establishing contact, which added to my frustration because the Egyptian was still neither interested in me nor curious to find out whether I was at least from the Middle East. I became more interested in him because he was not like other visiting Arab tourists who normally preferred to congregate with other Arabs or Arabic-speaking persons.

One evening I decided to take the initiative and request a light for my smoke. He was glad to offer it to me, but then he went sulking into his chair again. I asked, "Where do you come from?" He replied, "From Egypt" and turned his face the other way. At the time I thought it would be appropriate to leave him alone. I achieved something, anyhow, in exchanging a few words with him but, nevertheless, I felt that I was insulted and decided to leave him to himself for awhile.

For the next few days, I made it my duty to be there at the usual time and place. I began saying hello until a more tangible conversation with him could ensue. One evening, he asked me to join him at his table, which I triumphantly and gladly did.

He asked me why I was in Austria, and I obligingly recited my cover story. He introduced himself as Hussein Hassan Mohammed and added that he had already been in Austria for a long time, which sounded like a cover story. He did not say why he was there or what work he was actually doing there. He did not even mention where he was staying. There were many alleged Egyptian students in Vienna, but I could not place him in that category because he was much older.

Every piece of information I could extract from him was properly passed on to my control agent in Vienna. One day my controller surprised me with the information that Hussein, with whom I was beginning to become rather friendly, was a colonel in disagreement with Egyptian President Abdel Nasser, for whom he worked as assistant and confidant. He had differences with the chief and, voluntary or not, he was sent abroad until things returned to normal. That was rather a bizarre self banishment, but I kept this opinion to myself when my control added that they knew him long before I met him. They kept this secret from me in hopes of recruiting him for our service.

My role from then on was to strengthen our friendship in order to find out more about him. It was a tall and time-consuming order for me to fill. From that moment on, I took a different course in befriending Colonel Hussein. I first tried to interest him in my alleged business and, looking for clues or motivation for his love of fortune, I asked him to join me in my venture for profit and an easy life. He did not show any enthusiasm toward my suggestion but also did not say that he was not interested. This attitude did not deter me from persisting to meet him again and again.

In order to deter any suspicions about me, we decided to skip our meetings for a week or two and operate on other subjects, contacting other Arabs on our agenda. I was given the name of a person about whom they knew virtually nothing, except that he might be dangerous and also very interesting to us. The only clue my controller could give me about this person was that he was possibly working as a teacher or Imam (prayer leader). I also received an old faint picture of him with no references or name on it. My instructions were specific: to confirm and deliver his address and telephone number. That was like looking for a needle in a haystack.

Vienna, one of the largest cities in the world, has one and a half million inhabitants. The quarters I was supposed to search for this Arab were large enough to make me feel dizzy. It was as large as the New York City borough of Queens. My first step was to look at the telephone book, pick out Arab names at random, check their addresses and see which section of that borough of Vienna had the greatest number of Arabs. My target's name or profession was not in the telephone book, which would have been too easy a solution. I decided to approach one of these Arabic names and tell him I was looking for a room to rent for a certain period. This way I might stumble on some information.

The first Arabic name I chose ended up being not an Arab but a Turkish Moslem who could barely speak Arabic. After several attempts during the next few days, I found an Egyptian in one of the buildings. When he answered the door and talked to me, I discovered that he could hardly express himself in Arabic because he was the child of an Austrian mother and an Egyptian father. Nevertheless, he did give me the names and addresses of a few real Egyptians who could help me. After I had called some of them, one mentioned the address of someone whom he thought would be willing to share his apartment. His name was actually the same as the one we were looking for. However, most Arab and Moslem names are similarly repeated by many of the Islamic faith.

At his apartment, he was glad to see someone who could speak Arabic. I told him that I was new in Vienna and since I planned to stay in the city for a while, I was looking for a vacant room or an apartment near this decent neighborhood. He said he could not help me because his wife and children would be joining him soon. However, he referred me to another Egyptian who lived nearby.

To my surprise, it seemed that I had hit the jackpot. The name and description of this new person fit the scant information I had about my target. It could be him.

At the new address, I went up the staircase to the fourth floor, rang the bell and waited. Nothing happened. I tried again and after a moment or two, I noticed that someone was peeping through the hole at me. He hesitantly opened the door with a perplexed look on his face. I immediately greeted him in Arabic, as Moslem Arabs usually did. When I told him the reason for calling upon him and about the gentleman who gave me his address, he relaxed and requested that I sit down with him for a while to have coffee. I was surprised that his place was bare with very little furniture. He served coffee and we had a brief conversation. Then he expressed his regrets that he could not let me rent a room at his place, which I expected.

We parted warmly. During my next meeting with my controller, I recounted all the information I obtained about my target. I was told to return to him and make sure that he was indeed our person. I had no choice but to comply and call on him the next day.

I could have been in danger without knowing it when I went up the stairs that second time. I really did not know what to expect from someone who was mysterious and living alone. I was fully aware that I was going into the lion's den instead of attracting the lion to mine. I figured that my superiors were so desperate to know this Egyptian's whereabouts that they did not hesitate to risk my life. I felt as if I was given an order on the battlefield to go forward and attack. It would be sheer luck if I came out alive from this operation. Once again the thought of being kidnapped by the Egyptians crossed my mind, but I overcame my fears and accomplished my task.

When he opened the door, I apologized and said that I came to the building by mistake. After chatting with him for a few seconds, I again confirmed that he was the person in the faint photograph whom my controller had meticulously described. When relieved from this assignment, I drew a deep breath and waited for new instructions.

After an absence of over two weeks, I went back to my original assignment involving Hussein Hassan Mohammed, or Abu El Hassan (his nickname). I went to the Arondo Café, chose a table at the same place and ordered supper. He was already there so I joined him after he welcomed me and inquired where had I been all that time. I had earlier convinced my controller that in order to eliminate any suspicion of his knowing our target, I would tell him the truth about looking for a place to rent. I did not really expect that they knew each other or that we would run into each other, but it was possible. When I finished telling Abu El Hassan why I'd been absent, he indeed said that he knew the person I visited. My telling the truth in this case thus served two purposes — to find out more about our target, and to learn about the link between the two Egyptians.

It was a tough task for me. How would I be able to bare his real intentions, feelings, and character? The first clue came when I realized the link between our target and Abu El Hassan. I kept the idea to myself because if I expressed doubt about the wisdom of recruiting Abu El Hassan, it would antagonize my controller who was set on this action. He had already put so much time and work into it. I was determined to find the truth even if it meant shocking privileged people of the Labour Party like my controller. By then I also realized that Vienna was worse than Istanbul when it came to international espionage and intrigue. It was close to the Eastern Bloc and was full of KGB secret agents as well as CIA operatives.

My main objective became to strengthen my personal ties with Abu El Hassan and get as close to him as possible. We went out together at night to the few dance clubs in town frequented mostly by tourists and Arab students. One club in particular — the Volksgarden — was a favorite.

One evening at the Volksgarden, Abu El Hassan introduced me to another Egyptian whom he called Mahmoud. This new acquaintance claimed to have just arrived from Cairo on business. He was, like most Egyptians, very charming and pleasant to be with. He was witty, talkative, and always ready to tell a joke or two. After knowing Mahmoud for a while, he seemed to be of common rather than business stock. I never heard what kind of business Mahmoud was connected to or engaged in.

Abu El Hassan introduced me to more of his friends — students, tourists or employees of some Egyptian agencies in that country. I was always dubious of those who claimed to be just tourists because very few Egyptians could afford such a luxury. Many could have been officials of the Egyptian government under the pretext of being tourists. What amazed me most was that there were a disproportionate number of patriotic students. The same was true in Turkey; I believed that the new Arab generation aimed to correct the past and enhance their image by putting forward waves of educated generations for the future.

One evening Abu El Hassan came to the Volksgarden accompanied by two Viennese girls. They acted very nonchalantly, which led me to believe they were brought there for a special purpose. I was determined to figure out that purpose. I feared that I was a target of some plot of which the girls were a part. Meanwhile, my doubts about Abu El Hassan became stronger. I believed he had to be operating for a higher authority, but my controller constantly refuted this suggestion.

I insisted to my controller that my report be transmitted to Tel Aviv in full, which it was. My final remark to my control agent was that Abu El Hassan was not all he seemed to be and could not be kosher for our services. Upon hearing this, my controller became tough and rather abusive about my inference.

The next evening, Abu El Hassan told everyone at dinner that Israel was spreading the cholera germ in Egyptian waters to harm the civilian population there. Only yesterday I had heard this from our target at the casino. I kept my cool, though, and said nothing while the others debated this news for some time. Abu El Hassan gave this stunning news so effectively and matter-of-factly that I nearly doubted myself and believed him.

I was sure that Abu El Hassan was acting as instructed by superiors and was directed to say what he did. It was no doubt part of Egypt's psychological warfare, but I had no proof of this to present to my control agent. That proof, though, was soon made available to me through the media.

Three or four days later, in a little corner on the second page of the English-European newspaper, the *Herald Tribune*, a short article stated that "The Egyptian Embassies throughout the world are spreading through their agents at large the false accusation that Israel was contaminating the waters in Egypt with cholera." I cut it out and put it in my pocket for my controller to read for himself if he had not already.

I was more convinced that Abu El Hassan was in daily contact with the Egyptian Embassy and worked for Egyptian Intelligence. My control agent believed that Abu El Hassan chose to live in Vienna on his own volition because of a disagreement with his boss, President Abdel Nasser. His cover story was full of holes that began to show during and after the many months I was continuously in contact with him.

One evening I was invited by him to a casino outside Vienna at the shores of the Danube River. The invitation was sudden; I could not refuse. I was already in the car and the four of us (we picked up Mahmoud and a friend at the Volksgarden) drove to the casino, which was about ten to twelve miles outside of Vienna. On the way I detected nothing out of the ordinary, which made me feel better. Surprisingly, we didn't stay long at the casino, and we left early after Abu El Hassan met one of his friends there while we waited on the side. This bizarre visit was probably made to enable someone to see me and recognize me at a future date. The stranger who came along with us spoke only English. I first feared foul play, but when we returned to the city I felt better and was glad to be back.

That evening I was supposed to meet a new temporary control agent who arrived to replace my regular one who allegedly left for Israel on vacation. Incidentally, this time I missed the fixed meeting and could not reach the place on time. I went into a public telephone booth on Ring Strasse near the Austrian Parliament, far away from where we were supposed to meet, to call the embassy about my delay. After getting no reply from the special number I was given in case of emergency, Dov, the new replacement control, was suddenly in front of me, screaming in my face, "Where the hell have you been? We turned Vienna upside down looking for you fearing that something wrong had happened!"

I realized then that my encounters with Abu El Hassan were very serious and dangerous and that I was being carefully watched and followed. I forgot about all this for a moment and was amazed that he could find me so far away from our meeting place. I yelled back in astonishment, "How the hell did you know where I was at this particular booth?" Vienna is a big city and I could have called from any of thousands of telephone booths. Then I explained to him the whole story and that I was in no position to call him (which he probably knew already) until I left them. I remained amazed that Dov managed to locate me. He never explained it to me and we just laughed about the incident.

When I finished my report, he warned me to be extra careful, but he did not elaborate. I wondered why he was cautioning me. I began to understand why he was in Vienna. As the man in charge of all the operations at headquarters, he came to wrap up a case that was apparently shrouded in mystery and contradictions.

At my next meeting with him, he showed me a secret letter written by prime minister David Ben-Gurion which jubilantly informed all agents about the success of the Israeli Defence Forces in building a rocket called Shavit that would be launched very soon. Ben-Gurion told us to pay special attention to the reaction of our Arab neighbors and to include this with our regular reports. I was ecstatic at this news. This also signaled our initial development of the atom bomb. A few days later, the newspapers throughout the world ran full reports of our new rocket, which was said by the Israel government to be a meteorological research missile.

My meetings with Abu El Hassan continued as usual. The more we met, the more our relations became more relaxed after news about the Israeli missile.

One day I was with Dov at a remote restaurant that was always full of customers because of its low prices. Food was served at long tables accommodating ten to twelve people at a time. We had hardly sat down when Mahmoud arrived out of nowhere and sat at the table beside me. Dov immediately realized what was happening because Mahmoud spoke as a friend in Arabic. Dov and myself had not, as yet, spoken a word in Hebrew. When the waiter asked Dov what he would like to have, he told the waiter that he had just finished and would be leaving. This gave the impression that we were not together. It was a casual and natural reaction, because the dishes of the people who had sat at Dov's place before him and who had just finished their meal served by a different waiter were still on the table.

When Mahmoud asked who that was, I answered that I had never met him before. I doubted if this answer satisfied him. No other questions were asked. Actually, Dov and I had sat close enough to be discovered by Mahmoud, who could have belonged to the Egyptian Intelligence operating in that area with Abu El Hassan. It was really a close call and Dov's presence of mind saved the situation for the time being.

So far, all we knew was that Mahmoud was a good friend of Abu El Hassan. His presence at the far-away restaurant indicated that I was perhaps being followed. After reporting my activities to Dov at the next meeting, I was asked for the first time what I thought about Abu El Hassan. I gladly told him I believed that Abu El Hassan was an Egyptian patriot who would not betray his country and that my regular control agent was dreaming if he thought that he would come and work for us.

I was flabbergasted when Dov told me that Abu El Hassan already was working for us and that he agreed with my opinion that Abu El Hassan was a double agent. I felt somewhat relieved because I realized that I was right in my conclusion after being told that Abu El Hassan was ripe to be inducted into our service. I was then told to carry on my work as usual until other instructions were received.

My next encounter with Abu El Hassan and his friends came a few days later at the Arondo Café. I was extra careful and conscious of my actions and surroundings. Curiously, one evening a blond Swedish girl sat alone next to our table. She soon accepted our invitation to sit at the table with us.

The next morning I made up my mind to ask Dov about her and say she was our agent. As soon as we sat down at the table for our routine meeting, I blurted out to Dov, "How is the blond Swedish girl you sent over to our group?" He did not seem surprised that I discovered her, which I took for a compliment. He asked, "What girl are you talking about? I did not send any girl."

I repeated my question and told him that he could not convince me that she was not one of ours. I insisted that I knew and asked how he could do such a thing without telling me first. He changed the subject to our daily business, which convinced me even more that my assumption was true.

He then smiled widely and said, "Yes! She was sent to help you and join your net until further notice." He added that I was responsible for her and she would be working with me. I thought at the moment that I was barely capable of taking care of myself, much less looking after a girl, too. I nodded my head, bearing in mind that my agreement with them was about to expire very soon and I would be heading back home in the matter of a month.

When our group met again the next evening — to go dancing at the Volksgarden — I had a chance to dance with the girl and took her to the far side of the dance floor.

She immediately asked me, in perfect Hebrew, "How the hell did you discover my true identity?" She was upset that she had failed to fool me in her role. She made another mistake in speaking Hebrew with me on the dance floor. I immediately hushed her up and also calmed her by saying that it was no mistake on her part that I knew who she was. She was okay as far as I was concerned. In fact, I acted upon a mere hunch in discovering her true identity. I could not explain to her how this hunch always worked for me in my line of work. She told me that her name was Sara, she came from Jerusalem, and her mother taught her Swedish.

She reported that Mahmoud begged to accompany her home later. I just reminded her that no one should know where she lived and hoped that she could handle that. She answered, "Don't worry; I can take care of myself." From the way she said it, I was sure that she could. When she returned to our table, I completely distanced myself from Sara. When she left, she went away with Mahmoud.

The camaraderie between Abu El Hassan, myself, Sara and Mahmoud continued for a little while more. One day, Abu El Hassan and I met as usual at the Arondo Café. Before we sat down, someone suddenly greeted me in Hebrew and asked if I were not Mr. Horesh who lived in Ramat Gan, Israel. In Hebrew, he said that he lived not far from my home at Hapodim Street and that he was glad to meet me here. Perhaps I could be with him as neighbors meeting on foreign soil. The truth is: I did not recognize him or remember him at all. I interrupted him before he finished his next sentence to tell him in English that I did not understand what he was saying because I did not speak Hebrew and was not from Israel. Abu El Hassan stood there with his mouth open. The Israeli continued in Hebrew, "Come on, don't you recognize me? We are neighbors. Don't you understand Hebrew?"

Abu El Hassan continued to watch with wide-open eyes while the Israeli obnoxiously continued the conversation in Hebrew with himself. As trained, I did not lose my control, but I was tense. With some irritation in my voice, I repeated in English what I told him before. When he started speaking again in Hebrew, I told my Arab friends that I could not help him because he did not speak any other language but Hebrew. I turned my back to him, stepping toward our friends at the table who were within hearing range. Then he began again, this time in English, repeating what he told me before. I told him that he was very mistaken because I had never been in Israel and knew no Israelis. I don't know whether he believed me or not, but he left.

Later, I strongly suspected that Dov sent him deliberately to convey a message to Abu El Hassan — that he knew about his real intentions. Perhaps he did that because he knew that my agreement with the service was about to expire and that I had no intentions of renewing it. So he decided to burn me out. If that is true, I don't know if he succeeded.

The next day Dov told me and Sara to leave for Munich, Germany. It seemed that some fateful decision had been made regarding Abu El Hassan.

The last day I was doing some shopping on Maria Hilder Strasse when suddenly Abu El Hassan came up from behind and, before we exchanged greetings, a Middle Eastern–looking person with a tiny, almost hidden camera came in front of me taking pictures. I was sure that a couple of photos were snapped of me. Abu El Hassan told me that he heard that I was leaving Vienna. It did not surprise me to hear him saying that even if I did not tell him so. I said that some urgent business prompted me to go to Paris, regarding French films. Before I could add that I contemplated calling him before I left, he interrupted me, saying, "You are running away, *ya maaras* (you pimp)." I pretended I did not hear his derogatory remark and excused myself by crossing the street and bidding him goodbye.

From his mood that morning, he sounded beaten and I could understand that he already knew that he was burnt and could not carry on his role as the high-ranking Egyptian Intelligence officer in the area. He also knew that his exposure was partly if not mainly because of me — hence his insulting remark. He was surely frustrated and probably had plans for me, but my people were smarter this time. Dov ordered me to leave Vienna immediately, even without Sara, who was supposed to accompany me to Munich on the same plane.

At the airport a few minutes before departure, the controller who accompanied me handed me $500 and asked me to sign for it. Since I had already been paid my salary and expenses I asked what it was for. I told him I would not need it because my agreement had expired and I was heading home. He claimed that he was told by Israel to pay me that much. I repeated to him that Israel owed me nothing and technically I was already out and had drawn all expenses due to me. I almost missed my plane when our argument became very heated and he pushed the $500 into my pocket and forced me to initial a ready receipt in his hand.

The plane took off for Munich and within a couple of hours I landed there until my next flight to Paris.

In Paris, as in Austria and Germany, there were many Arabs. I realized that Arabs — whether students, workers or tourists — were all over Europe.

I visited a cousin of my wife there, Rachel, whose husband Shimshon Ambarchi from Basra was posted there by the same Intelligence section. A few days later, I finally boarded the El-Al plane direct to Tel Aviv.

My homecoming was emotional and I had a hard time establishing rapport again with my children and wife. It took my youngest son Ouri over a week to get used to the idea that he had a father. He was eight months old when I left him and about 2 years old when I came back. The first day, he called me Uncle. When I corrected him, he thought for a few seconds and then called me Uncle-Dad. I was told that my elder son, Moshe, had trouble at school adjusting himself with other kids who teased him because he did not have a father at home.

Listening to all this, I was determined to never again leave my family for any long period of time. When I was approached after a while for another term in some other country, I requested to do it for short periods only and to be accepted as a permanently employed official. So far, I was employed only under a one-sided agreement, which held few benefits and was renewable every year.

In light of my service, I was entitled to such benefits but was turned down instead. The same thing was done to many other employees in the government, contradicting the *hisadruth* (labor union) regulations that state that every employee be considered permanent after one year of service.

The government employers who were socialists insisted on granting a one-year renewable arrangement that enabled them to fire those who were unsuitable or not a member of one of the ruling parties. While the first reason was reasonable and just, the latter was discriminatory and the real reason for the arrangement. When I fell into the second category and was refused permanency, I left my job.

Realizing that I would have little means to live on and support my family if I left, my ex-boss, Mordechai Almog, who was also in charge of the Mossad operations in Europe while I served there, called me and asked me to see him and tell him that I was not interested in rejoining. Then he said the real reason he called was to ask for the $500 that I took rather unlawfully in Vienna. I was mad and nervous in hearing what he said and demanded to meet him immediately. He agreed, probably thinking that I was beaten and broken and would soon begin working again for them.

At his office, he noticed that I was mad. He calmed me down and said, "Perhaps you drew this amount by mistake, right?"

I said, "No! Wrong! It was forced upon me."

When Mordechai insisted on his version, I demanded to have Dov there with us to settle this assumption, since he had been present with my control agent at the airport. Upon hearing this, Mordechai backed up, probably realizing that the trick would not work, and conceded that I could pay back the money in Israeli pounds. I made sure that we were talking about the equivalent in Israel currency and not United States dollars, because the law in Israel forbade its citizens to carry foreign, undeclared currencies under penalty fines and prison. Still, I had the $500 with me for such anticipated accusations against me. We agreed that I pay it back in small monthly installments. I thought at the time that it would be better to serve Israel as a patriotic national rather than to seek a career in this field. How wrong I was, because this was not over yet.

# CHAPTER 27

# Severing Ties with
# the Secret Service

I have mentioned that in an Istanbul restaurant I had met (perhaps not by accident) an Iraqi Jew who drove a Volkswagen car around the city. This incident had its repercussions in Tel Aviv after I terminated my services with the Mossad. This Iraqi-Israeli saw me in the Ottoman Bank (now a mercantile) in the corner of Achad Haam and Shederoth Rothchild in Tel Aviv while I was meeting the bank's manager, my friend and former Alliance classmate and Army colleague. As soon as this Iraqi Jew noticed me, he ran out to the street and within few minutes came back with someone from security who approached me and, after he pointed at me, asked me to step outside. I cut my conversation short with my friend, who probably thought that the man and I had security business to attend to. He was my colleague in the unit after all. When I stepped out of the bank, I noticed a near-full battalion of plain-clothes agents as well as uniformed police officers. About 50 feet away, a man who seemed to be their commander was laughing his head off. As soon as he saw me coming out with his deputy, two secret agents and the Iraqi Jew surrounded me. I recognized him as soon as we were near. After we greeted each other by our first names, the Iraqi Jew told the officer in charge that I was the Moslem Arab whom he reported to the security bureau as a possible spy or saboteur. I did not know at the time whether to congratulate myself on a job well done or to get mad at my ex-bosses who had probably cooked up this contraption. My friend, the commander of the security unit, calmed him down and told him that this matter was now in his hands. After a few greetings and meaningless bits of information about the incident, he apologized and I departed amicably. I am still not sure if this incident was not staged for some other reason.

In 1964, my brother-in-law, who by now had made a small fortune by disregarding financial regulations and laws, established a small bank for Iraqi Jews. Our third child, a daughter, was born in October 1964. Nirit was the joy of our life, because our family had mostly sons. My two sons almost went wild when they learned that a daughter had been added to the family. Meanwhile, my financial situation at the age of 45 was not promising, and my prospects of finding a job that met my expectations were remote.

In 1966, Israeli Intelligence achieved one of its highest honors when a Russian MiG-21, desperately sought by the West, was smuggled here. But no written or filmed account of this operation mentioned that it was initiated and executed by two Iraqi-born Jews.

In 1961, the Russians, under extreme secrecy, began to introduce this aircraft to the Middle Eastern Arab nations. We had gathered through Intelligence that they had previously supplied MiGs to the Egyptians. Security was extremely tight. Pilots were carefully selected for training.

In December 1964, someone called the Israeli Embassy in Paris and urgently asked to speak to the military attaché. He said he had a message from a friend in Iraq—"If the Israelis want a MiG-21, they should telephone a certain number in Baghdad and ask for Abraham (an alias)." The man abruptly hung up.

No one took the message seriously; it was forgotten for almost a year. General Amit then decided to follow up on it.

At first, it was thought that the caller was an enemy agent trying to lure the Israelis into a trap. Everybody in the Mossad realized that it was dangerous for an Israeli agent in Baghdad even to attempt to check that telephone number. It became necessary for someone who knew the country well to make an assessment of the contact, if it really existed. That person would be like a sacrificial lamb; if captured, he must not betray the Mossad, even under torture.

The person chosen for the task was a *sabra* of Iraqi Jewish origin, fluent in Arabic (Iraqi Arabic) and English. After having passed a crash course with the Mossad, he flew into Baghdad and checked into a hotel on Saadoon Street under the assumed identity of a health equipment salesman. He first made the rounds to hospitals and health ministry officials, pushing his articles. All the while he prepared himself for a single telephone call—his sole reason for coming to Baghdad.

As part of his cover, he invited two Iraqi health officials to dinner at one of the best restaurants in Baghdad. While at the table he excused himself for a few seconds, supposedly to make a business call. He dialed the number, and his legs trembled when he heard this question from the other end: "Who is speaking?" He asked for Abraham and said that he was an out-of-town friend. About a minute later, Abraham came to the phone. Our agent awkwardly asked, "You are the Ibrahim [Arabic for Abraham]?" Ibrahim saved the situation by responding very calmly, "Are you the gentleman who met my friend?" Our agent said that he was and they set up a meeting in a café the following day.

Our agent had forgotten the instructions regarding secret meetings in enemy territories. Luckily, though, nothing happened and Ibrahim arrived on time at the meeting place. Ibrahim was about 60 years old and had snowy hair. He opened the conversation by saying it was nice of our agent to have come. Being in Iraq with a forged passport made our agent fear for his life. Amazingly, Ibrahim's presence calmed him for the first time since arriving in Baghdad.

Our agent told the old man that he was most interested in the merchandise he was selling. Ibrahim replied, "You mean the MiG-21?" Mansour nodded. "It would cost you a lot of money," Ibrahim added. Mansour said that he thought it could be arranged.

When they met for the second time, Ibrahim told our agent his story. He had come from a poor Jewish Iraqi family and at 10 was working as a servant in the house of a rich Christian Maronite family. He never attended school and could hardly read or write. As the years went by, his parents died and he established himself in a special position in the household he worked. In theory, he was still a servant, but the whole family came to rely upon his advice and guidance. He looked after the head of the house with lavished love and care and he became part of the family. Up to then, he existed only as a member of their family; the only other identity he possessed was as a Jew. Now he set forth in search of his heritage. The Jews of Iraq left in the fifties and only a few remained — one was a rabbi who instructed Ibrahim in the Jewish faith. Then he felt profound ties with his people and Israel.

The Iraqi government was putting pressure on the Christian minorities, like it did before on the Jews, and it became difficult to manage any business due to government interference. The Christians were financially squeezed and many of their friends were being imprisoned on fabricated charges. The oldest son became deputy squadron leader and was chosen to fly the new Russian MiG-21. Ibrahim knew that the West and the Israelis were ready to pay $1 million for one of those jets, as already reported throughout the world media. He thought this could help the whole family to escape and establish themselves somewhere else in the world, starting a new life. Thus Ibrahim used his influence on the boy to fly his MiG-21 to Israel. Ibrahim persuaded a fellow Iraqi Jew friend to leave his message with the Israeli Embassy in Paris.

Our agent, back in Tel Aviv, reported to General Amit all he had learned. He then went back to Baghdad to set up a plan, but Ibrahim wanted assurance that all the family would be out of danger before anything took place. He also requested that an advance against payment be deposited to assure their survival after leaving Iraq. A trusted relative would soon leave for medical treatment and tell them whether or not the advance was paid. The Israeli government approved of the operation. They sent back our agent with a radio operator and four men covered his every move.

The regular Israeli networks in Iraq were temporarily removed to make sure there were no risks if something went wrong. Our agent continued his cover as a health equipment salesman. Three more men were dispatched to serve the family through electronic means; six more were established in the Kurdistan region of northern Iraq to keep in contact with the Kurdish revolution there and to transport the family out of the country. Still another team was stationed in Ahwaz, Persia (Iran) to help the evacuation of the family.

A special team was sent to Washington, D.C., and Turkey to seek landing and refueling rights. The Russians, aware of the dangers of pilots on training missions flying their aircraft to the West, kept fuel tanks only half full, thus making a journey from Iraq to Israel impossible.

Because of the risk of being caught and killed by the Iraqi authorities, the family could not know of their imminent departure and were only told that they would spend the summer as most Iraqis do—in the north at the mountain resort. The Israelis were on good terms with the Kurds and the Kurdish rebels in that area made arrangements to fly the whole family to Ahwaz.

All this became a gigantic operation for Israel when General Amit decided to bring in the CIA to help. The United States was delighted to assist and the operation got the green light.

On August 15, 1966, the pilots' duty roster showed that squadron leader Munir Redfa would be on an early morning training mission from his base in Mosul. Once in the air he banked his plane, put on his afterburners and was over the Turkish border before anyone knew what had happened. With United States Air Force Phantoms flying escort, he put the plane down at a secret CIA base, refueled, and with more fighter escort planes made his way out over Turkey and the Mediterranean, where Israeli fighters waited to escort him to Israel. The whole family was already being escorted over the border to a prearranged spot where Kurdish guerrillas picked them up. They traveled by mules through the night, a journey which many Iraqi Jews had made before the *aliya* of 1952. From there they were taken by a helicopter to safety. They were given new identities to enable them to disappear into thin air and live happily ever after.

The whole affair was initiated by three Iraqi Jews: one who lost his heritage and found it again; another who was prepared to risk his life in the planning of the venture; and one who conveyed the message to Israeli Intelligence. All three were simple persons, untrained Israeli Jews, who found simple solutions to a worldwide puzzle. Assisted by none, they helped initiate a gigantic leap forward for the free intelligence of the world.

# CHAPTER 28

# Seeking Magnanimity

In 1966 there was again one of the many recessions that plagued Israel for a long period with the yearly inflation rate at 100 percent or more. Most of the banks were in trouble, including Credit Bank which owned a knitwear factory in Afula. Every sign indicated that some drastic measures had to be taken to resolve the situation.

Pinhas Sapir of the Labour Party managed the finances of the country almost since its establishment like Jewish committees in the diaspora used to handle their finances with personal rules and regulations. It was not a secret then that Sapir had created two kinds of signatures. His sympathy and help to others were well known except that some were real and some were for political purposes or subsequent refusals by his subordinates. When help was solicited from him and the petitioner was of his party and had the prime minister's graces, Sapir's real signature and seal were affixed. Should the solicitor be in disfavor with the minister, he would never refuse to help but would affix his negative signature and seal. His knowing subordinates then put such bureaucratic obstacles in the way until the receiver of the supposed help got tired and abandoned the idea altogether. In that manner he kept a portrait of himself as savior of needy people, enterprises, and other business firms.

Many Israeli banks were in danger of closing down. Some obtained help from abroad with the blessing of the finance minister because they were sympathetic to or supporters of his ruling party. Others, because of party politics, received support from the government and continued their business as usual, even when they failed.

Two small banks fell into the category of semi-independent — Feuchwanger and Credit Bank. The officers of the former, like the other bank officers, were Ashkenazi. The latter officials were the only ones of Iraqi-Swiss origin. Feuchwanger, like other banks, bent some government financing rules and was, probably due to disfavor in the minister of finance's eye, condemned to close. Credit Bank was looked down upon because it was feared that it would give sectarian financing concern for the Iraqi Jewish community in Israel. Also disfavored by the ruling party, it was ordered to close.

During a news conference with the minister of finance regarding the closing of the two banks, one of the reporters dared to ask why Credit Bank, which was the only Sephardic/Iraqi small bank, did not get any help and why the minister had not acted evenhandedly in the matter. Sapir replied that he acted evenhandedly on a fifty-fifty basis in dealing with this matter.

The victory of the Six-Day War in 1967 ran like alcohol into the heads of the Israelis. The Israeli people began to savor the victory and also enjoy the monetary compensation paid by Germany to almost every Ashkenazi individual in Israel. All this created a gap between one part of the Israeli people — whose dead loved ones could not be compensated by any amount of money — and the others who were in worse financial shape.

I desperately realized that I was 48 years old and had three children to take care of. The Israelis, after the 1967 war and the compensation from Germany, became aloof even toward Labour principles. Those who lived in the kibbutzim (settlements) received their compensation payments abroad, in order not to turn it over to the Socialist system which held them accountable for everything they ever owned. The money paid by Germany went to everyone who had a relative, even to some who had none. The Socialist Labour indoctrination became so embedded that it became synonymous with the State of Israel itself. Any Israeli who spoke out against Israeli Socialism and Labour was labeled as a traitor. Terrorists affiliated with the Palestine Liberation Organization (PLO) began to strike randomly at children, old persons and other civilian targets. In March a children's bus was blown up by a mine and an Israeli airplane was hijacked to Algiers. (The passengers and crew were released later by the Algerians.) In Athens another El Al plane was attacked; one passenger was killed and another was wounded. In November a car explosion killed 12 and injured 50 in a Jerusalem marketplace.

The intoxicated Israelis did not realize the dangers resulting from the Six-Day War. The Socialist government of Israel made sure it strengthened its grip on everything and boasted that any opposition party would be unable to function even if victorious. Anyone who broke through that "grip" did so by transferring all his financial and personal belongings to a foreign country. This was the natural reaction in protecting oneself from worse things to come. The people of Israel continued to be hypnotized by the failing Socialist government of Israel.

The situation had changed since we were all struggling to realize Herzl's dream and risking our lives for the State of Israel and the Jewish people before thinking of ourselves. Now it was quite different.

I asked myself what personal benefits arose from putting one's life on the line for Israel. This attitude compelled me to seek my remaining future in another place. I had no intentions of staying away very long from the land I hoped to live in and love.

My application to leave for Canada was quickly approved, which made me hesitate before I took this desperate step. A friend of mine heard of my intentions and suggested that we work together and try our luck again in the same line of business. I was skeptical because I knew that without government help nothing would tick. Since my friend was unaffiliated like me, I had the feeling that our work would be doomed.

I put everything on hold and took another chance in exports, a most encouraging activity for the State of Israel. I tried my best to establish myself in the country that I had helped for most of my life. With other partners, in 1968 we registered our business legally, unlike others who got rich by operating outside the law. A reasonable investment by a few people was secured and we selected about $100,000 worth of different styles of knitwear and other garments intended for export to the United States. After completing the legal procedures, we were told that we had to certify our price list with the ministry of commerce and industries to keep track of all exports and also to become entitled to export benefits after payments from overseas. We did everything according to the instructions we received for our first export deal. After a few months, I had to be in New York with one of my partners to close out the entire deal.

It was my first time in New York and I was looking forward to seeing the country about which I heard so much all my life. After admiring the magnificent buildings and the multitude of New Yorkers filling the streets of the city and the thousands of cars and trucks moving over the streets, my partner and I busied ourselves disposing of the remaining merchandise. Unfortunately we were not able to do that, so we decided to return to Tel Aviv and compensate by moving another already-bought shipment. In the meantime, perhaps, our agent in New York would be able to dispose of the remaining balance of the exported goods.

A day or two upon our return to our humble office, three persons visited us. We suspected one to be with the Shin Bet (Security Department of Israel), but he declared himself to be an economic policeman and announced that we were all under arrest, our office would be closed, and documents would be confiscated for evidence. Gathering my faculties and self-control, I asked him if he would kindly explain what this was all about. He announced that our firm exported and accepted gratuities without certifying a price list as required by law.

I said that it was not true and pulled our certificate from the file. He looked at it, read it carefully and, to my complete surprise, threw it to the floor and said that this certificate was wrong. I protested and told him that if he wished he could verify the signature of the deputy minister of commerce and industries. I also explained that this was what he and other officials advised us to do in order to operate within the laws of the State of Israel. He looked at me with a laconic smile and said, "The certificate should have been given by the ministry of finance and not commerce and industry." Immediately I thought of Pinhas Sapir, the finance minister.

Arguing, pleading, and explaining did not help; I was taken with my partner to the police station and a file was opened against the firm. Dazed, I could not believe what had happened. Was it possible that I was a victim of a dispute between two Israeli ministries struggling for power? It was possible, because each ministry was controlled by a different party in the coalition. Or perhaps my previous bosses woke up all of a sudden and believed that they could drag me back to my previous job by using intrigue instead of a direct approach. Both assumptions were possible, but in either I remained the innocent victim.

An anonymous caller from Jerusalem offered his help, saying that he did not know it was me who fell victim to this sorrowful situation. I fiercely rejected his help, telling him that this state of things was not on my agenda when I faithfully worked and served Israel. I was so mad that I could not express my disappointment.

I obtained permission to go back to the United States to conclude what we had begun. Once in New York again, I worked hard with my partner to dispose of the exported goods while feeling betrayed, vis-à-vis my ideal convictions. That was the straw that broke the camel's back. I decided to resign from the firm I helped establish, collect the money and pay back our creditors and the Israeli government to close the file with the infamous Israeli economic police.

I suddenly found myself without a job again, but this time I was in the United States. I worked on my papers to legally stay and work in the United States. Even though my papers were approved, I never talked with or met any official dealing with my case. The only time we were asked to meet an immigration officer to verify our identity was after my sons and daughter had already learned to speak fluent English.

After we settled in and were working like everyone else, news of dissatisfaction with the state of affairs in our Israel reached us. In 1973, the War of the Day of Atonement (Yom Kippur) shocked everyone. Thousands of men, including myself, volunteered to go back to join the Israeli Defense Forces lest Israel be destroyed. Israel, in retreat, was taken by complete surprise by Egyptian and Syrian forces. If it were not for Ariel Sharon, a patriotic general who saved the day by acting on his own, perhaps the Israeli Defense Forces would have withdrawn to a line near the borders of Rehovot, about 20 to 30 kilometers from Tel Aviv. Because of this, Sharon became the villain of the Army.

It is estimated that over one million Israelis have either left for good or are living and worrying abroad. They chose that in preference to being frustrated by the semi-democratically elected officials of the State of Israel. While abroad, we were disturbed when terrorism increased and the media took the side of the PLO without understanding the real purpose of this organization. When media throughout the world disregarded the true intentions of the PLO and went all out against Israel to the extent of calling it an imperialist nation, we were all angry. It prompted me to write the following open letter:

> This letter is addressed to all the media and I wish to bring to your notice — what prompted me to write it — the straw that broke the back of the camel. Your report last night on the Beirut crisis was, allow me to say, very biased.
>
> Being a 62-year-old Jew and an Israeli, I consider myself as knowledgeable on what is happening as anyone, because I was born in one of the Arab countries and lived there until I was forced to decide that I was not intended for free living with my fellow countrymen. Luckily for me, because I did not have to suffer the humiliation of my fellow Jews after I joined the forces fighting for the freedom of the world in World War II.
>
> I call your reporting biased because of the pictures I see on TV make the PLO look like freedom fighters being put down by the Israelis by alleged methods of cruel fighting to destroy them. Well, like our President says, I cannot understand your broadcast of Arafat many times with a baby (I wonder if the baby was his and if he is married at all) at least four times always hugging and kissing him or her like another leader in my time who did the same under the advice of his propaganda minister who committed suicide with his children and family later to avoid judgment. I wonder if the broadcast was not done on purpose to portray the alleged leader as a family man who loved children. We portray our politicians the same way to gain support from the voters. It would have been enough and natural if you showed him once. But three or four times you showed him smiling in spite of the beating he had taken; now the world believes he is a strong leader (who won the battle). You call this unbiased?
>
> The network reported by John Chancellor that Israel is waging "savage attacks" on the PLO in Beirut, adding that Israel today is not the Israel we need to know. I say: You bet your life, Mr. Chancellor. We are no more sheep to be led to slaughter or be turned down from landing and sink to the bottom of the sea because we were helpless then and nobody said anything about it.
>
> It is time to stand and say "You asked for it Yasir Arafat," who does not even recognize the name Israel not to mention the State of Israel. He is like his predecessors in this field whose leaders he surely admires and who slaughtered five million Jews as a result of such reporting and propaganda methods, which cultivated in the mind of the people of the world that we are bad and we do bad things.

At long last, Mr. Chancellor, you mentioned the word, long said before you by our arch enemies, that Israel is becoming an Imperialist State. Congratulations! This surely is a different tone that the United States and Israel is all about, and you want to say that you are unbiased? A persecuted and suffering people who are looking to for peace for the last 2,000 years are Imperialists. It does not make sense.

Your broadcast of wounded civilians touched us all — including me, my kids and wife — but we never in our own mind blamed Israel for it; we put the blame squarely on the PLO and company, who brought about this misfortune to those unfortunate people who were naive enough to believe in what their leaders said to them. We pity them very much.

As I said, I lived through the period to witness World War II and the underground fighting to create the State of Israel. I can recall that Mr. Begin and his group (though I am not of their party) fought honorably as soldiers, as can be proven by many records and how the media compare him with Arafat and company as an ex-terrorist. He was extremely careful to spare the innocents, even at the risk of giving advance notice of his attacks, as can be verified from many sources. Now, how could you accuse the same person of savagery like you reported?

I recall well when our prisoners fell into their hands, they were not only savagely killed but they delighted in such savagery. Such instances are horrible to recall — like those who were executed, and their cut-off heads were used for a football (soccer) game by their leaders and fellow terrorists. Thousands of atrocities were committed by these people, not only against Jews or Israelis but against Christians and Moslems and their fellow countrymen.

Gentlemen, let us not kid ourselves. These are the people we are dealing with now. Every other method was tried to no avail and there is only one way to eliminate this evil. The sooner the better, so that the Middle East might breathe easy again. I am sure millions of Arabs and heads of states share my view but are afraid to say it.

Josh Horesh
August 3, 1982

The leaders in Israel, especially all the Labour ones, threw accusations at Israelis and Jews in the United States as if we were escaping the State of Israel. Maybe this would be healthy because it is about time to stop being flatterers or sycophants and seekers of benefit. Everyone agrees that it is time to stop the crazy running after begging and ruling.

Those of us who wish to visit Israel must be encouraged and even helped instead of harassed. Otherwise, hundreds or maybe thousands will visit other places and not return; Israeli leaders must become open and more faithful to the love of Israel and less to power, position, and property. One *yored* (emigrant) was asked by a journalist in New York why he decided to remain in the United States. His answer was, "I came here to find meaningful work and go back with some extra money! But, I found freedom instead, so I decided to stay."

I found my peace of mind and magnanimity in the midst of the most noisy and active city in the world and decided to stay in the most accommodating country, the United States. After my first trip out of Baghdad — which was my whole world at the time — in 1937, we became United States citizens almost four decades later, in 1976.

Today I am semi-retired. In Israel there is still the dilemma of standing up against irreconcilable neighbors. Israel must secure itself by continuously being strong. The minute Israel shows any weakness, it will be devoured by its enemies just for the pleasure of destroying it, with or without a treaty.

Surely, such a treaty would lessen the threat and lower the burden on this beleaguered, tiny nation. Though Israel cannot rely on pacts, such pacts could help. Let not Shomer Israel, the watcher of Israel, become drowsy or fall asleep. As long as Israel has to deal with Arab nations who cling irrationally to the concepts of honor and dignity, ready to kill whether wrong or right, there will inevitably be war and hostilities. Sometimes, this could be forgotten, but Jews and Israelis who review their recent past have every right to expect and believe that this small nation could become prey again to anti–Semitism and anti–Israeliism. We are always aware of any prejudiced society that might spring up from nowhere to destroy us.

# Index

# Index

# Index